DATE DUE

DEMCO 38-296

The Art and Science of
Computer Assisted Ordering

The Art and Science of Computer Assisted Ordering

METHODS FOR MANAGEMENT

Barbara V. Anderson

QUORUM BOOKS
Westport, Connecticut • London

Library of Congress Cataloging-in-Publication Data

Anderson, Barbara V.
    The art and science of computer assisted ordering : methods for
management / Barbara V. Anderson.
        p.   cm.
    Includes bibliographical references and index.
    ISBN 1–56720–049–4 (alk. paper)
    1. Retail trade—Management—Data processing.   2. Industrial
procurement—Management—Data processing.   3. Inventory control—
Data processing.   I. Title.
HF5429.15.A5   1996
658.7—dc20   95–41390

British Library Cataloguing in Publication Data is available.

Library of Congress Catalog Card Number: 95–41390
ISBN: 1–56720–049–4

First published in 1996

Quorum Books, 88 Post Road West, Westport, CT 06881
An imprint of Greenwood Publishing Group, Inc.

Printed in the United States of America

The paper used in this book complies with the
Permanent Paper Standard issued by the National
Information Standards Organization (Z39.48–1984).

10 9 8 7 6 5 4 3 2

Contents

Acknowledgments

A special word of thanks to the people who have taken time from their busy schedules to review this book. I especially want to thank Marvin Woods, founder of Marwood Systems, whose ideas and input on replenishment and logistics have been so helpful; Bob Cohen, founder of Logistics Data Systems and the author of the Spaceman Planogram System, for his insights into the future of planograms and the importance of top-down corporate philosophies and functional integration; Terry Donofrio, president of Retail Systems and Services, for his advice on the interfaces to planning; Larry Buresh, former CIO/vice president of Frank's Nursery and Crafts and Ben Franklin Stores, and currently of Chief Auto Parts, for helping me keep this book applicable to real-world situations; Peter Abell, president of Abell Automation Technologies, for his input on future technologies; Donald R. Mowery, director of Customer Response/ECR for Ralston Purina Company, for his insights to the needs of manufacturers; and Warren Thayer, editor of *Frozen Food Age*, for editing the book and targeting it to you, the reader.

Introduction

Do you want increased consumer service levels and reduced safety stock at the same time? How about better control of seasonal products, and a single system that integrates all your planning functions?

Of course you do! These are just a few of the benefits of CAO, or computer assisted ordering. CAO is one of the most misunderstood and underutilized strategic weapons available to retailers today. Yes, "available."

If you think CAO is just another ivory tower industry buzzword, this book is designed for you. CAO is here, and its use can dramatically improve your business in measurable ways. Moreover, it can be implemented in cost-justifiable stages.

In a limited sense, computer assisted ordering simply replaces manual ordering—the order clerk—at store level. But CAO in its full sense is much more. We like to think CAO is *the optimization of manufacturer, supplier, and retailer distribution to the retail store, based on consumer and store data and corporate policy.* CAO must be integrated into your current operating environment, and steps must be taken to ensure that it is a part of your future plans.

Consider the obvious: each day, retail management makes multimillion dollar decisions in less than five minutes, without the benefit of any real analysis. Most of the time, the potential impact of these decisions is never even known.

Should minimum presentation stock be two or three units deep? Should planogram default be a case and a half? How many weeks of supply do you need for a specific product, and exactly when should orders be triggered? The truth is, many retailers wing it.

During a meeting, the system installer unexpectedly asks, "What weeks-of-supply should we use?" All heads turn to the highest ranking person in the room. He or she answers, "I don't know, what do most retailers do?" A well-paid consultant answers, "They mostly use three weeks." "Okay, we'll start off with three weeks." And there it is—a multimillion dollar inventory decision in less than three minutes. *Many retailers suffer from a lack of integration in their systems and their thinking.* We will discuss CAO as an integrated project that is, in fact, part of a larger vision of retail.

This book provides:

- A framework and checklist for implementing CAO
- An understanding of key terminology
- Suggested solutions to problems you're likely to encounter
- Ideas to make your CAO implementation successful

First, it's important to keep several key points in mind:

1. *There is no one right system, product, or approach for successful CAO.* CAO is successful when it works with the individual merchandising, product, and system environment.

2. *CAO is too big a leap to make in one step.* It can be achieved using small incremental steps. Each step is cost-justifiable on its own.

3. *CAO consists of a set of modules and functions that can grow in sophistication over time.* CAO is developed with simple methods initially, and with more sophisticated techniques over time.

4. *Not all retailers and not all categories within one retailer will use the same methods for forecasting and ordering.* However, all the systems using these methods should be integrated.

5. *The distinct separation of replenishment product from planning product is artificially imposed.* Basic products such as grocery and hard goods are thought of as replenished and planogrammed. Non-basic product is considered product that is planned initially and restocked only through the plan. However, a retailer may have many products that have attributes of both planning and replenishment, and all products should be managed under one flexible system. Planned product can be tracked using replenishment analysis; traditional replenishment product benefits from using planning strategies. *Differences between planning and replenishment should be considered primarily in terms of length of time rather than different systems.*

6. *The distinct separation of headquarters from stores is artificially imposed.* Headquarters and distribution center systems should be fully integrated with the store systems, and systems within the stores should be integrated with each other. Systems that address replenishment to the distribution center as separate from replenishment to the stores are incomplete.

7. *Integration does not mean integration of separate systems, but rather the integration of business functions.* The current definitions of systems as we know them will change dramatically. The final goal is a full integration of bottom-up information with top-down business strategies.

One final point—none of this is going to come easily. You'll need lots more than off-the-shelf software. Successful CAO requires clean scanner data, working warehouse pick and load systems, electronic store receiving, manageable store-level planograms, integrated planning systems, and a global approach to logistics management.

Let's go into a little more detail on some of the benefits you can achieve:

- Increased consumer service level. By automating the ordering process, missed orders due to clerical errors are eliminated. Planogram product is often "faced out," creating the illusion that product is available when it is not. Orders are missed when there are no apparent "holes" on the shelf. Store forecasting and ordering includes trend, seasons, and promotions that may be overlooked by clerks.

- Reduced in-store stock levels. CAO limits the product in the stores during normal demand, seasons, and promotion to the product needed for consumer demand and store presentation. With most planogram-type products, manageable store-level planograms are a necessity to accomplish this goal.

- Seasonal product control. CAO orders products coming into seasons. CAO also balances the cost of ordering additional product against transferring product at season end. Seasonal transfers can insure availability of product no longer available from the supplier or not available in time. The real benefits occur when transfers and returns are automated.

- Reduced warehouse stock levels. Warehouses currently hold not only safety stock on top of in-store safety stock, but also product that could and should be flow-through. The opportunities available for intelligent logistics explode with CAO. Unfortunately, many CAO installations continue to treat the warehouse as a separate business and a logistically separate function.

- Product availability. Long-term forecasts available at all points of the distribution chain assist manufacturers in producing and supplying sufficient product quantities. Improved long- and short-range forecasting, intelligent order generation, and electronic communication are necessary.

- In-store reserve storage control. Products are lost, damaged, and aged in uncontrolled back rooms. Product is reordered from floor stocks when there is product in the back room. CAO provides the potential for reducing and controlling back room stocks. For those retailers where the back room is a needed part of storage, the back room can be managed more like a warehouse.

Chapter 1, "The Future of Retail," is presented to help you, as a retailer, to place CAO on a development timeline in the context of your current environment.

Chapter 2, "The Retail Environment," is designed to help you identify the characteristics of both your merchandising philosophy and your products. The best starting point for CAO is a clear definition of your own environment and goals. Before you can select strategies, you must define the problems.

Chapters 3 through 7 discuss in detail each of the major components of CAO and the myriad of possible approaches. The "best" methods will depend on your environment as defined in Chapter 2.

We'll cover the spectrum of retailing, including grocery, drug, general merchandise, specialty retailers, and discounters. We are concerned with processes and functions. To avoid the confusion of terminology that may have different meanings to different segments of the industry, we will not use the terms *ECR* (Efficient Consumer Response), *Quick Response,* and *JIT* (Just In Time).

The terms ECR and Quick Response connote the ability to flow goods through the distribution pipeline efficiently without excess costs. JIT is the ability to produce and distribute product on an as-needed basis without excess costs or inventory. Although this book addresses these concepts, it does not use this terminology.

We also do not use the term *best practices,* so as to avoid confusion between best practices as a concept and the several defined functions labeled as best practices. Best practices is a goal. We intend to lay out several different methods that can be used to achieve best practices on the realization that many companies will need to walk or even crawl before they can run.

Finally, the terms *wholesaler, distributor, manufacturer,* and *vendor* are purposely omitted. The functions that they perform in the distribution pipeline vary greatly. For this reason and to avoid confusion, we use the term *supplier.* However, wholesalers and distributors are in excellent positions to provide the necessary functions and processes discussed as third-party logistics providers.

We will discuss techniques of CAO logic, but not the specifics of hardware devices, system platforms, software packages, or communication options. Although there are discussions of differing formulas, anyone who is not already familiar with mathematics will not be able to "code" a system from the formula explanations. The explanations of formulas are meant for management, system users, and the information services (IS) staff that must investigate software products and design the surrounding systems.

Implementing CAO involves the integration of several software systems and requires changes to in-store procedures. Each of the components requires not only the logic to manage it but also the ability to interface with adjoining systems, improving them if necessary. Additionally, CAO requires changes to key performance indicators by including the store-level inventory and service level in the evaluations.

If all retailers and suppliers used all the latest technology, many of the problems discussed here would never occur. There will, naturally, be tradeoffs over time, since it is impossible to change all methodologies at retail headquarters, suppliers, and the stores overnight. Most retailers will make a long-term plan where they will "live with" certain problems until it is possible to fix them. Some solutions will be temporary means to allow old systems to continue functioning until replaced. For this reason, we will discuss "old fashioned" methodologies as well as newer ones.

We hope this book will help you get started with CAO and help to develop a solid foundation for profitable implementation.

The Art and Science of
Computer Assisted Ordering

CHAPTER 1

The Future of Retail

OVERVIEW

CAO does not exist in a vacuum. It must be integrated into the current retail environment and into the retailer's vision of the future. CAO is a long-term development that can take several years to fully accomplish. The outcome must coincide with the retailer's future objectives.

Each retailer must consider their own vision of the future. Suppliers, software vendors, and consultants are all introducing various approaches to streamline retailing. It is important to understand that each of these approaches is also making an implicit statement about the future. It is equally important to have one's own (flexible) vision when embarking on a project as extensive and long-term as CAO. We don't claim the monopoly on crystal balls, but a brief analysis of current directions may help you form your own ideas.

In this section we discuss three different aspects of the future.

Current Environment is a description of the way things have been. For some retailers it is the way things still are. These are implemented, existing technologies and systems.

Leading Edge is a description of many of the new concepts and technologies. Retailers have implemented some of these systems or are in the process of implementing them.

Future Paradigms are the possible future directions for retail, including:

- Integration of functions
- Dynamic rather than static basis for decision making
- Consumer-based, real-time systems
- Global optimization of logistics
- Top-down strategies, bottom-up information
- New levels of data

CURRENT ENVIRONMENT

Products

Basic Products and Planograms

Initial sets for grocery, drug, and basics are created with planograms. Planograms (shelf management systems) are non-integrated, one-off analyses. That is, planograms are run in a stand-alone environment, one time, and not referred to again until a new season begins or there is an obvious problem. Normally, planogram creation involves a simple forecast using a "selected" period of time during the past year(s). The initial set often defaults to a pack size basis when the pack exceeds the product need (sales demand). POS (point of sale) data provides a history of actual consumer sales. Store demand is derived from the store orders, delivery quantities to the stores, or store receipts. Planograms do not always have the POS data that they require and are at times forced to use store demand. Store planograms are almost always created centrally for the standard store within a store cluster. Actual store-level planograms are rare. There are both management and philosophical problems with store-level plans. The actual control of individual store managers over the stores versus central control is unresolved. Planogram problems and maintenance are identified manually.

Non-basic Products and Planning

The overall merchandise plan provides the initial sales forecast, as well as inventory position for all categories. This sales and inventory forecast then drives the expected receipt flow. CAO drives the flow of goods for basic products within the context of the original merchandise plan. The plannable categories—such as fashion items—are bought and distributed based on the merchandise plan and allocation of non-basic products or non-warehouse items to the stores. Open-to-shop or other allocation methods are driven by the merchandise plan for these effected categories. Planning, like planogramming, is primarily a one-off, non-integrated analysis.

Stores

POS Data

The quality of the POS data varies by retailer, and is often directly related to how much the retailer uses it. Initially, retailers didn't use the POS data themselves, but only sold it. Many retailers could not even bring their POS data to their central computer. Those retailers bringing the data into a central location often only accumulate the data across product lines or stores. In this way, many of the problems of error or "noise" that would be present with store-level data are (rightly or wrongly) ignored. POS data is primarily used centrally by headquarters or suppliers.

Forecasting

Forecasting is used by distribution center replenishment, supplier-managed product lines, labor management, planograms, merchandise planning, store forecasting, and several other retailer systems. Each of these systems has its own separate forecasting module. These forecasting systems use different methods, different sets of data, and rarely interface with each other. They use historical demand, from which seasonality and promotion data is analyzed. Few systems use other factors in the forecast analysis.

Store Perpetual Inventory

Store perpetual inventory—available for use at the store in a timely fashion—is rare to nonexistent for grocery and drug. GM (general merchandise) retailers' perpetual inventory systems are maintained and controlled centrally. These systems are timely on a daily basis. Grocery and drug continue to measure turns, service level, and safety stock at the distribution center as though the retailer was a wholesaler. Grocery and drug measure total store inventory by calculating the dollars in the stores in contrast to GM and specialty retailers who measure their total investment in inventory across the stores and distribution centers. The store P&L (profit and loss statement) for grocery and drug is based on estimates of the stock position.

Consumer Data

Consumer data is primarily demographic data by store cluster obtained through surveys (quantitative analysis), focus groups (qualitative analysis), and government reports. Products are varied in mix and quantity by the store cluster. Merchandisers set assortments by demographic store clusters.

Logistics

There are several generally-accepted classifications of product delivery. These include distribution center (warehouse), DSD (direct store delivery), DSP (direct store purchase), rack jobber, and supplier-managed (partnerships). Once a product line has been identified under one of these delivery methods, it usually takes something just less than an act of God to change to another method. Some retailers are tied to computer systems with separate databases that are based on the product delivery method. Products are overstocked on the retailer shelf, in the distribution center, and at the supplier. Some slow movers are shipped and picked in sellable units (repack), which reduces the inventory at a cost of increased labor.

Distribution Center (Warehouse)

There are two primary methods of ordering to the distribution center.

1. *Manual Ordering.* Store orders are made by reorder clerks who are re-filling the shelf. The reorder clerk uses a hand-held wand device that can scan the tag for the bar-code. Some of these tags also advise the clerk about the target shelf quantity for this product as well as order pack size. The clerk enters the order amount. Some order systems round to pack for the clerk. Some systems expect the order clerk to round the order.

Frequently, when a shelf tag is missing, needed product is not reordered. If a product space has been "faced out" with other product, the clerk may not notice that product is needed. Replenishment orders are sent to the central processor either daily or on a specific store/category schedule. Clerks sometimes bypass certain slow-moving categories on the scheduled days in order to save time. Fast-turn products such as grocery use primarily manual ordering.

2. *Automated Ordering.* Using a store perpetual inventory, the system orders up to a preset or maximum level. The order quantities are usually reviewed either at the store or at headquarters. Automatic ordering is used primarily in slower-turn environments, such as soft goods (clothing, linens, etc.).

Both manual and automatic orders are batched with other stores to maximize distribution center picking cycles and to allocate limited supplies. There are store "available to order" edits. Reasonability edits are made on the order amounts, but there is often a problem establishing completeness of data. Completeness of data ensures that all the stores and the categories within those stores that were expected to order, have indeed placed an order.

The better systems link related bar-codes under one SKU (stock keeping unit). These systems link together substitute SKUs and promotion SKUs with the primary SKU.

When product is insufficient to fulfill the total store orders, there are a variety of allocation routines to decide which stores get how much of the limited product.

New product, some in-and-out product, and some promotion products are "pushed" by the buyers to the stores. Promotion need is difficult to determine. The initial need is often determined by the merchandiser. The merchandiser may or may not have the corporation's historical references. Some promotion data is provided by third-party vendors or the suppliers. Normally, the stores determine the continued needed amount after the initial "push."

Overbuying by the stores or even forward buying by the stores is a continuing problem during promotions. Forward (investment) buying is buying long on discounted product to maximize future non-discount sale profits. Since stores are measured on sales and not on inventory overstock, store personnel err on the side of overstock rather than understock. Automated forecasting is limited by lack of data, and thus it often produces merely a ratio distribution based on store type. Additional forward (investment) product is bought into the distribution center to take advantage of the supplier's reduced cost.

Buys into the distribution center are determined using store order history and time series forecasts. *Most distribution center buy calculations do not take the stores' inventories into consideration.*

Product that is stored in bins (slots) at the distribution center has a fixed designation as warehouse product. Currently, warehouses are thought of primarily as storage centers. Flow-through (cross-dock) is considered an operationally different function from warehousing. (To cross-dock is to deliver product [flow-through] through the warehouse to the stores without the necessity of putting the product away into warehouse bins—therefore, "crossing over the dock" from one delivery vehicle to another.) The distribution of the product is predetermined by the system at order time. These guidelines are set by the assortment plan or by actual store orders. Some retailers find that neither their distribution center construction nor their logistics systems are capable of managing cross-docking.

DSP (Direct Store Purchase)

When a retailer and a supplier determine that product is best delivered by the supplier or a third party directly to the stores, product is set up as DSP or supplier direct. Stores order as they would with distribution center product but either the stores or the central processing system builds the orders to the supplier minimums. (Store personnel may build the orders manually.)

There are two versions of DSP. In one version, central headquarters creates a purchase order for every store and the supplier (or third party) delivers the product directly to the store. The purchase order is created by polling the store orders and combining them centrally. This polling function may or may not be integrated into the ordering system. The buyers often spend time reviewing and redistributing these orders.

In the second version, the orders are created by the stores and sent directly to the suppliers (or through the central system for invoicing but without the need for joining with other orders or buyer review).

In both versions, the supplier responds by delivering the product directly to individual stores (normally on a scheduled delivery cycle). Invoicing is almost always to central headquarters and, depending on the supplier's system and the retailer's systems, invoice matching is a nightmare.

DSD (Direct Store Delivery) and Rack Jobber

Some 25–45% of the product on the grocery retail floor is DSD. Other types of retailers use this method considerably less. DSD product is brought directly to the store by the supplier without a purchase order. Payment is based on the received amount. By definition, the DSD supplier does not place the product on the shelf and the retailer creates the planogram. By definition, the rack jobber places the product on the shelf and creates the display. However, there are many shades of gray between these two definitions, especially where freshness or extreme high sales affect the product.

The DSD receiving system is the key to successful DSD. There are many successful backdoor receiving systems on the market, but not necessarily as many successful installations. There are no forecast routines or suggested orders.

Supplier Partnerships (Managed)

Supplier-managed product lines are forecasted by the supplier from the retailer's data, planned by the supplier, and delivered directly to the retailer by the supplier. In some cases the retailer gives the supplier forecasts instead of demand data. POS data is used for supplier-managed lines delivered direct to the stores. For supplier deliveries to the retailer distribution center, the supplier uses the store orders to the distribution center. The supplier's materials requirement planning (MRP) system uses the information to control its production cycle. Excess inventory storage and handling is reduced from the production cycle.

Communications

Communication between the supplier and the retailer are partially manual and partially automated. Standards of communication exist and third-party suppliers provide the infrastructure, but not all retailers and suppliers have made the investment necessary. Most retailers are communicating partially electronically on some functions with some suppliers. Using all electronic communication functions with all suppliers is rare.

LEADING EDGE

Products

Basic Products and Planograms

Planograms are still a one-off analysis. Planograms are based on POS data at the store or store cluster level. The most advanced of these store-level planogram systems are maintained with a hierarchical logic. Central or district planograms can be modified at lower levels to reflect actual store layouts. Planograms are generally feeding information to other systems such as CAO. The most advanced systems are fully integrated with planogram maintenance determined by forecasting and CAO. Increased attention to store-level planograms, continual monitoring of the planograms, category management, and pack size analysis create ongoing maintenance and analysis of store inventory.

Non-basic Products and Planning

Planning down to the class and subclass level in both dollars and units provides the basis for complete inventory and profitability control. Bottom-up planning is propagated through to the financial and/or management plan. Automating the planning process allows changes to be made quickly and easily. In-season tracking of plan versus actual provides the basis for operational decisions and replanning. Planning is fully integrated into retail operations.

Stores

POS Data

POS data is used for central category management. A passive monitor or the POS system itself accesses the data and makes it available to the individual stores. This data is reviewed by the systems for completeness and reasonability and is used to continually monitor for store-level problems. It can also be used in store-level CAO systems. Because the stores are using the POS data, store procedures are implemented and enforced. Data cleaning formulas insure data quality.

Forecasting

Store demand and promotion forecasts are created for each individual store. Managing of store forecasts is one of the challenges of the new CAO approach. Forecasting formulas begin to use factors besides sales history, but these factors are limited by the ability of the retailer to gather and retain additional information electronically. POS data quality improves due to data cleaning formulas, increased usage, and observed benefits. Sales influences including weather, promotions, pricing, and data about companion and competitive products are used in the forecasting. Although the techniques of forecasting are more sophisticated, retailers still have as many different forecasting methods as they have systems using forecasts.

Promotion history is collected centrally and by store-level electronic devices, including electronic marketing systems. Using promotion, pricing analysis, and forecasting, the system recommends quantities for each store.

Store Perpetual Inventory

Stores keep a perpetual inventory. This requires improved receiving and better controls on the distribution center pick and delivery accuracy, as well as clean POS. Transactions such as transfers, supplies, and damage are recorded in an accurate and timely manner. Store discipline is extremely important. Various hardware/software devices are used to aid store personnel in making the scheduled and exception-based audits required by the system.

Turns, service level, and safety stock are measured at the store as well as at the warehouse.

Consumer Data

Frequent shopper and electronic marketing programs have created the opportunity for micro marketing. The retailer and the supplier are able to direct their marketing efforts at the individual customer. Customer buying habits can be tracked and predicted via the customer database.

Energy is directed toward store-level decision making using store and customer data, but controlling micro merchandising is an unresolved problem for mass retailers.

Logistics

All product for all stores makes use of the same static definitions as explained in the "Current Environment" section. That is, product is warehouse, store direct, or flow-through. The difference for leading-edge retailers is the increase in the supplier-managed lines. Retailers with store-level supplier data can calculate suggested orders for DSD, DSP, and supplier direct orders. Retailers without store supplier databases use a central supplier database or turn these lines over for supplier management. Because of data cleaning and because the stores are using their POS data more, the quality of the POS data provided to the suppliers has improved.

Distribution Center (Warehouse)

Store orders are created by a CAO system using store-level forecasting and the store perpetual inventory. Automated orders are not necessarily reviewed before order fulfillment. Suggested orders are reviewed and released by store personnel before order fulfillment.

Distribution center logistics systems manage flow-through (cross-dock) orders as well as warehoused product. Flow-through is ordered as both pre- and post-distribution.

1. *Pre-distribution.* At the time of ordering, using either an automated ordering system or manual orders, the system produces a supplier order. This order may or may not be palletized by the supplier to meet the store requirements. Pre-palletized product is easier to handle at the dock. The precise definition of cross-dock is pre-palletized flow-through, but in common usage the terms cross-dock and flow-through are used interchangeably.

2. *Post-distribution.* At the time of arrival or arrival notification, the system calculates the product distribution based on current store need and the merchandise plan. Post-distribution product is initially ordered using long-term forecasting. When the delivery arrives at the distribution center, a short-term

forecast and store-need determination is calculated. The product is allocated to the stores accordingly.

DSP (Direct Store Purchase)

DSP and supplier direct orders are electronic and automated. Using CAO systems these orders are automated and controlled from order time through order receipt.

DSD (Direct Store Delivery) and Rack Jobber

DSD suppliers can use POS data in the same fashion as supplier-managed lines. Retailers use their forecasting and perpetual inventory systems to audit the DSD deliveries. Retailers with supplier/store-level files can calculate their own suggested order for their DSD suppliers. In this way DSD become DSP. Calculated forecasts can be used to transmit order quantities to traditional DSD suppliers if there isn't a freshness factor. Alternately, forecast calculations can be used to create an after-the-fact audit on DSD deliveries.

Supplier Partnerships (Managed)

As with DSD suppliers, retailers can audit supplier-managed deliveries using their own store-level forecasting systems. Suppliers have access to improved POS data and to store-level perpetual inventory. Some retailers calculate their own store orders but continue to transmit POS history and promotion data for the supplier's use in production and logistics. Many suppliers still ship to the distribution center but can use cross-dock techniques.

Third-Party Logistics Managers

Third-party logistics managers can, in some cases, take over the management of some supplier lines in specific regions. If they gain a saturation level in a region, they can eliminate the need for warehousing certain lines in these locations. Third-party management varies from simply managing the communications to actually managing the delivery vehicles and the staging warehouses.

Communications

Communications between the supplier and the retailer is standardized, complete, and electronic.

FUTURE PARADIGMS

What is the future of retail? There is a lot of talk about electronic malls, supplier-to-consumer direct sales, and a customer who prefers to stay home and order rather than go to the stores. What percentage of product will be delivered directly to the consumer (bypassing stores altogether), and when will this evolution (or revolution) be completed?

Retailers are told to prepare themselves for two major demands. First, consumers want more than shopping electronically—they want to be second-guessed. They want to be provided with their merchandise before they've even realized they need it. They want systems that mother them, take care of their needs, and even suggest new needs to them.

Second, we are being told that the store must be a satisfying event. If consumers are going to go into a store, it's going to be for a very good reason. Consumers want service, quality, price, and ambiance, all at one location. They want complete shopping and boutique shopping. They want a warehouse of product as well as personalized attention. They want low prices with high variety. Consumers will have no tolerance for an unpleasant or disappointing shopping experience.

We're the first to admit not knowing what percentage of the shopping dollars will bypass stores, or when. We do know that this movement will vary dramatically by industry, product line, and consumer demographics. We also know that as much as people are attracted to the convenience of electronic shopping, we are still social beings who are attracted to social events which can include shopping.

What is interesting and important to us, as we look to the future, is that the requirements to fulfill CAO are a subset of the requirements that are needed to achieve this new version of retail. Demographically rich data and a streamlined delivery pipeline are required to support CAO as well as direct-to-consumer delivery.

Integration of Functions

System integration, the total system approach, is a concept that has been in our vocabulary for more than 20 years. System designers have attempted to produce systems that "did it all." But "doing it all" meant separate systems for the supplier, distribution center, the stores, or headquarters. Even when limited to one segment, there always seemed to be a new technology, a new idea, a new system that was added on later. And these new systems usually sat on different databases, if not different platforms. The last thing the IS (information services, data processing) departments were going to do, when they had time, was to integrate those systems.

The problem lay in the concept of system integration. The function of replenishing product to the stores was treated as a distribution center replenishment system, a store ordering system, a logistics system, and a supplier production system. When we begin to think in terms of functional integration, many systems as we know them change.

For example, forecasting, as a function, is a *single* engine that drives all the systems. Instead of using different forecasting techniques for every system, forecasting is considered one function. As new operations are added, the question is asked: Does this require long- or short-range, item- or class-, store- or region-level forecasting? All the efforts to forecast are concentrated into the same function.

The replenishment function is no longer seen as store replenishment versus warehouse replenishment versus supplier production. The warehouse is defined as a distribution center that may house product. Replenishment is not divided into separate functions on separate platforms. Are we integrating suppliers and retailers? OK, that's the ideal, but there are some philosophical battles to be fought here. (Perhaps alleviated somewhat by the third-party logistics managers.) Supplier/retailer integration depends on the individual supplier and retailer, and is an important component in streamlining the delivery pipeline.

However, without making that quantum leap, we must discuss the integration of replenishment between the retailer's own distribution center and stores. Much emphasis has been placed lately on the partnership of supplier and retailer, but another important change will be a functional integration of the retailer headquarters (and distribution center) and the stores.

Planograms and planning are not just fully integrated but are active and responsive. They are no longer one-off, analytical functions that, once performed, are frozen in time. Planning and planogramming are reactive to changes in store and consumer needs as well as to management strategies. Planning and planogramming react to bottom-up information. The functions of planning and planogramming are central drivers to other operational decisions. Top-down management strategies are implemented through planning and planogramming.

Dynamic Rather Than Static Basis for Decision Making

Dynamic decision making means that both the data and the analysis techniques will be evolving constantly. .

Forecasting will be based on statistical or artificial intelligence methods that can vary and learn over time. Rather than determining the forecasting model at the time the system is initially set up, the system itself can select the best model. AI (artificial intelligence) has the ability to use information over time to become "smarter" about the relationships and effects of the variables.

Order determination and logistics will use flexible delivery methods, times, and amounts. Rather than defining product by its delivery method, the delivery method can be selected on an as-needed basis.

Planogram- and planning-type functions are dynamic rather than static. Planogramming and planning are no longer one-off functions, since there is an ongoing interplay. As bottom-up information changes, planograms and planning replan. As top-down management philosophies change, planning and planogramming extrapolate that information into the operational functions.

Consumer-Based, Real-Time Systems

POS data is used at store-level and in real-time (up to the minute). Consequently, store-level procedures are strictly monitored and enforced. Consumer-targeted marketing plays an increasing role in promotion planning and promotion forecasting. As ordering is automated and store forecasting improved, both the supplier and the retailer will use POS history rather than store orders in product need determinations, product space utilization and mix, order generation, pricing and promotion, and replenishment.

Real-time perpetual inventory and sales data are used to monitor the stores. This data can be used in the stores, at the store cluster, and centrally. Electronic devices—such as hand-held devices, electronic shelf tags, and portable computers—direct store personnel to the audit area and can be used to transmit corrections. Real-time, store-level POS and perpetual inventory systems monitor inventory and personnel problems. In essence these systems become electronic store managers, communicating problems to store personnel.

Consumer data bases, created from frequent shopper cards and other electronic marketing approaches, may remain jealously guarded by the retailer. These data bases describe individual shopping behavior, and can be used to create programs for both store and direct merchandising. By understanding both the existing consumer base and the area demographics, retailers determine the customer base they are not attracting and can structure their merchandising accordingly.

It isn't clear whether the future of bypassing the stores by delivering product directly to the consumers' home and office will be controlled by the supplier or the retailer, or a partnership of the two. It is clear that these demographically-rich consumer data bases will be the key to both consumer-direct sales and consumer-relevant store merchandising.

Global Optimization of Logistics

Logistics systems have traditionally been limited to optimizing deliveries within very limited, defined structures. Analyzing delivery methods was usually done up-front as the product line was first assigned to the system. Therefore, every product had a designated delivery method. Logistics of the future will be a global optimization based on multiple stores, multiple sources, and multiple delivery methods.

The concept of a warehouse as a storage location is gone, and warehouses are redefined as distribution centers. Product delivery methods are dynamic rather than static. The system would dynamically define product as slotted, flow-through, or direct delivery. That is, product can be delivered in the most effective way for the quantity of product needed. The logistics systems use the stores' perpetual inventory, store planogram, store/supplier data, and store forecasts to decide when and how much to order for the stores and how that product is to be delivered. The order size is maximized. Product can be brought directly to the stores during high season (with safety stock in the distribution center) and brought through the distribution center as flow-through during low season. Not all stores define all the product the same way. Stores take advantage of their proximity to supplier distribution points. Actual product delivery may be the function of third-party logistic managers or improved retail systems.

The logistics system must be dynamic enough to evaluate store forecast and store stock level, and then decide when and how to order and deliver the product to the store. It also decides how to allocate limited or unallocated flow-through, and which stores, seasons, or orders should be supplier-managed.

Top-Down Strategies, Bottom-Up Information

In recent years, much energy has been devoted to the concepts of micro marketing and micro merchandising. This has been assumed to be harmonious with bottom-up decision making. But there is another side to this equation. Corporate strategies of mass merchandisers personify the retailer to the consumer. This personality identity is of central import to bringing the consumer into the retailer's many outlets. Store look, merchandise mix, service level, and pricing philosophies are determined at corporate and modified at region and store level. This requires the ability to filter corporate philosophies from the top while using bottom-up information, such as consumer and store data. Corporate philosophies are defined, cost-analyzed by the system, and driven down through all the appropriate functions. This requires a functionally integrated system which can understand and use corporate strategies throughout the operational systems. One approach is to extend the definition of planning and planogramming to include the task of extrapolating top-down decisions into operational functions.

How important is this? Which systems are affected if management decides to eliminate products it defines as extreme slow movers? The planning, planogram, forecasting, and replenishment systems are all affected. What if management plans to deemphasize designer women's clothes in future advertising and begin emphasizing medium-priced women's business clothes? Again, all of these systems must react to this directional change.

But can these management decisions really be quantified? Yes, they can and should. Too often, management makes decisions that are quantified at lower levels and implemented without analysis of the total impact on costs. What types of decisions does management make that should be quantified and extended operationally? The most fundamental of these decisions is store size and variations on store size. This translates into costs, ROI (return on investment) on space, facings, and a myriad of other store layout and merchandising decisions. Other examples include:

- The stores will keep all (by rank) products in top shelf reserve
- Aisle width will be narrow/wide (actual size)
- Presentation stock for planogram product will be three units per facing, etc.
- Shelf height or shelf depth in our B stores will be _____
- Pricing will be based on obtaining a target ROI, will be low cost based on a given calculation, will be low cost only on A items, etc.
- Weeks-of-supply for planning, order point, or safety stock will be "X"

New Levels of Data

Currently systems are thought of as store-level or headquarters. There are normally reporting levels of regional and district management. These reporting levels often receive information in an ad hoc fashion. "Here's a new store report. Should we give copies to Joe, the district manager?" "This exception report is going to the merchandisers. Should we give a copy to the store operations?"

Channels of input and output must be created between stores and head-quarters management. When we consider the importance of extending top-down decisions throughout the operational functions, we realize that this will include information that comes in from the region, district, and store cluster.

What, specifically, do these new retail paradigms mean for CAO? CAO will be impacted by bottom-up information, including:

- Consumer data base
- Store layouts and planograms
- Store perpetual inventory
- POS
- Store forecasts
- Detail cost factors

CAO will be implemented by management strategies, including:

- Store look
- Merchandise mix
- Service level
- Presentation stock
- Pricing strategies

Operational functions will be implemented from top-down business strategies and impacted by bottom-up realities. Forecasting and order determination will be dynamic models based on both bottom-up data and top-down decisions.

Logistics will be dynamic, streamlining the flow of goods from supplier to consumer. These functions will be fully integrated across the retailer and will include the supplier. One-off, analytical functions such as planning, planogramming, and category management will become integrated into the functional operations.

CHAPTER 2

The Retail Environment

OVERVIEW

All CAO implementations are different, but all CAO projects should have the same starting point: defining the retail environment. There is absolutely no reason to buy software until after defining your own needs and philosophies. This chapter will help you define your philosophies, merchandise mix, product and promotion characteristics, and ordering strategies. In Appendix B, there is a sample worksheet for you to analyze departments within your company. Use the information in this chapter and these worksheets to identify the problems that your company must resolve. Subsequent chapters will refer to your findings in explaining the forecasting and order determination formulas.

This chapter enables you to define the environment before studying the various strategies in later chapters. As we explore these options, it will be clear that many different approaches will work. What is important is to select the most applicable methods for your products and suppliers.

There are important reasons for making clear definitions of these top-down business strategies.

1. *Minimum costs are measurable.* Once defined, store look, aesthetic minimum, and consumer service level have measurable costs of doing business. Using fully integrated systems, the "ripple down" costs can be estimated before being implemented. Currently, major decisions about weeks-of-supply and presentation stock which drive order determination and forecasting are often made without guidance.

2. *There is a measurable goal for the CAO system.* CAO is bringing inventory as low as possible and turns as high as possible *within the boundaries set by management.* As we will discuss later in this chapter, this is quite different from the concept of the lowest inventory to satisfy sales expectations.

3. *The consumer has consistent expectations from the retailer.* Many discussions of CAO emphasize:

- Using POS sales, planning, and ordering decisions that are consumer sales–driven
- Using store demographics and smart card technologies, marketing decisions that are consumer-targeted

- Using store-level layouts and planograms, merchandising decisions that are store-specific

This bottom-up information is imperative for successful CAO. What is often overlooked in today's discussions is that the retailer's image is set at the corporate level and that merchandising, store look, and pricing philosophies drive business functions. There is a balance and partnership between central management philosophies and bottom-up information. Consumers require a clear perception of the retailer selection and pricing and a continuity from store to store. This is achieved by propagating central philosophies throughout the total system.

MERCHANDISING PHILOSOPHY

To get started with CAO, you need to have an understanding of key merchandising components—including store look, merchandising mix, and expected consumer service levels. For every retailer, these components can and do vary greatly depending on individual marketing strategies and positioning efforts. For this reason, we can't advise you on how many SKUs (stock keeping units) to carry, for example, or what service levels should be for specific products. But we can give you a framework that will help you define and achieve corporate merchandising goals.

Setting a store to optimize costs is very different from setting a store for merchandising. We're talking a difference between art and science here. The art of merchandising is to create the store look, merchandise mix, and acceptable service level using various tools—including computer systems. *The science of CAO, on the other hand, is to deliver product as efficiently as possible in order to provide for management's merchandising philosophy.*

Note: Although we are discussing CAO as a replenishment method, shouldn't a CAO system deliver reports for management review? Absolutely! These reports analyze the profitability of the merchandising philosophies and are an integral part of CAO. They warn management about potential problem areas, *but they don't change merchandising philosophies.*

After all, retailing is not just about efficiency and mathematics, but about attracting customers. An efficient, low-inventory store without customers is not a successful store.

Everyone who has been in retail for a day and a half has heard about the 80%–20% rule: 80% of the sales result from 20% of the product. In traditional, high-variety retailers, this is generally true. What isn't often mentioned are the other equally interesting rules. For instance, 60% of the sales result from 10% of the product; the 40%–4% rule; and the 20%–1% to 2% rule. This means much of the product in traditional high-variety stores is not going to be sold today, tomorrow, this week, or possibly even this month. Much of the product at the average high-variety retailer is for creating the store look.

When the discounters reduced inventories to only the fast-moving 20% and reduced prices accordingly, they created a unique problem and opportunity for retailers still offering variety. Discounters satisfied the customer's desire for low price, but not variety. Customers still wanted variety but now they didn't want to pay as much for it. Among high-variety retailers, cutting costs through efficiency in operations and more careful merchandise management surged in importance. However, efficiency alone cannot erase the fact that carrying variety and presenting a full store look simply costs more money than not carrying variety.

What does this 20%–80% rule mean to CAO? It means that probably 50% to 80% of the product is purchased for reasons other than immediate store sales, and CAO is purchasing product for other than strictly store sales.

Before we proceed too deeply into the mathematics of CAO, let's look at the "cost reduction scientist's" perfect store. The perfect store would be set only with product that was needed to sell in the immediate future. Probably only 10% to 25% of the product would have a traditional "full shelf look."

The "pure scientist" would negotiate extended payment terms resembling consignment sales, and pallets and packs sized and mixed for each store. Much more product would be shipped in retailer packs rather than warehouse packs. For the really high-variety retailers with multiple stores in one geographic location, the "pure scientist" would just put a picture of the product on the shelf (or in the catalogue or electronic mall) and keep limited product in a central staging area.

The store would look barren by today's standards, possibly of both product and customers. Profit is sales minus cost. When we try to optimize results solely by cutting costs, we use only half the equation. Since the "pure scientist" can't affect sales, all of the optimization is aimed at cost. As the store becomes less attractive, a death spiral is created as fewer and fewer customers require less product until the retail doors are permanently closed.

Merchandising is the other half of the equation. There are, in some ways, built-in conflicts between merchandising and the cost of inventory. Consider a grocer carrying a large assortment of jams and jellies, where 60% to 80% of the flavors are classified as slow movers. Yet it is this high variety that attracts the consumer to shop with this retailer. *CAO helps you keep an eye on these conflicts, allowing you to implement your business philosophy.*

That is why it is so important to understand the corporate strategies for store look, merchandise mix, and service level. These philosophies are seeking to create a satisfied and loyal customer base.

This leads to the question: When is the customer satisfied or dissatisfied? There is no correct and universal answer. The answers vary by retailer, market positioning, and product category. *We do know that consumers expect their experience at the store to match their expectations based on their perceptions of the retailer's image. Establishing clear strategies provides a uniform retail image and a mathematically measurable base on which CAO can build solutions.*

Let's look at the individual components of a merchandising philosophy:

- store look
- merchandise mix
- service level

Store Look

What makes a store attractive to a customer? The answer differs by planogram and non-planogram product. The aesthetic minimum is the minimum amount needed to create the desired consumer appeal. This aesthetic minimum is also known as presentation stock.

Planogram Product

A planogram is a mathematical approach optimizing the use of space based on projected sales and ROI for one category, class, or subclass. Because pack (shipment units) often exceeds store need, the planogram is often based on the pack size rather than on store sales. Planogram systems vary, particularly in their use of ROI analysis and whether the plan is made centrally or at store level. However, most have user-defined constraints of minimum facings, minimum weeks-of-supply, shelf depth, and space available. Planograms select the number of facings based on the product and the depth (number of units per facing) of the shelf. User-defined constraints, central planogram creation, and product pack cause these systems to create more facings than are required for actual customer demand.

What is the minimum presentation stock to create the desired store look? One, two, three units per facing? At what point does the store begin to look understocked? Often one unit per facing looks like the product is not actually available. Does this vary by size of the product? Large product may not need as much depth as small product for the shelf to look full.

Does presentation stock vary by the number of facings per SKU? Planogram product is normally defined as one SKU per facing. If the product has four or five facings, does it require less presentation? Not necessarily, since the look created by thin settings is the same whether the product has one facing or 10 facings.

Does the product depth vary by the SKU rank? SKU rank is the mathematical division of products into fastest movers, medium movers, slower movers, and very slow movers by unit or dollar sales. Is a hole on the shelf—any hole—unacceptable? Is it all right to have holes on the shelves for slow- and very slow-moving products? Be careful here. It's a convincing argument that a few holes on slow-moving items are not a problem. But not when you begin to consider that over half the products in the high-variety store are probably slow movers, and empty shelves on the slow movers create the impression that this retailer is about to go out of business.

What is your corporate philosophy for presentation stock? Your corporate philosophy for presentation stock may never have been articulated. The company president, however, can be counted upon to clearly articulate this philosophy to you if a CAO implementation puts the presentation stock below desired levels. That's just one of the reasons why it's important to first state the corporate philosophy for the store look and minimum shelf fill. This will also give you a look at the costs inherent in your plan, allowing you to make adjustments ahead of time.

For planogram product, stating the presentation stock policy may be as simple as "the minimum is three units per facing." It may be "three units per facing for my A and B rank items, but only one unit per facing for the C, D, and E rank items." Of course, policy can vary by department, product size, number of facings, item rank, cost of product, or a number of other factors.

Non-Planogram Product

Non-planogram product often does not have a one-SKU-per-facing relationship. Therefore, an out-of-stock does not cause the look of an empty shelf. Only when all the product that shares the space on the shelf is out of stock is there an empty look. That is not to say that an out-of-stock doesn't create an unhappy customer. Customer service level and store look are considered separately here. Although both concepts play a role in determining the minimum product in the store, store look creates the aesthetics minimum and service level creates the sales minimum. *The aesthetic minimum for non-planogram product is based on the entire category, not just a single SKU.* A clearly articulated store look philosophy is the acceptable minimum presentation of planogram and non-planogram product.

Merchandise Mix

The merchandise mix sets the tone for the retailer, and is designed to attract a targeted customer base. It provides the product definition to meet the expected customer need. Merchandise mix is uniquely related to the "image and look" that you are trying to establish. The relationship among different categories of product is a key element of the overall merchandise plan and the assortment plan. The basic assortment, fashion impact, and seasonal product flow are all ingredients of the mix dimension.

There is a big difference between the retailer who carries only the top 20% of items and the retailer who is carrying full variety with depth in each category. The term high-variety retailer refers to retailers who carry depth of assortment within a category, not retailers who carry a high variety of product categories with little depth. Category depth can include multiple brands, sizes, colors, fragrances, flavors, price ranges, and/or ingredients. It is possible for a retailer to have a limited number of categories and still be a high-variety retailer. Variety of categories does not create the in-store sales cannibalization that depth within a category creates. In-store sales cannibalization occurs when the consumer desire for product is limited but the options and assortments are substantial.

Examples of high-variety categories include a large assortment of soups or yogurts, multiple color choices of turtleneck sweaters, or multiple brands of toaster ovens. Consumers may buy extra soups because they are attracted to the choices, but if the soups are not on price reduction, consumers will not buy more soup than what meets their immediate needs.

Yogurt varieties can attract a consumer to eat yogurt more frequently and on more occasions, for breakfast, snack, dessert, and dieting. The shelf life of yogurt (or with frozen yogurt, limited home freezer space) prevents the consumer from buying in excess. At some point the various yogurt flavors and brands cannibalize each other's sales.

Turtleneck sweaters may be presented in a selection of colors that entices the consumer to purchase extras, especially if they are offered in multiple units for one special price. However, depending on the retail price, the consumer may only buy one sweater, and the variety cannibalizes its own sales.

A large toaster oven selection may be the reason the consumer shops this store, but the consumer will buy only one toaster oven. So the toaster oven assortment is both the merchandising draw and the sales cannibalization.

Product such as five-pound bags of sugar only cannibalize, and multiple brands do not increase sales although they often provide the store buyer more opportunity to obtain products at reduced prices. Therefore, the consumer may buy sugar from this retailer because of pricing, but all the sugar sales are a cannibalization by each other.

There is some sales cannibalization across categories, such as between fresh and prepared foods. This type of cannibalization is the most difficult to track. The retailer may not even realize it is happening.

You can offer product depth in a single brand within a category, or depth with several brands or price ranges within a category. It is possible to appear high-variety to the consumer by extending one brand into all possible configurations, but limiting the other brands to a limited assortment. For example, in gourmet ice cream, both the sales demand and the retailer freezer space may limit the amount of product, but all flavors of one brand and the top flavors of the other popular brands tell the customer you can always find your favorite brand here and you can always find your favorite flavor (just not necessarily your favorite flavor in your favorite brand).

These differences translate into very different approaches not only to CAO but to service level, safety stock, forecasting, and ordering. There is probably nothing more difficult to forecast than a category with heavy in-store cannibalization caused by promotion and pricing variances. Forecasting of individual products depends on reliable sales history. In-store cannibalization makes the sales patterns difficult to discern. If we look back at the five-pound bag of sugar example, we see that total category demand is divided with one-third to the house brand, one-third to the national brand, and one-third to the cheapest that day. If the cannibalization is between many products in one category, actual demand shifts with price and promotion activities. If cannibalization occurs across categories (or departments), category managers may not even realize that their sales are about to be impacted from within their own retail outlet.

CAO implementation and strategies depend heavily on the merchandise mix. CAO benefits will be limited by the system's ability to manage the problems created by the merchandise mix.

Service Level

Service level is the percentage of time product is in stock for the customer. What we forget much of the time is that a 90% service level translates to a potential 10% out-of-stock rate. At the store, this means that when the consumer desires to buy this product, it won't be available 10% of the time (lost sales).

Service level measured at the consumer level is very different from service level measured at the distribution center. A distribution center out-of-stock does not necessarily have a direct relationship to a dissatisfied customer. Usually when product is ordered from the stores to the distribution center, there is still product on the store shelf. Products may be below the aesthetic minimum in the store but still have sufficient product for several ordering cycles. The store buyer may be annoyed when the distribution center does not fulfill the store's orders. However, the consumer is content with the service level, since there was a relatively high stock level on the shelf when the store buyer placed the initial order. (Remember, facings, pack, and presentation stock create a minimum set that can be well above consumer demand.)

An out-of-stock on a particular product in the store does not necessarily translate to a dissatisfied customer, either. Service level for the consumer may or may not be by individual item. In some situations the consumer readily takes another similar product. Is it acceptable to be out of one brand if another brand is in stock? Is it acceptable to be out of one size if another size is in stock? Is it acceptable to have less than 100% of all the available colors, fragrances, or flavors?

You can see why clearly stated corporate philosophy on service level is required. The most basic definition of service level says that this product, brand, size, color, or fragrance must be in stock X% of the time or my customer will be dissatisfied. High-variety retailers carry multiple sizes, brands, fragrances, and/or colors of the same product. When is service level by a product group and when is it by an individual item? Only by understanding the customer and the product can the question of substitution on service level be answered.

Does service level vary by item sales rate (item rank)? At store level is it as important to be in-stock on the slow mover items as it is on the fast movers? What are the consumer expectations?

Does service level for your consumers depend on your ability to fulfill the customer's desire rapidly? If the blue dress isn't available in a size six but you have on-line computer access to the inventories of your other stores, is your customer satisfied if you have the dress to her house on next day delivery? Is she satisfied if you must "call around to the other stores but you'll be sure to get back to her by Tuesday?" Is individual store service level dependent on the quality and access to perpetual inventories? Which products will the customers wait to buy and which products sell primarily as impulse buys? *By definition, no one waits to buy an impulse item.*

Does service level vary by product category, season, or promotion? The only acceptable service level during a promotion is 100%. The acceptable service level at the start of a season and at the height of the season is very different from the desired service level at season end. Depending on the type of season, consumer expectation at season-end may be accelerated or complacent. A clearly articulated service level philosophy is necessary by product, category, season, and so on.

A clear definition of the merchandising philosophies creates a clear problem definition for CAO and a measurable cost of inventory. Once the store look, merchandising mix, and service level are clearly stated, they can be analyzed for a cost of inventory. Once cost of inventory is established, it is important to recognize that this cost will not be eliminated through operational efficiencies. When these corporate philosophies are implemented, there is a measurable cost of the sales minimum.

CAO and other operational efficiencies bring down the costs of *supplying* the aesthetic and sales minimums, but they do not eliminate the cost of *carrying* the aesthetic and sales minimums. CAO can reduce the overstock supporting the store look, merchandise mix, and service level, but CAO will not take the inventory costs lower than the minimums. CAO can and does analyze and report on the cost of carrying these minimums, but it should not and does not dynamically change basic merchandising philosophies.

PRODUCT

As important as understanding the corporate philosophies is the understanding of characteristics of various products. The ideal CAO system for a book retailer will not solve the problems of a drug retailer. Product characteristics vary by retailer and category of product. As you read this section, analyze your own retail environment. You may need to consider each department separately. This foundation is necessary to determine which forecasting and order determination strategies are appropriate for you.

Product Types

Basic products are individual items that are carried year-in and year-out. They may be affected by trends, business cycles, seasons, and promotions, but there is a measurable sales history. These items include cans of corn, men's white shirts, aspirin, and diapers. They can be highly seasonal, such as nutmeg, Christmas tree tinsel, spring garden fertilizer, and cough syrup—as long as the product and the season repeat every year.

Non-basic products are within categories that are carried year after year, but the individual items are always different. They are controlled in plannable categories via a merchandise planning system. Plannable categories have trends, seasons, and measurable sales history at the category level. They include fashion, cosmetics, bedding, plants, and holiday decor. The product can be similar but the fashion, color, or pattern changes in popularity, such as decorative paints or linens.

One-time only products are strictly merchandising in-and-outs for a current consumer interest or a special supplier offer. This may be product that never existed before and may never exist again, such as items associated with a local sports team's championship. Local special attractions such as a major sports event (World Cup soccer, track and field finals) create a one-time opportunity to sell related products. One-time only product can also be product not normally carried at this outlet, but purchased because a one-time buy opportunity is too attractive to ignore.

There are important questions to ask about these product types. The answers affect the type of forecasting and service level expectations that should be selected.

Within basic products, *how many items actually own their history?* How many items have reliable history that represents this item in the same format and without variable packaging or presentation? When product UPCs (EANs) are redefined in the headquarters' systems, when and how is the history reassigned? (UPC is universal product code. EAN is European article number. They represent the product bar-code.) When products are repackaged or reconstituted but the UPC (EAN) is not changed, does the existing history still pertain?

How many items have a sales history that exists without the influences of other similar products sharing in their demand for this item? The answer varies considerably by the amount of variety carried within the category. High-variety categories normally have in-store cannibalization of sales. The more selections customers have, the more likely they are to select an alternate choice. Some products (and this varies by geographic region) have tremendous brand loyalty. Other products are completely price sensitive. Most products are somewhere in between. Brand loyalty and price sensitivity play an important role in forecasting.

Where there is a variety of colors, flavors, or fragrances, the consumer may change buying habits on whim. A low price or an out-of-stock of one product can affect the sales pattern of its competitive offering. Multiple offerings such as multiple flavors of one product may increase the consumers' purchases of that product or simply cannibalize the sales of an already saturated market.

Reasons why products may not "own" their sales history include:

- In-store cannibalization (products that fight for a single customer purchase)
- Price sensitivity (products where consumers buy the least expensive choice)
- Category depth (multiple choices of brands, sizes, colors, fragrances, flavors)
- Repackaged and redesigned products (product loses its history by changing the consumer appeal of the packaging without changing the bar-code)
- Disconnected SKU and bar-code (the headquarters database is not properly coordinating the multiple bar-code assignments to the central SKU)

The answers to the above questions may differ by individual department and will help you select your approach to forecasting strategies.

Major Sales Factors

What are the major factors affecting consumer sales? What is the role of weather, news reports, promotions, and price? These sales factors are discussed in detail in Chapter 5. For now, we'll just list the potential factors for you to review in relation to your own product. Some of the factors relate to individual stores or clusters of demographically- or geographically-related stores. Other factors are more relevant to the type of product. Why product is or isn't selling must be reviewed in the light of *all* potential influences. Using the sample worksheet in Appendix B, try to rate these sales factors based on their influence to sales. Which factors are electronically and historically saved?

These are some of the major sales influences.

Store influences

Competitive store openings and closings

Companion store openings and closings

Street repairs and traffic volumes

Impediments or improvements to transportation

Weather

Labor unrest

   Competitive store labor unrest

   Competitive density

Store layouts

   Store traffic flow

   Product positioning

   Shelf height

   Facings

   Hanging and table products

   Number of locations within store

Corporate influences

   Major marketing strategies and promotions

   Pro or adverse press

   Merchandising strategies

Overall business and cyclical economic influences

   Overall business climate

   Cyclical economic influence

   Merchandise strategies

Product influences

   Errors

   Trends

   Seasons

   Stocking level

   Pricing

   Promotions and advertising (see also "Promotion Influences" in Chapter 5)

   Brand loyalty

   Product repackaging

   Adverse and positive news stories

   Appearance

   Fashion

Item relationships

   Companion marketing

   In-store cannibalization

   Shared bar-codes across single SKU

   Shared items across department

   Bonus pack

   Special ads/holiday pack

Set sales

Catalytic sales

Demographics

Brand loyalty

Purchasing power

Shopping habits and preferences

Age

Education

Family size

Ethnic background

Sex

Income

These sales factors do not apply with the same weight to every retailer. Some may have little or no bearing on sales at some stores. The first step is to identify the sales factors that have a role in your product sales. The second step is to determine if these factors are electronically captured and stored. If so, has this process been consistent? And finally, have these factors been quantified, or is the data simply free-form? (Some of this information is provided by third-party suppliers, such as the data on weather and promotions.)

MAJOR ORDERING FACTORS

In Chapter 6, we will present several different ordering strategies. It is necessary to first define your current ordering and supplier environment. All of the ordering strategies work, but not all will work in your environment.

Is the product available product or requested product? *Available product is continuously and readily available to the retailer. It can be ordered when the retailer needs it and the retailer can depend on supply.*

CAO normally assumes that most product is available product and attempts to order product on an as-needed basis. We must recognize, however, that not all product is available product and if we wait to order, there may very well be no product available for ordering.

Product that is not available product is requested product. *Commodity-based products, imported products, fashion, and highly seasonal items require advanced planning, purchasing, and possibly early delivery.*

Weather-based seasons often require early store set-ups to be in a merchandising position for the earliest possible season start. Complete CAO provides for both available product and requested product.

CAO forecasts and manages orders, optimizes ordering and logistics, and analyzes the process. With requested product there are no ordering choices and, therefore, no possibilities to optimize the ordering process. There is, however, category forecasting, planning, order management, and analysis that can be used to coordinate and manage inventory.

Order and logistics optimization relies on flexible ordering options and supplier reliability. Supplier reliability includes reliable: lead times, purchase order fulfillment, costing, and carrier dependability. Your ability to analyze supplier reliability plays an important role in successful CAO.

What are your major ordering factors?

Suppliers

- Who and where are the product suppliers? Are these products supplied from several regional distribution centers? Are the products imports?
- Are there alternate suppliers? Are there alternate sources for this product, as with commodity-type products? Are there wholesalers, distributors, or third-party logistics suppliers providing this product in your area?
- What role are the suppliers currently playing in the product logistics, and what role do they want to play? Does the supplier have supplier partner relationships? Have you been approached to work with the supplier more closely?
- Which product is available product and which is requested product? Requested product uses very different ordering logic than available product.

Commodity based products	Requested
Imported products	Requested (normally)
Highly seasonal products	Requested (normally)
Fashion	Requested (normally)
Turn product	Available

Logistics

- What role do the suppliers take in the product logistics, and what role do they want to play? Are the suppliers partnering? Are they delivering direct to the stores? Do they palletize by store?
- What role do third parties take in the product logistics, and what role do they want to play? Are third-party logistics providers in the area?
- Who are the carriers and what are the delivery methods? Is delivery on your own vehicles, the supplier vehicle, or independent carrier? Can your system track carrier performance?
- What is relationship of order size to supplier/carrier minimums? Are the stores struggling to meet minimums? Is the distribution center struggling to meet minimums? What are the minimums based on? Are they negotiable?
- Are delivery times fixed days? Does the supplier require fixed delivery days? Why?

- What are the lead times? Are there variable lead times? Are the lead times dependable? Do you measure lead time dependability? Can you discern the difference between supplier lead time problems, carrier delivery problems, and lead time variability caused by your own distribution center rescheduling? do you have supplier-to-store lead times?

- Where are the suppliers? How many distribution centers are there? What is the relationship of the stores to the supplier distribution centers? What is the relationship of the retailer distribution center to the supplier distribution center?

- What is the dependability of the suppliers and carriers? Are delivery time and order fulfillment tracked?

- How much extra product are you ordering for full truck? What is the effect of LTL (less than truckload)?

- What are the opportunities to cross-dock? Can your ordering system handle cross-dock? Can your distribution center system handle cross-dock? Can the physical layout of your distribution center handle cross-dock?

Pack

- What is the relationship of pack to product turn? Are other pack sizes available? Can ordering units be dynamic? Supplier pack versus retailer pack?

Pack is the number of units that are shipped to the stores. If there are twenty-four tubes of toothpaste in a case and the supplier ships only in full cases, one orderable case of toothpaste will provide the store with twenty-four sellable tubes. If the retailer distribution center or a third-party logistics provider intervenes and decides to ship individual tubes to the stores instead, the store orderable unit now is one sellable unit. Often both the distribution center and the supplier are able to offer multiple sizes of orderable units, but are restrained by the retailer ordering and inventory systems.

Ordering and delivery methods are presented in later chapters. Substantial benefits are possible with well-designed logistics. In this section you have defined your starting position. You can use the checklists provided in Appendix B before going forward to define (by department if necessary) your current retail environment. *A successful CAO implementation is not about picking the "best" formulas; it is about selecting the most appropriate strategies for your environment.*

CHAPTER 3

System Overview

In this book we will look at the individual components of CAO and the integration of CAO into the total system. Each component is necessary to implement CAO, but each component can be implemented independently with its own system integration and benefits. CAO should not be viewed as stand-alone and separated from other systems and procedures.

The four main system components are:

- Perpetual inventory
- Forecasting
- Order determination
- Logistics

Perpetual inventory is an actual reflection in units and dollars of the product at single retail location. Perpetual inventory is updated by POS, receiving, transfers, supplies, and returns.

Forecasting is the engine that drives not only CAO but also planograms, labor management, merchandise and assortment planning, and allocation. Forecasting is the ability to analyze current data and use history to identify patterns and predict future sales. Forecast modules use sales history as a base, with a selection of other factors that influence the sales rate.

Order determination is the stand-alone, store-level calculation of how much product to order (and when) for a specific retail location. Order determination includes product need determination, order generation, and order management.

Logistics is the global optimization of multiple sources, multiple destinations, multiple costs, and multiple methods of delivery. Logistics is the ability to deliver product to the right place at the right time, in the right quantity and at the most effective cost for both the supplier and the retailer. This section provides a discussion of the integration of purchase order generation into logistics.

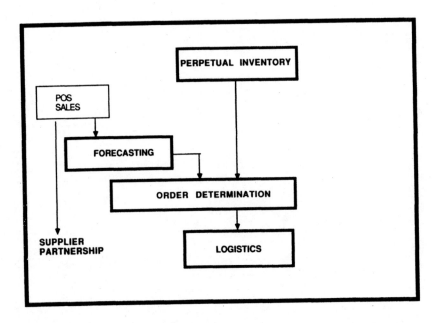

Each component is a replaceable module in the CAO structure. Each component also has its own system interfaces and benefits that relate to functions other than CAO. Part of the full implementation of a CAO system is to decide which modules will be implemented in which order, and when a simple module will be used as a stop-gap measure or stepping stone. A CAO implementation strategy includes the improvement, enhancement, and/or integration of these interface systems. Each module can and should be cost justified on its own merits as well as being a part of the overall CAO implementation (see Appendix C).

Implementing CAO involves the integration of several software systems and requires changes to in-store procedures. Each of the components requires not only the logic to manage the component but also the interfacing with and, if necessary, improvement of, adjoining systems.

CHAPTER 4

Store Perpetual Inventory

OVERVIEW

Store perpetual inventory is an accurate picture of a store's product on hand. All changes to inventory, increases and decreases, apply to a base inventory initiated through a physical count. Perpetual inventory can represent both a quantitative and a financial picture of a store and is a statement of the store condition.

Depending on product type, the store perpetual inventory can be real-time, with all increments and decrements applying immediately, daily, or weekly. Store perpetual inventory systems may exist on the store platform, headquarters platform, and/or at a third-party site. Perpetual inventories can be used in daily store management for immediate problem resolution.

A shadow perpetual inventory exists when a third party, such as a supplier, keeps a store perpetual inventory using *assumptions* of actual increments and decrements. A shadow perpetual inventory is normally an off-site attempt to mirror receipts and sales in a particular category. This is necessary when the supplier is making the order determination and the retailer does not have an accurate and available perpetual inventory. The shadow perpetual inventory cannot provide the benefits of an actual perpetual inventory.

The location and system that maintains the perpetual inventory is less important than the usefulness of the system to the stores. Since the majority of the procedures necessary to manage perpetual inventory are at store level, the majority of the benefits should also be at store level. This means that perpetual inventory must be thought of as an independent function, not just an "adjunct" to store ordering. A warehouse perpetual inventory would never be considered a mere adjunct to ordering, but store perpetual inventories are often treated indifferently. *Many unsuccessful implementations of CAO can be attributed directly to the lack of attention to the perpetual inventory.*

COMPONENTS

There are three main components to a store perpetual inventory system:

- Initial physical count
- Increments and decrements
- Audits

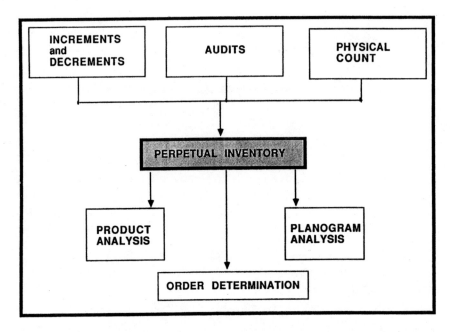

Although the perpetual inventory is a key component of CAO and order determination, this is not its only function. The perpetual inventory provides important input and audit controls to forecasting, planograms, and product and category analysis.

Initial Physical Count

The initial physical count can be made by store personnel, trained corporate personnel, the supplier, or a third party hired specifically to make these counts. Blind counts discourage counters from "eyeballing" the section rather than completing an accurate count. Blind counts are made without knowing the system-calculated balance on hand. The count can also be made as a part of initial store planograms.

Products situated in multiple locations, either in the retail selling space or in reserve locations, may be difficult to locate and count. It helps to use floor plan systems that identify all the planogram locations in the store in conjunction with portable hardware devices that identify alternate sites.

Eliminating and/or locating as much reserve product as possible before the count is always helpful. Since reserve storage is often not well organized, the same product may be located on several shelves and behind other products in the reserve area.

Store planograms and floor layouts can be used to organize and audit the counting process. Initial counts and audit counts have a natural affinity with the planogram function. Initial category sets are a good time to take inventory. Portable electronics (hand-held devices, electronic shelf tags, portable computers) can order the count into planogram sequence.

Products that vary only by flavor, color, size, or fragrance are difficult to count. These products often only vary slightly in appearance. These can include products such as flavored sodas, jams and jellies, soups, jeans, and t-shirts. If the merchandise is set as one item per facing, product should be moved into its correct location before counting. Managing the counting process or paying for the counting process based solely on the units counted per hour encourages carelessness in these "lookalike" sections.

For many specialty retailers, there is a one-for-one relationship between the SKU and the UPC (EAN). That is, there is only one bar-code representing one product. For many retailers such as grocers and drug stores, however, there are many bar-codes representing one product. Accurate counts depend on the retailer's ability to relate these multiple bar-codes to the single product.

The timing of the count, count audit, and the entry of the count into the system is extremely time-sensitive. No increments or decrements can be made without reconciliation. The system can be used to make reasonability checks as audit counts are entered. Sections are recounted that fail the audit check— which is the physical count compared to expected balance on hand. Portable data terminals communicate directly to the system, allowing for real-time reasonability checks in the counting process.

Increments and Decrements (Addition and Subtraction)

The addition and subtraction to perpetual inventory must be complete, accurate, and timely. This requires:

- Interfacing store and central systems that are not normally interfaced
- Interfacing systems in which data accuracy has not been of high importance
- Creating new in-store procedures
- Creating a continuing in-store training program

Each of the systems in the following diagram creates the updates that must be applied in the correct sequence before the perpetual inventory can be used for analysis or decision making. When the application sequence is questionable, increment and decrement audits are difficult and the system must allow for "negative" inventory. Therefore, it is best if the application sequence can mimic the real-time occurrence of the updates. This diagram is not sequential, since the application order varies by retailer.

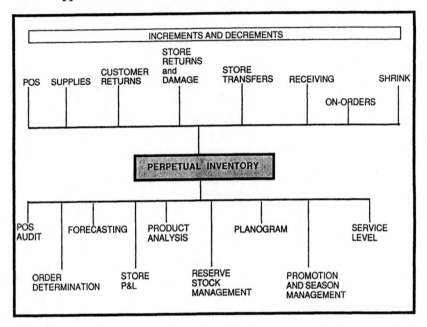

POS

POS is the basis for perpetual inventory decrements, forecasting, and category analysis. For many retailers, obtaining accurate POS data represents a switch from merely collecting (or sometimes selling) the data to actually using the data.

Even retailers who were previously collecting the data and using it centrally find that CAO requires POS data to be more precise and accurate. The quality of POS data cannot be resolved solely through improved systems. Moreover, poor quality data cannot be ignored simply by implementing advanced mathematics or data cleaning technologies. *Although these systems are helpful, there is no substitute for good in-store procedures and a commitment to continued personnel training.* Significantly, POS data improves with use. Some retailers are afraid to implement CAO because the POS data is not clean. The reality is that POS data improves when it is used extensively and real-time in-store. Today's POS systems, data collection devices, and passive monitors allow the retailer to use the POS data to manage the store.

Use of POS data directs a level of attention to the data that previously did not exist. These are the important keys to improved store procedures:

• Creating personnel rewards and a store P&L system at store-level that will insure the enforcement of regulations

- Day-to-day store management based on information from the POS system
- Continued in-store training
- Regulations that are workable at the store during prime shopping hours and high-season

POS data problems stem from several causes, including:

- Scanner misreads
- Cashier errors
- Manual keying
- Register adjustments
- Support system errors
- Headquarters POS control and communication

Scanner Misreads. When today's POS hardware is kept in clean, operational condition, scanner misreads due to equipment should not be of concern. What can be a major factor (and this varies greatly by industry) is packaging. This is particularly true of packaging from new companies and for imported product. New companies use duplicate bar-codes, have spacing and color problems, and change bar-codes without notifying you. There remains a ramp-up time for the new companies entering the market. All new products should be scanned on acceptance at the retailer and at first receipt. When the package cannot be read and the operator must enter the bar-code, there is a margin for error.

When packages are shrink-wrapped into an assortment or bonus-offering, there is a possibility of scanning the wrong bar-code. Shrink-wrapping for assortment combinations and bonus packaging remains a popular if unfortunate form of promotion. Although there is a bar-code especially for the promotion pack on the outside of a shrink-wrap assortment, the individual item bar-codes are often still visible and are mistakenly passed over the scanner. This creates quite a nice bargain for the customer, who will now buy the assortment of five jars of art paint for the price of one jar rather than the promotion price for the five jars.

Another source of misreads is the attempted mark-out. Experienced managers not used to the quality of the current POS readers may attempt to "mark-out" the price, in order to reduce selected products of a particular item, usually due to freshness issues. A simple felt tip mark rarely prevents the newer POS machines from reading the bar-code. This usually results in an irate customer who has purposely selected the dated product, only to have the cashier "attempt" to charge full retail. These types of errors—which are so easy to make and understand for people inside the industry—appear as particularly devious to consumers (and their lawyers). Bar-codes must be fully covered to prevent POS reads.

Cashier Errors. Cashier errors result from lack of ongoing training, regulations that don't match reality, incompetence, and theft. Probably the most-discussed cashier error is improper use of the multiple key. Unfortunately, the product that is most often scanned out incorrectly due to use of the multiple key is also hard to physically count because the product is normally multiple colors, fragrances, sizes, or flavors in identical packaging. Some retailers choose to disable the multiple key. Other retailers find this solution unacceptable. Another solution has been to limit use of the multiple key to multiples in excess of a constant such as 10 or 12 coded into the POS device. Still other retailers dismantle the key for products prone to abuse such as baby food.

There is no substitute for continued training and in-store, real-time POS data use. Mathematical approaches analyze the normal ratio of multiple scans and distribute the purchases according to normal buying habits. This approach has some value when data is massive, as for a manufacturer reviewing a market area. The problem for the individual store is that consumers do some very unpredictable things. A class project or a church bazaar creates an unusual demand for orange flavor or turquoise color. Ratio mathematics does not replace improved procedures. An improbable buy of popsicle sticks may be an error or it may be a sixth grade class creating a replica of a pioneer village. Ratio mathematics at store level is useful in:

- Identifying cashiers misusing the multiple key
- Auditing the POS data
- Directing store personnel to potential problem areas

Cashier incompetence or actual theft can be controlled by using one of the several systems that analyze POS data by cashier. These systems use the POS data to identify personnel problems.

Regulations at the check-out needed for clean data must also work when the cashier has a line of ten impatient customers. There is an unfortunate history in retail of creating and attempting to apply store regulations without conferring with store personnel and without considering the problems of the peak shopping hours. There is a balance and a compromise that must be established between what is needed in the computer systems and what will work at the store.

Manual Keying. Other sources of errors include default bar-codes, mismatches of the product to POS, missing bar-codes on POS, cost errors on POS, store-assigned PLU (price look-up number), and other causes resulting in manual entry. Whenever manual bar-code entry is substituted for scanning, the possibility of error increases. By improving the POS support systems and eliminating PLU numbers, most manual entries can be eliminated. Forbidding the use of default entries results in the cashier's adopting the use of an actual bar-code with price override as its default. Too often, decisions made at head-quarters in order to preserve the integrity of the data are not workable at the stores. The way the POS system should work at the store is not necessarily the way the POS system actually works. *You really can't eliminate manual entry by fiat; the way to eliminate it is to get rid of the reason clerks have for using it.*

There is a problem when the supplier does not initially give the correct bar-code with new item data. *There is no substitute for breaking open a pack upon first receipt (especially of new items) and verifying the package bar-code.* This includes new items, new suppliers, diverted product, or special promotion packaging. Problems explode exponentially when bar-code problems are not recognized early in the distribution chain. The best time to find the problem is with the supplier and at new item acceptance. The next best is at the distribution center receiving, verifying the bar-code at first receipt. The next best after that is at store receiving before the customer brings the product to checkout. The last and worst scenario is when the cashier must correct the problem while the customer is waiting.

Register Adjustments. Register adjustments are caused by register resets in the middle of the collection cycles, store price changes, store manual entry of new items, or updating of UPCs (EANs). These adjustments interfere with data collection, but stores make these adjustments out of necessity. Reasons for the manual updates include providing suppliers with data at midday, correcting for poor central system interfaces, and adjusting for untested bar-codes. Third-party systems that specialize in data cleaning analyze and correct these errors.

It is important to correct the reasons for these midday adjustments. Resolving support system errors and regulating supplier data collection is imperative. As more suppliers attempt to manage shadow perpetual inventories and switch promotion payments to a sales-based approach, more midday collection requests are being presented to the stores. Every supplier-managed product line and promotion must have an agreed-upon, regulated system to share information.

Data cleaning provided by third parties analyzes the POS data for reasonability and researches the actual POS journal entries to debug and change data that has been recorded incorrectly due to midday changes and in-store errors. Data cleaning uses advanced mathematics to determine if the data is complete or if there has been a transmission or reset error at store level.

Support System Errors. Support system errors are an enormous source of POS problems. Often, headquarters item master files were designed before the importance of POS was recognized. As a result, these systems do not support clean POS data and are incapable of timely and accurate updates of the POS system with new items, item deletes, cost changes, and special promotion prices. When the headquarters systems do not support the stores, too much store intervention is required. Where store intervention is required, the margin for error increases.

This can, obviously, become very confusing. Headquarters has to insure that the stores have all the bar-codes for all the products it carries, and that prices are consistent both within the store itself and chain-wide. With all the potential pitfalls, it's easy to see how things can fall through the cracks. Headquarters must see to it that orderable products, and bar-codes for that product, match up.

There are many reasons for the confusion between bar-codes and SKUs.

- When multiple suppliers exist for one product, multiple bar-codes represent one orderable product. Each supplier creates its own, unique UPC (EAN) for product that to the consumer and the ordering system is only one product.

- The bar-code changes due to product lines being sold from one manufacturer to another. Part of the UPC (EAN) is the manufacturer code. Therefore, even when nothing about the product changes except the conglomerate that owns the division producing the product, the UPC (EAN) will change. To the consumer and the store order system, the product is the same.

- The bar-code sometimes changes due to slight repackaging. This is a gray area. Some manufacturers change the UPC (EAN) after repackaging, some do not. Depending on the extent of the repackaging, the product may or may not be considered the same product.

- In the grocery and drug industries, manufacturers use the bar-code to identify diverted product. Manufacturers began using alternate bar-codes to track when the product they were promoting in Texas started showing up in California. Retailers who didn't check the bar-code on products received from diverters into their distribution centers ran into tremendous problems at the stores where the UPC was not in the POS system.

- In Europe, multiple manufacturing sites located in different countries create multiple bar-codes for the same product. Part of the EAN is the country of origin. Multiple manufacturing sites for one product create multiple EANs for that product.

The master item file's relationship between the orderable product and the related bar-codes (sellable product) is the way that the headquarters system insures that the store system has all the bar-codes associated with this product and that the prices are consistent.

For the retailer embarking on a CAO project, it is very disheartening to realize that its headquarters system will not support its CAO goals. Unfortunately, there is no band-aid or patch that will hold over time. The best and only approach is to resolve the problems with the headquarters systems.

Headquarters POS Control and Communication. Finally, transmitting data accurately and completely to and from central headquarters is of utmost importance. With today's technologies, a well-planned system has little trouble transmitting the planned data within the window of data transmission time.

But problems occur for two major reasons. First, due to increased sales, promotions, seasons, or other factors, the transmission data exceeds the planned quantity and cannot be transmitted within the window. Second, the interface systems fail or are misused. Recovery systems and audit controls are imperative for successful POS transmission. So many new techniques are being introduced for moving the consumer more efficiently through the check-out process that by the time this section is read, some POS issues may be obsolete. However, reasonable regulations, the reduction of manual interface, improved headquarters support systems, cashier and data auditing, and ongoing staff training will likely remain the keys to quality POS data for some time to come.

A note on POS and perpetual inventory: When POS data is used to evaluate the store and the cashiers in real-time, the data can be corrected for the perpetual inventory updates. The perpetual inventory is also useful for auditing POS.

For example, when sales push the perpetual inventory into negative inventory (in a system where negative inventories are not a timing problem), there may have been an error in the headquarters systems or usage of the multiple key. The system issues a request for an audit of the item in negative inventory and tracks the cashier. Store personnel may find that product is being sold from the back room due to delayed receiving or that there has been incorrect receiving. If the product is not available, and similar items in the section also have incorrect counts, then there is probably a misuse of the multiple key.

When the perpetual inventory is in both units and dollars, and the unit and dollar update during a non-promotion period is not within expected error tolerance, the POS cost and units fields can be reviewed. There is an expected unit price which is known to the system. The total units and dollars sold should relate to each other reasonably.

For those retailers who do not have a one-for-one relationship between orderable and sellable product, the perpetual inventory must by definition be SKU-based rather than bar-code–based. During the POS update, POS data is audited for accurate relationships and for consistent pricing. When POS and perpetual inventory are real-time, these problems are addressed and resolved immediately.

Supplies

Store personnel routinely use sellable product for in-store maintenance or as an unscanned component product or ingredient. This can include products such as paper towels or window cleaner used for cleaning, or packaging or ingredients used for food preparation demonstrations. Delis, salad bars, and bakeries sometimes take ingredients from the store shelves. Marking pens make their way into store staff usage. Normally, supplies reduce inventory but are not scanned out as a sale. Products that become components of another sale often do not correctly deplete inventory. When the system still thinks that this product is on the store shelf, the system does not reorder, and ultimately this results in an empty shelf. An example is plant saucers placed under house plants, which are then sold. Supplies must be scanned out as supplies and allowed to decrement the perpetual inventory.

Supplies are not normally added to the forecast. However, if there is no actual "supply ordering mechanism," supplies used on a consistent basis need to be considered carefully in their relationship to forecasting, category management, and ordering. If store personnel are continually removing the private label plastic garbage bags for use in the stores, the forecast system must account for both sales and supplies. The question regarding supplies and CAO is always whether the ordering is only for sales or also for supplies.

Customer Returns

When a customer returns product to the retailer, that product may be returned to the shelf (to a sellable status), returned to the supplier, or discarded. In return, the customer may be given a refund, credit, rain check, or a replacement product.

The product is tracked as a return. If the product is replaced for the customer, the system depletes the inventory by two (the original sale and the replacement product) but counts the sale as one (one sale/one return).

Product staged for supplier returns is placed into a "system return status" and held for the supplier. This usually requires staging the product in the back room.

When a customer is refunded with a rain check, the original sale is canceled. There must also be a rain check system that collects outstanding rain check transactions for use by the ordering system.

Refunds handled as credits cancel the initial sale. Obviously, credits create a more complex accounting transaction. There is a dollar sale without a product sale.

Many systems do not have adequate ability to take in information on returns. Store personnel require training to insure that returns information is processed in a timely fashion. Systems will create problems by delaying perpetual inventory updates if they are based on sending paperwork to headquarters, which enters information days or even weeks later.

Store Returns and Damage

Stores can return products to the supplier or the retail distribution center due to overstock, damage, or incorrect product delivery. Product overstock can be due to promotion pushes, end of season, or incorrect ordering. Whatever the reason, the store return procedures are the same. When the product is removed from the shelf and staged in the back room for pickup, it is moved to a system staged (transfer) status. When the product is actually moved out of the store, it is subtracted from the staged status. The store return system depletes the perpetual inventory without affecting forecast.

Headquarters can identify existing overstock at store level for the central buyers. Central buyers make a decision at season-end to purchase more product for their stores or to shift product from overstock stores to understock stores. After promotions, retailers may allow their stores to return product to headquarters. This incoming return amount affects current merchandising and pricing decisions on that product. Unfortunately, the distribution center buyers are often working without information on store inventories.

Store Transfers

Not all retailers cost justify store transfers, but some do. Since systems are not integrated, transfers cannot be evaluated on a case-by-case basis. Store transfers are products that are needed by one store and are in excess supply at another store. Store transfers are made for several reasons.

- The supplier cannot supply in time to prevent service level problems at a store.
- Product that will have no sales after a season is over is equalized across stores toward the end of a season.
- After a promotion, a store is overstocked and other stores need product.

Cost justification of store-to-store transfers depends heavily on product type, size, weight, cost, and store locations. There are times that store transfers cannot be cost justified on hard dollars alone but are necessary to maintain service levels on promoted or seasonal products. In many ways, catalog sales that pull directly from the stores operate as transfers (although sometimes stores are credited with the sale).

Store transfers begin by communicating overstocks to a transfer system. Store-to-store orders are booked. Much like store returns, store transfers deplete the physical inventory and remain in a system staged (transfer) status until they are received by the ordering store. Store transfers should not update the receiving store perpetual inventory until the product is received. Store transfers require auditing between what the sending store sent and what the receiving store received. Transfers update perpetual inventory without affecting forecasting.

Receiving

Product is received directly from the retailer distribution center, the product supplier, or from a third-party logistics supplier. Receiving is the primary means of increasing the perpetual inventory.

Retailer Distribution Center. One of the primary difficulties in maintaining a clean store perpetual inventory is shipment accuracy from the retailer's own distribution center. The solution lies in the quality of the retailer's distribution center and logistics systems, and personnel training. Hardware/software systems that control the distribution center's pick, outbound control, and ongoing audits will improve accuracy. Some retailers are able to count all product in and out, but this is obviously not practical for fast-turn product. The headquarters system should be able to update the store perpetual inventory with the accurate shipped amounts. The store perpetual inventory should not be updated at time of shipment but at time of receipt. This cannot be overlooked. Fixing the distribution center system can be the key to correcting the store perpetual inventory.

Product Supplier and Third-Party Logistics Managers. There are many effective backdoor receiving systems on the market that handle scheduling, receiving, and paying for supplier shipments direct to the store. These systems should be used with a perpetual inventory system. Some product lines are difficult and time-consuming to receive accurately. The unfortunate scenario at the store is usually that at some point a customer asks for the product that is being slowly received into the back room. A helpful clerk then runs to the back and fetches the product, and it is sold before it is entered into the system. Working with suppliers to improve shipment accuracy, installing sophisticated backdoor receiving systems and electronic communications, and using store personnel scheduling systems to insure that the personnel required are available combine to improve the receiving from the product supplier. The simple fact is that most suppliers have invested more in scanning systems to insure accurate deliveries than have many retailers.

Where partnerships between retailers and suppliers exist, receiving counts may consist of only periodic audits on the received product. Communicating advanced ship notices and in-transit tracking greatly benefits the receiving process.

Shrink

Shrink is often the retail euphemism for theft. It is obviously impossible to track each theft, but theft can be tracked over time. Theft is often the unexplained difference between expected balance-on-hand and actual balance-on-hand. The differences are detected manually by locating "holes" on the shelf or shortages at product put away time. The differences are also detected when sales fall below expected levels when there is product in the system. When these differences cannot be explained, they are assumed to be shrink. This shrink can then be tracked over time. When shrink is large enough and consistent enough to form its own pattern, it must be considered in forecasting. Shrink affects the ongoing actual perpetual inventory. Tracking shrink can cost justify acquiring the security controls needed to prevent it.

Spoilage of product that has a freshness or dating factor is also considered shrink. Where possible, account for spoilage separately as both theft and spoilage need to be understood and contained. Some shrink, as with display case fresh fish, really does shrink. The poundage sales of fish can be less than were originally brought into the store. This is due to dehydration rather than actual spoilage.

On-Orders

On-orders, which are discussed extensively in Chapter 6, are the amount of product scheduled to arrive at the store. On-orders are created when there are open purchase orders or partial purchase order receipt. On-orders include distribution center backorders, partial receipts, and late purchase orders. A store-level purchase order management system is required.

On-orders are, of course, necessary for accurate order determination. Additionally, tracking on-order quantities and expected delivery dates is useful in analyzing inventory problems. For example, when there are sales into negative inventory and the on-order delivery date was today or even yesterday, there is a strong indication that this product has not been properly received.

Audits

The ability to audit inventory is of utmost importance. Audits can be either scheduled or exception-based. Physical inventories are scheduled counts used to begin a perpetual inventory. Cycle counts are scheduled partial counts, based on events or perceived need. Audit counts are reactions to identified problems in one or more SKUs.

Examples of when cycle counts can occur:

- Every six months
- Halfway through a seasonal sell down
- Weekly on the 2% of the product doing 20% of the sales
- With selected problem categories or planograms
- At the end of a large promotion

Examples of when audit counts can occur:

- Product is in the perpetual inventory but sales are below the error tolerance expected (with real-time perpetual inventory this check can be made during business hours)
- Sales are greater than the product available in the perpetual inventory
- Product on hand is greater than the planogram or order determination maximum
- Product on hand is less than the planogram or order determination minimum
- Forecasted product on hand will not meet service level before next order date
- Empty shelves or shelves with less than acceptable presentation stock

A workable audit function must be able to:

- Recognize an exception audit situation
- Manage and schedule exception and cycle audits
- Direct store personnel to the audit location and indicate the problem

- Receive and apply count changes in a timely fashion
- Track and edit the audit changes

The audit function is most successful when using software and mobile two-way communication devices, such as hand-held units. In this way, audit problems are investigated and resolved immediately. There is a myriad of store shelf electronic devices and portable terminal communication devices (and more are being created almost daily) that can be used to create audit efficiency.

Using the store-level planogram to control the audit is an excellent method to structure the audit procedure. The audit is easiest when it follows the planogram. The store personnel are able to work in the order of the store set.

TOTAL INVENTORY

This chapter so far has focused on the store perpetual inventory. When a retailer has distribution centers, there is also a distribution center perpetual inventory. There are many excellent mainframe- and distributed-warehousing systems on the market for maintaining distribution center inventories. When there are multiple distribution centers and potential transfers between warehouses, some of these software systems function better than others. As with the stores, all of the updates to inventory must be applied in an accurate and timely fashion.

Supplier deliveries are the primary source of distribution center inventory. Product is received, counted, and put away based on the retailer-defined SKU. Increased use of case codes to scan in product has helped receiving accuracy. The use of advance ship notification aids receiving, labor management, and order determination.

Product is shipped to the stores, supplied for catalog or consumer direct purchases, returned as overstock or damage, and sometimes stolen. The ability to track these decrements accurately is key to distribution center perpetual inventory.

Major problems occur at the distribution center for these reasons:

- Installation of cross-dock functions without proper system support. With flow-through product, the system must receive and ship the product into the distribution center, even though it is never slotted.
- Shared bins (slots). There are inevitable problems when different products are placed into the same slot. Eventually, the wrong product will be picked.
- Promotion pack. There is often confusion in the warehouse when the manufacturer creates a holiday or bonus version of a product. This product is too often slotted with the regular product. Managing the sell-down of this product before pulling the regular product—as well as insuring that the stores are receiving the promotion product—is difficult for many systems.

- Dated product. Many warehouse systems have no ability to manage and track products by lot.

- Partial shipments. When the supplier makes a partial shipment, there is usually a question of how long the purchase order remains open, awaiting the completion of the shipment.

- Returns from stores. Often the distribution center buyers are working with an incomplete picture of the total retailer inventory. As a result, they buy product on top of overstock at the stores. Managing store returns is a necessary part of any warehouse system.

- Damage and supplier returns. Staging and managing damaged, dated, and returnable product scheduled for return to the supplier can be managed by the warehouse system or by an auxiliary returns system, but it must be managed.

- Investment (forward) buys. Forward buys should be tracked separately in the system when managing distribution center inventories. When this is not done, it is impossible to distinguish product turn problems from forward buy investments. Forward buys can also overcrowd a warehouse, reducing efficiency across all product lines.

Distribution center inventories and store inventories should be seen as total retailer inventory. These combined inventories are needed for order determination at both central and store.

OUTPUTS AND BENEFITS

The perpetual inventory provides a basis for managing the store with electronic data. The closer to real-time the perpetual inventory is, the more useful is its data in managing the merchandise.

Perpetual inventory provides input to:

- Order determination
- POS audit
- Forecasting
- Store P&L
- Product analysis
- Planograms
- Reserve stock management
- Planning
- Service level
- Promotion and season management

Order Determination

With few exceptions, order determination systems use either an actual perpetual inventory or a shadow perpetual inventory as the basis to their ordering formulas. If the perpetual inventory is not real-time, it must be accurate at the time that the order determination module calculates the product need. This allows the system and the buyers to optimize inventory levels across the entire enterprise.

Order determination is dependent on a clean perpetual inventory to establish the product need. (In Chapter 6, we discuss the concept of product need and timing.) The perpetual inventory at the end of a promotion allows management to identify the actual promotion sales against the excess product remaining unsold in the stores. This knowledge can also be used to evaluate the systems for push or promotion forecasting. The perpetual inventory, approaching season-end, allows the buyers to determine if the product should be transferred from store-to-store or if more product needs to be purchased to last throughout the season. This information also gives management the opportunity to reduce the price on overstocked product.

POS Audit

When the perpetual inventory is real-time or accurate on a scheduled basis throughout the day, the actual sales can be compared to the product available to sell. For example, let's say we normally sell fifty of a certain product every day in a store. It's now 11:00 A.M., and we haven't sold any. However, the perpetual inventory shows that there are three cases of product in the store. This means that the chances are very good that this product is still in the back room and not out on the floor.

The system can warn store personnel when sales are lower than expected even though there is still sufficient product in the store. In this case, the product may be in the back room or poorly merchandised. The product may have an incorrect SKU-to-UPC (EAN) relationship, so it is not being identified correctly. The system can question a multiple sale that doesn't match the product available to sell, or all sales that create negative inventory.

Forecasting

Forecasting uses sales data. The POS audit determines usability of the data. The forecast module reacts accordingly.

Store P&L (Profit and Loss Statement)

A perpetual inventory in dollars instead of units is a store P&L. The store P&L is used to help the store work as an individually-managed unit. A store-level P&L by item, by category, or by department provides a basis for product management and personnel payment rewards. It moves the focus for decision making to the store level. Store performance based on POS data also brings the POS data to the immediate attention of supervisory personnel.

A perpetual P&L allows both store and central management to carefully monitor a particular store or cluster of stores. When management bonuses depend on the profit and loss of specific stores, a perpetual P&L gives the store personnel the tools to make necessary changes. The perpetual P&L is most important when stores and departments within stores are functioning with some autonomy.

Product Analysis

Product analysis uses the perpetual inventory to evaluate actual product turns, ROI, and return on space. A real-time perpetual inventory, combined with a well-designed exception reporting system, lets you manage inventory, service level, and labor. Moreover, such a combination of systems lets you flag trouble spots precisely when they occur, allowing immediate corrective action. The perpetual inventory system aids in the management and pricing of discontinued items, end-of-season, and end-of-promotion items.

The perpetual inventory gives the category management systems specific store information and greater depth of knowledge on actual ROI on dollars and space, as well as turn ratio.

Planograms

Planograms tied into perpetual inventory can identify ordering and forecasting problems, as well as the need for resets. One of the basic problems with planograms is knowing when the planogram isn't working. A perpetual inventory shows when a plan is under- or over-planned for a specific location. With a perpetual inventory, actual turns and ROI to space can be measured.

By calculating the actual ROI on space, the quality of the planogram in relation to the actual inventory can be evaluated. The return on space is the actual dollar sales over time per square foot of space. This can be done at the product or the category level. Normally, we measure return against the dollars invested in inventory by measuring our turns (units sold against average units' inventory over time) and dollars sold against average dollar inventory (cost) over time. By measuring the return against space, we can establish how effectively we are using the selling area.

Reserve Stock Management

Reserve stock management is a natural part of perpetual inventory. The system should keep track of which products are allowed to be placed into reserve storage and how much of that product is in reserve storage at the store. When the reserve storage product is moved to the selling floor, the reserve storage units are decreased and the selling floor units are increased. This is relatively simple using wand devices.

The perpetual inventory system informs floor personnel when the restocking of the shelf space needs to occur. The calculation of needed transfers contributes to labor management calculations. The continual tracking of reserve storage inventory and movement provides the basis for cost analysis of reserve inventory.

Note: Philosophically, CAO can be used to greatly reduce the use of in-store reserve stock storage, but this is not practical for every retail situation. The level of sophistication of reserve stock management must match the complexity and size of the in-store reserve stock facility.

Planning

The perpetual inventory system provides the basis for developing the merchandise plan. Historical monthly inventory values are used to support the development of a new inventory plan for the upcoming season. BOM (beginning-of-month) or EOM (end-of-month) inventory values at department and class level will be key to developing these new plans. As you move into the season, actual inventory values are needed for comparison against the plan. This "plan versus actual" comparison provides information for in-season tracking. Also, the most recent inventory position is used with the future plan to generate ongoing inventory projections and updated OTB (open to buy).

Service Level

Customer service level is improved in two ways. First, the store in-stock position has many more audits and warnings on both current in-stock and delayed on-orders. Second, when product cannot be carried in full assortment at all outlets, access to the inventories of all the stores allows quick transfers of product to where it is needed.

Promotion and Season Management

Store sell-through is the only true measure of promotion and seasonal effectiveness. Overstock at season or promotion start and end can be balanced with the knowledge of its existence. Potential store out-of-stocks can also be prevented.

Real-Time Perpetual Inventory

If the perpetual inventory is real-time, the audits can also be real-time and used not only to maintain a clean perpetual inventory, but also to produce warnings on insufficient inventories. Real-time perpetual inventory tied to electronic communication devices creates an "electronic manager" in the store, able to communicate problems to store personnel.

CHAPTER 5

Forecasting

DEFINITION

Forecasting is a mathematical means of analyzing the past and the present in order to predict the future.

There are three major components of forecasting:

History. Forecasting uses historical data to search for patterns and trends.

Math. Math, whether simple or complex, is the series of calculations attempting to predict the future based on data from the past.

Judgment. Mathematical forecasting cannot reasonably be expected to handle all possible situations. Good forecasting evaluates itself and determines when human intervention is necessary. Therefore, people using the system must use judgment, and a form of judgment must be built into the system. *Forecasting is both a science and an art.*

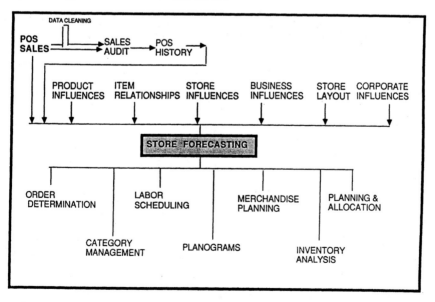

As shown in the diagram on the previous page, sales forecasting provides input to many different systems. In this chapter, we are addressing sales forecasting in general. The level of the forecast and the importance of certain sales influences may vary depending on the operational function.

A forecast's timing—but not its characteristics—is different for the distribution center versus a store. Promotions, seasons, and so on influence store as well as distribution center forecasts.

The difference is that the distribution center is forecasting for the time when the stores will want the product and the stores are forecasting for when the consumers will want it.

If this is true, shouldn't distribution center need just be a lead time (DC-to-store) offset of consumer demand (POS sales)? Not necessarily. Early season set-ups, promotion set-ups, and displays in the stores require that stores pull product from the distribution center much earlier than actual consumer demand. Initial set-ups of new planograms or new products create a store demand considerably larger than consumer demand in order to fill the pipeline.

Forecasting is often confused with order determination. Forecasting only predicts future sales, while order determination is the actual creation of supplier orders. Forecasting does not look at actual on-hand inventory except to establish the quality of the historical data. It is not concerned with available space, vendor lead time, order cycles, delivery methods, current on-orders, or suggested orders. The forecast interval and the order determination interval may not be related. The type of forecast formula used and the rate of sales determine the frequency of the forecast interval.

Forecasting is not a one-size-fits-all proposition. As discussed in Chapter 1, it is important to understand the product before selecting the "right" forecasting method. Forecasting complexity can grow over time, and there is a learning curve for both the system and the personnel who must use it. In this section, there is a review of the many factors that influence forecasting. The inability to obtain the needed sales influence factors causes some forecasting problems.

It is a long-held belief in retail that the best forecasting method is the one that can easily be understood by the personnel using it. That belief stems from a time when retail was less event- and promotion-driven, and retail personnel were not used to computers driving both operational and analytical decisions. There is surely a trade-off between complexity and ease of understanding. However, ignoring the necessity to incorporate the most important influences on sales—just to keep the forecasting methods simple—is a dead-end solution.

Forecasting can be applied successfully at different levels and in a combination of levels. Forecasting feeds many different systems, which require forecasts at various levels.

Forecasting levels include:

Item/SKU (EAN) Level: orderable and/or sellable unit of product.

Item Group: items grouped by like attributes such as color, fragrance, brand, flavor, size, and style. Items can be grouped by supplier delivery route. Item groups are any linkage that brings information to the analysis process. One SKU may exist in a variety of item groups.

Category (Classification) (class, sub-category, subclass): items that share a selling space in the store and are promoted and merchandised together.

Department: sections of the store that often have their own separate managers, P&L, personnel, and even support systems.

Store: a single individual retail outlet.

Cluster: a group of demographically similar stores.

Region: a geographic grouping of stores.

Forecast times include:

Time-of-Day: primarily used for labor management, scheduling in-store promotion activities, and identifying inventory or operational problems.

Short-Term Forecasts: used to forecast for the next few days for high-turn, frequent-order items, or the next few weeks or even months for slower-turn items—used for replenishment and to distribute past allocated flow-through.

Long-Term Forecasts: used for requested products, merchandise and assortment planning, planograms, ordering post-allocated flow-through and materials requirement planning—long-term forecasts, like short-term forecasts, vary in length depending on the product turn.

Forecasts compared across different levels increase the value of the individual forecast. For example, forecasting both at the item level and at the category level indicates if this item's trends and seasons are functioning like other products in the category or differently.

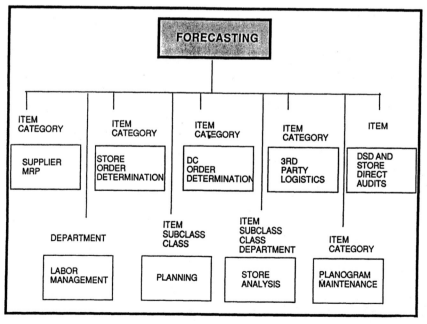

High-turn retailers emphasize short-term forecasting for replenishment. Fashion retailers concentrate on long-term forecasting for planning. Each industry segment can learn much from the other. High-turn retailers need to use long-term forecasting to reduce overstock in the supply pipeline. Fashion retailers, although committed early to advance purchases, can use short-term forecasting to allocate flow-through and for in-season merchandising strategies.

Currently, retailers perform various types of forecasting and run multiple forecasting systems, not all of which are appropriate for their product. Today, most software systems are sold with embedded forecasting techniques that perform the functions of CAO, distribution center replenishment, labor management, planogramming, merchandise planning, and allocation. For example, the CAO process requires store/SKU forecasts several days or weeks into the future. Merchandise planning uses monthly sales forecasts at various merchandise levels (department, class, etc.) that exist six to eighteen months into the future. Labor management requires short-term department forecasts by time of day. Instead of spending time improving the quality of one set of formulas, the retailer spends time maintaining a myriad of different forecasting modules and databases. *Forecasting should be a single engine driving many different machines.*

The trade-off in forecast implementation is to select the level of complexity appropriate to the product, but that is still manageable by retail personnel. There is no single forecasting method that is right for every circumstance, every product line, and every retailer, but various strategies can exist within one forecasting function. Implementation is most effective when there is flexibility to handle the majority of the retailer's product situations and product types.

FORECAST SITUATIONS

What is the "situation" of the forecast? In each of these major "situations," the forecast techniques may vary. Any one item at different times of its product life cycle can be in one of the situations discussed here. Each forecast situation must be considered.

Demand Forecasting

Demand forecasting is used at the item level for basic products, and at the category level for basic and non-basic products. For example, we can forecast both Campbell's tomato soup and the entire soup category (as well as all Campbell's soups, all tomato soups, and/or canned soups versus dry soups). For categories such as women's blouses carried every year, we forecast just the category, since the individual blouse styles change every year. Demand forecasting is used for normal, repeatable sales.

Demand forecasting predicts future sales of product with accumulated history but little promotion activity. Mathematical forecasting searches for past repeatable patterns and applies them to the future. Good forecasting requires complete data, an understanding of the data quality, and methods tailored to the situation.

Demand forecasting uses two major sources of history (data):

- Store demand. Store demand can be thought of in three ways: the orders generated by or for the stores; the store receipts; or the shipments to the stores. It is not a direct representation of consumer sales, but simply the frequency and quantity of store orders.

- POS data. POS data is a historical log of all POS transactions for a selected product and is the most accurate representation of individual store sales and consumer demand. (These data frequently are stored weekly or monthly.)

History of sales and/or orders constitutes the *base* of forecasting, but should not be considered the only factor. The degree to which other factors play a role in product sales depends on the product type and the merchandising philosophy. These factors are discussed in detail in "Influences on Sales," later in this chapter.

Slow Movers

Slow movers are simply products that sell very slowly. In fact, slow movers normally sell less than one per week. They defy most complex forecasting formulas, especially at store level. (Slow movers may even be slower than the file definition for forecast as they may require more than one decimal place—selling only .05 per week, etc.) When selecting the formula, the reason for the slow movement must be considered.

Reasons for product slow movement include:

- Unpopular
- Out-of-Season
- Cannibalized
- Overpacked
- Completes a set, line, etc.

Unpopular

Unpopular products are the ones on your "most likely to discontinue" list. But keep in mind that some forecasting techniques move up the demand on these products during their category's high season. This can happen even though there's no way volume on these products is going to rise—people just don't want them.

It's a common mistake to allow category seasonal indices to move the entire category with the high-season index. Some would argue—erroneously—that slow movers aren't affected much by all this. But slow movers can be affected significantly depending on the size of their pack and the seasonal index. Imagine if the system orders just one extra case of an unpopular item for every store. In-season or not, that item is not going to move any faster than your old Aunt Mathilda. And worse, it'll have to be dumped at the end of the season. Multiply the loss by a few hundred stores, and consider the damage.

Where category profiles are used, recognizing and discontinuing unpopular items before going into a season is imperative. Consider children's books. Children's book sales rise dramatically during the holidays. Expensive children's gift books, which are very slow movers most of the year, sell very briskly during the holidays. Other books are simply not appealing. Christmas alone is not going to cause these books to sell. Using indices that increase the sales volume of these books equally is an error.

Out-of-Season

Out-of-season slow movers are products that may be carried year-round but sell well only during their season. These products respond effectively to forecasting techniques that inflate the demand during high season. CAO can report the problems with slow movers, although it cannot resolve them. First, out-of-season slow movers are often overpacked for the out-of-season period. Second, the planogram during the out-of-season period may be overgenerous. In the garden section, a small amount of snail bait is carried year-round. But during the prime growing season, gardeners buy large quantities. On the other hand, spring fertilizer is available only from early spring through mid-summer. It is removed completely from the stores during its out-of-season. So we must have a replenishment plan for the out-of-season snail bait, which is carried as a courtesy to customers with winter gardens. The decision for the retailer is to invest the manpower to reset the shelves in order to reduce inventory which is selling as "slow as snails" and free up shelf space for other products.

Cannibalized

Cannibalized products are under intense price sensitivity. The consumer buys only when the product is the cheapest or on promotion. This is a merchandising problem that forecasting cannot resolve. In-store cannibalization of price-sensitive product spreads actual demand for product across several brands. Each individual item may have a steady share of the total sales; but a high percentage of total demand moves to the cheapest or most-promoted product. The forecast is for the total product group. Demand for the category is constant, but individual item sales are not. A product may become a slow mover due solely to a competitive product's temporary price reduction or promotion.

Overpacked

Overpacked product has a reasonable sales rate but low turns because the supplier pack is too high for the outlet. (This definition of slow mover reflects low turns. The normal definition reflects slow sales.) Often, products are offered in a variety of pack or in a pack determined to be appropriate for the retailer. Unfortunately, the selected pack is often determined with the fast-selling stores in mind. *If you want to avoid this problem by ordering different pack sizes for different stores, you'll have to make sure your ordering and logistics systems can keep up. They'll have to have the capability of ordering and shipping a variety of packs. Often, this is beyond what the typical retailer's inventory control and ordering systems can manage.*

When pack cannot be reduced to match actual sales, the retailer and supplier can negotiate payment terms. *Extended payment terms can create reasonable dollar turns where unit turns do not exist.* The problem again is whether the retailer payment system can manage purchase orders with line-item payment terms. For example, a product containing 24 items to the pack, which sells two per week, will take 12 weeks to sell through one pack of product. Because of the makeup of the supplier's production line, he does not want to reduce pack on these items. Instead, he extends payment terms of six weeks—the supplier does not require any payment whatever for six weeks instead of the usual ten days. By the end of that time, the retailer has already sold half the product, and realized half the profit before actually paying for the product. At the end of 12 weeks, all the product has been sold, but the retailer was able to reinvest his profits during the first six weeks before he repaid the supplier. This has, in effect, created an acceptable rate of dollar-turns where the unit-turns were below the store's target rate.

Completes a Set or Line

Slow-mover product which is sold in individual units is often purchased by the consumer in *sets*. Sales of items such as pillow cases or table napkins are normally in units of two, four, or eight. This requires multiple separate rings at the register, but to the customer, buying just one would make no sense. For this reason, traditional smoothing forecasting techniques would never provide sufficient product when the consumer wants it. The forecast is used to evaluate the cost of having this product in the store and establishing potential turns. The amount of product in the store, however, represents the buying component that the consumer expects.

Slow movers often complete a *line*. High-variety retailers want product to show a variety of flavors, colors, fragrances, or sizes. The pack for the slow-moving segment of the line is often the same as for the high-moving segment. Some slow movers are simply a part of the cost of doing business. They don't sell enough to justify carrying from a purely financial viewpoint but the consumer expects the product to be available. The forecast for this product is used solely for evaluation.

Slow-mover forecasting and error evaluation must be considered differently from fast-moving product. Slow movers bounce from overstock to out-of-stock reports on a daily basis under traditional forecast error detection techniques. With slow movers, it's often true that the simpler the forecasting technique, the better the forecast.

Promotions

Promotion product is that which is affected by external merchandising. In this book, the term *promotion* is used to describe all merchandising activities with the goal of increasing sales and/or foot traffic. A promotion includes all the products that are affected by this activity.

Promotion forecasting is similar to demand forecasting, but it depends on many more factors. Available promotion history is more limited than demand sales data. Furthermore, the factors affecting the results of a promotion are more complex. With so many variables to contend with, it's difficult to get a handle on just what made or broke a particular promotion. Besides that, few retailers have mechanisms to record causal data, even when they know about key factors at the time. And promotions aren't an everyday event, so history is even more scarce. This combination makes promotion forecasting difficult, but not impossible. It is also difficult (and perhaps unwise) to separate promotion forecasting from pricing analysis. Prices before and after a promotion, price volatility, and price sensitivity are extremely important for most promoted product.

A subtle but important problem exists for retailers who collect data from POS systems weekly (Sunday through Saturday), but run promotions weekly (Thursday through Wednesday). For example, data processing has made the decision to keep store-level POS data only at the weekly level because of capacity restraints. Since the programmers go home on the weekend, there is more time on the computer for running large jobs. They decide the ideal time to back up all the store data is Sunday mornings. However, your ads break on Thursday. Now you want to analyze how you did the last time you ran a special on pink rain booties. Someone in information services creates an algorithm to figure out how much of the sales during week 24 and week 25 were due to the ad, and how much were normal sales. There is no way to tell what sold on the weekend and what sold right after the promotion began. And here is the scariest part: to build the algorithm there must be some assumptions—and these assumptions reinforce our assumptions for the ad. If it poured rain the four days before the ad broke and that's when we sold all our pink rain booties, we'll never know it. The assumption is that we sold those booties due to the ad.

An additional problem of weekly data is the variances by day of store traffic patterns. This variance can be consistent or can also vary by the time of the month. When we don't have daily data, the assumption of the traffic patterns takes precedent. This is not a problem for slower turn product, but high-turn products must be able to function on a daily basis.

The poor quality of promotion history, not the available forecasting techniques, is the biggest hindrance to good promotion forecasting.

Promotion forecasting begins with the implementation of systems that record the relevant data. Unfortunately, many retailers do not know what data is relevant. A good promotion forecasting system should provide not only the math techniques to analyze promotions, but also a way to easily collect the necessary data.

Several vehicles help capture promotion data:

- Electronic store promotions. Actually, these should be a better aid then they are. Too often, electronic promotions do not feed the appropriate level of data back to the retailer system. We find electronic store promotions existing on a myriad of unrelated platforms. In-store promotion capture is fundamental for promotion information.

- Automated store measurements. We have the central promotion information, POS data, possibly cart tracking devices, electronic shelf promotions, and in-store workstations that should be the central point of our promotion gathering. We only need to integrate and begin gathering this information.

- Supplier EDI communication of promotion offers. The initial capture of the supplier offer, the performance requirements, and the retailer response, are available via EDI. While these transactions capture what headquarters is planning, what actually happens at the stores may be quite different.

- Third-party suppliers of promotion information. Several third-party suppliers of promotion information manually collect data on actual in-store promotion activities. This can be an invaluable source of information while you are undertaking the task of full store integration.

There are many activities that make up a promotion. Common examples include:

Retailer-Planned

- Advertised Special. In-store and/or community promotion activities aimed at drawing consumer attention to this product and into the store.

- Unadvertised Special. Point-of-sale advertising draws customer attention when they are in the store.

- Reduced Price. Lower retail price, coupons and rebates.

Supplier-Planned

- Advertised Special. In-store and/or community promotion activities aimed at drawing consumer attention to this product.

- Reduced Price. Lower retail prices created by special packaging, bonus packaging, cents-off labeling, pre-price, shrink-wrapped sets, coupons, or rebates.

Other

- Post-Promotion. Promotions that create customer desire for a product after the promotion is over. If you never tried a certain diet cola before, but tried it during its promotion, and now you buy it every week, the promotion has hooked you. This is particularly important for products that we didn't know we couldn't live without because we didn't know what they were until we tried them.

  There is the opposite possibility when a promotion finishes. We can saturate the market so heavily that all of our customers have stocked up and no one wants any more of this product, or any similar product, for several weeks. This, of course, depends on the type of product. Products with limited shelf life cannot be severely overbought. Products that are "used up" at one time, such as boxes of flavored rice, frozen dinners, cans of tuna, or packages of soup may cause us to eat more rice, frozen dinners, tuna, and soup. But products that we can think of as "rip, tear, and scoop" such as sugar, coffee, and paper towels are used at the same rate as before, and the consumer simply stops purchasing. Fashion and non-basic products are interesting, as different consumers have very different attitudes about when they have met their saturation point for a type of product.

- Slump due to Competitive Product Promotion. Products that are price-sensitive or do not have brand loyalty can lose sales when a competitive product is promoted. This is particularly true with high-variety retailers. There are some products that share their demand with similar items, and promotions may increase sales of the total group of products or rob sales only from competing brands.

- Companion (Piggyback) Product. Companion product sells along with the promoted product but is not also on promotion. Examples include selling purses with shoes, crackers with soup, and paint brushes with paint. In some cases, the real profits come from the companion product. Consider the store that sells holiday turkeys as a loss leader. The idea is to bring more people into the store, in hopes that they'll buy their other needs for the holiday meal during the same shopping trip.

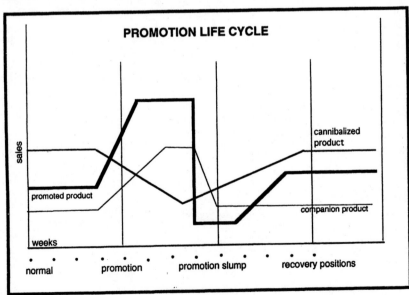

Promotion Factors

The following is a list of factors that can affect a promotion in *addition* to the ones that play a role in demand forecasting discussed later in this chapter. Not all of these factors apply to every retailer, every promotion, or in equal importance.

Store Location

Sales vary by the products' location in the store and on the shelf, as well as the number of locations in the store. Not all end racks give the same lift. Some aisles, end racks, or other locations are "hotter"—they get more foot traffic. Cart and basket tracking systems can tell us exactly where consumers travel in our stores and the sales saturation rate of each location.

Multiple locations
End rack
Special display
Center aisle
Check-out

Promotion Time

The time of year when the promotion is held, how long it lasts, and the consecutive promotion activities all play a major role in product sales during the promotion. Few seasonal sales can be clearly separated from promotions, and attempting to do so is pointless.

Time of year
Length of promotion
Timing of activities within promotion
Consecutive promotions

In-Store Promotion Activity

Promotion activity within the store can be passive or active. Active ones, such as those listed here, create an "event."

Demonstrations/fashion shows
In-store announcements
Samples
TV at POS
Electronic marketing

Coupons/Rebates

Coupon redemption and issuance should be tracked and analyzed. Coupons are issued by the retailer, the supplier, and by third-party marketing suppliers. All these sources add to the complexity of tracking the lift caused by coupons.

Newspaper

Magazine

Flyer

Register

POS

Product

Kiosk

Reduced Price

Various strategies draw the customer's attention to reduced price. The depth of the reduced price and the methods used to advertise it create differing lifts. Competitive prices and the differential between normal price and sale price impact the effect.

Advertised

On package

POS

In-store activity

Advertising—Print

Print advertising varies from small print, one-line (contract, obituary) ads to full-color feature ads. Contract ads are run in response to supplier requirements but do little to generate additional sales. Many promotion systems have insufficient information on print ads. This produces insufficient data for analysis since the size, coverage, and type all impact the effect of ads.

Level
  Feature
  Regular
  Contract
Coverage
  Geographic
  Flyers

Magazines: which?

Newspapers: which?

Picture

Size

Color

Advertising—Other

TV, radio, signs, and packaging all vary in their coverage and effectiveness. Like print ads, the depth and extent of these factors creates a different impact.

Television

When

Which

Type

Trailer

Coverage

Radio

When

Which

Type

Trailer

Coverage

Signs

When

Which

Type

Trailer

Coverage

Packaging

Special packaging

Bonus

Shrink-wrapped

Pre-price

Cents-off

Target Marketing

Consumer target marketing is becoming an increasingly important part of retail. However, with the many third-party providers participating in this type of marketing, it is often difficult to assess effectiveness.

Frequent shopper cards

Mailings

Bonuses

Special shopping hours

Advance sales

Reminders

Promotion forecasting requires that the retailer first identify pertinent factors and assemble necessary data. The next step is the selection of a forecasting technique that can weigh these factors. Various prediction techniques are discussed in this chapter.

Promotion forecasting is also heavily influenced by the merchandise plan. A major element of the merchandise plan is the estimate of monthly sell down dollars generated due to promotions (promo markdowns) or clearance (permanent markdown) situations. The merchandise plan provides the promotional emphasis by category and also determines timing.

A Note on Forward (Investment) Buys

Technically, if everything we've written about CAO was in full effect, forward buys would be nonexistent. But reality is often different from what we expect. As sophisticated as forward buy formulas were in the past, there was always an enormous hole in their logic. This was the assumption that product sent to the stores during the promotion was actually purchased by the consumer. A 10-week forward buy could turn out to be a 20-week forward buy if stores were over-stocked at the end of a promotion. Using store perpetual inventory systems and enhanced promotion forecasting should improve the retailer's batting average.

New Items

What is a new item? To discuss new item forecasting, it is important to understand all the ways this can be defined. Often, our default definition of new item is that which causes us to create a new record on the master item file.

Line Extension: New Size, Flavor, Color, Package

When a line is extended, there is a like item that can be used to base future forecasts upon until the extension item has its own sales history. Line extensions may increase sales or cannibalize them. The entire category can be affected.

New, But Duplicate: New for Manufacturer But There Is Existing Competitive Product

Duplicate product almost always creates sales cannibalization and creates the need to monitor both the new item and the category sales. Duplicate items will not necessarily mirror sales of the existing item.

Entirely New: Brand New Concept or Manufacturing Technique

The manufacturer sales predictions are the source for expected sales. New product may cannibalize other categories, such as a frozen line cannibalizing the sales from canned foods, or a new designer line cannibalizing another designer.

Pack Change: Discontinue an Existing Item and Introduction of a New Ship Pack (problem in some systems)

Pack changes are not really new items, but because some software systems define an item by its pack, it is necessary to create a new item in order to enter the new pack. Since these systems often retain order data by orderable pack instead of, or in addition to, unit sales, a pack change can produce a substantial alteration of the order unit history. Pack changes also affect the retail price calculation routines, since cost in these systems is maintained at the orderable pack level.

Packaging/Size Change: Change in Look or Quantity/Weight to Consumer

When the manufacturer changes the look or measure, the consumer's reaction can be unpredictable. Previous history may not predict future sales, even though the item UPC (EAN) and pack have not changed. This is particularly true when there is a substantial size change. Packaging changes may be made to advertise a flavor or ingredient change. This change may make this product more or less appealing to the consumer, and therefore the history more or less reliable.

Temporary New Item: Pre-price/Cents-off Label Temporarily Substituting for Existing Item

Temporary promotion and holiday packages are supposed to have unique UPC (EAN) but often they do not. The sales may be increased due to this packaging, although the sales cannot be used to predict future movement.

Supplier Change: Same Item Supplied by a Different
Manufacturer or Sell-off of a Manufacturer's Division

This problem is especially important in Europe, where the EAN varies between production source if there are producers in different countries. These items need to be linked together, since the sales history is the same despite a change in UPC (EAN).

Depending on the type of new item, there may not be sufficient history for the preferred forecasting technique. Managing forecasting exceptions, scheduled reviews, and simplified forecasting techniques are required for new items. How long a new item is still "new" depends on product turn.

For retailers who make assortment plans, new items are also dependent on the overall assortment plan for the category. New items, existing items, and discontinued items are the key elements of the assortment plan. This plan, which is below the category level merchandise plan, defines the mix of new versus existing items over time. In this case the percentage of new items are known before the actual items are identified. Forecast of the new items is a percentage of the category forecast.

As with promotions, the introduction of new items is not done in a vacuum. A new item may create new demand and generate additional sales. However, a new item may not be generating as many additional consumer purchases as it is cannibalizing existing product. For this reason, new item analysis should encompass like items within the category. The new item effect on planograms should be analyzed as part of ongoing planogram maintenance.

FACTORS INFLUENCING SALES

The following is a list of the possible forecasting inputs. Their relative importance will vary considerably by individual retailer and product category. Is it really necessary to track all this information to forecast correctly? No, but *it is necessary to track (or use a third party to track) all the information that is relevant to your sales.* As you read this section, compare it to the worksheets you have prepared on your own environment.

Product Influences

Errors

These are irregularities due to system or human error. All of the previously mentioned problems inherent in POS data create erroneous sales history.

Trends

These are one-time sales increases or decreases. Trends are not recurring. They reflect when an item's popularity is increasing or decreasing in a sustained fashion over time. Down-trending items may be those that are cannibalized by new items or whole categories cannibalized by new competitive retail outlets. Price-sensitive items that have recurring in-store cannibalization of each other's sales are not trends. Trends can be thought of by individual item or by category. They can be mathematically tracked and predicted.

Seasons

Seasons have sales patterns that regularly repeat each year. Seasonality can be identified separately from forecast, business cycles, and trend. Although seasons can be mathematically identified, not all seasons are the same, nor are product sales and merchandising handled in the same way for them. Seasons can be thought of as:

Holiday. Holiday seasons are responses to scheduled holidays, and are sometimes called "cliff seasons." That's because there is a steady rise in sales as the holiday approaches, and then an abrupt stop afterward. These patterns occur at exactly the same time each year, except for floating holidays such as Easter. Much of the product is in-and-out, and won't sell when the season is over—at least, until the following year. Different demographics and weather will have a bearing on what is actually sold. Some holidays, such as Easter, can be sensitive to the weather. For example, a rainy day will affect Fourth of July picnics, and cold weather discourages the spring fashions generally associated with Easter. Holidays can include the Super Bowl and Mardi Gras, depending on the region and whether or not the types of products you sell are associated with these seasons.

Calendar Events. Events range from back-to-school to football season. Events normally have a sharp rise (although not as rapid as for a holiday) and a long, slow decline.

Merchandise Event. This "event" is created by the retailer but is repeated year after year so that the consumer expects it. White Flower Days, Can Can sales, and others are heavily promoted events created by retail. The "event" product is always promoted, but the increase in foot traffic also leads to a season on the non-promoted product.

Weather. Weather seasons are extremely important to all aspects of retailing. Averaging the start time of a weather-related season over several years is generally an error. There is only one time to have weather-related product on-hand—when the weather for the season breaks. Generally, a weather set-up is needed at the earliest time that the weather might break. Weather seasons generally decline slowly. Of course, you could consider a storm warning a "weather season" of a sort, and expect sales of bottled water, batteries, and flashlights to spike.

Payments. In some demographic areas, the monthly issuance of social security checks, food stamps, and so on can create a significant spike in overall volume. A similar pattern may appear where a large employer issues all of the town's paychecks. Generally, these payment seasons are monthly.

Bubble. Bubble seasons are weather related, but are characterized by a one-time consumer buy that saturates the market until the following year. Product examples include spring flowers and fertilizers, umbrellas, rubber boots and rain coats, swimsuits, and outdoor tools. Once such items are purchased, there will be only a few more bought—no matter how long the season is. This makes bubble seasons different from weather seasons, such as the drug industry's cough and cold season. The drug industry does regular repeat business on cough syrup throughout this particular season, especially if the weather stays extremely cold and rainy throughout.

Foot Traffic. Store foot traffic has daily, weekly, or monthly patterns. These traffic patterns create increased sales volume on products that have no natural seasonality.

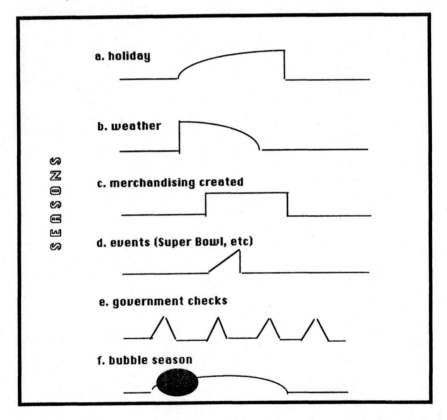

Stocking Level

If product is not available when consumers want it, the future forecast can be affected. This is particularly a problem for systems that have accurate perpetual inventories only once a week. These systems look at stock position and total sales at the end of the week. But if the product arrived on Monday, and the customers wanted it on Saturday, the accuracy of the actual forecast can be affected. Long-term out-of-stocks can also hurt demand. Consumers can lose their enthusiasm for the product, switch to another brand, or shop at an another store.

Pricing

Some products are basically commodities. They exhibit little or no brand loyalty and are extremely price sensitive. The demand is for a group of products and the sales vary by price point. But pricing includes more than cannibalization. When certain items become too expensive, they are viewed by consumers as luxuries rather than necessities. Obviously, the reverse is also true, as we continually see with personal computers and home electronics.

Promotions

As discussed in the promotion forecasting section, promotions are affected by a variety of factors with varying weights.

Brand Loyalty

Some products exhibit tremendous brand loyalty. For the forecasting system, these items "own their own history" and establish their own sales patterns. They may or may not follow the trends of the rest of the category.

Product Repackaging

Product repackaging is a type of new item, even when the UPC (EAN) does not change. Repackaging may have a positive or negative effect on appeal. There can be negative effects if, for example, the quantity of product is reduced, but the price stays the same.

Publicity

Publicity can create short-term trends which may or may not be sustainable. In order to forecast accurately, retailers must pay close attention to the products affected and be able to react quickly. Possible scenarios here include medical reports praising or condemning certain foods or medicines.

Appearance

Appearance includes the packaging, durability, color, and so on, and its appeal to the consumer.

Fashion

Fashion refers to the style's current popularity. This is product that is setting the fashion trend, in time with the current fashion, or a fashion miss.

Item Relationships

Companion Marketing

Some products are not advertised but experience sales increases when another item is marketed. Items affected by companion marketing can be the bean dip that is sold when the corn chips are on promotion, the mustard with the hot dogs, or the purse with the shoes.

In-Store Cannibalization

Product that is robbed of sales when another product is marketed or reduced in price is said to be cannibalized. Cannibalization also occurs when new brands, flavors, colors, or fragrances are introduced. This may occur within a category or from another department.

Shared Bar-Codes (UPC [EAN]) Cross SKUs

Problems can occur when there is one SKU with several different scannable items. Multiple bar-codes occur when there are multiple production sites, multiple suppliers, bonus or holiday packaging, diverter detection, or for a variety of other reasons. Forecasting must be for the group of bar-codes that are identified under one SKU.

Shared Items Cross Departments

Some products are located in several different departments. For example, in a craft store, glue may be set with wood crafts, with the glues, and with model planes. This increases impulse buys. However, some computer systems consider the product as actually being in different departments rather than just in different store locations. Systems that reserve a set of SKUs for each department may find the same product defined as two different SKUs. There is one product with one scannable UPC (EAN), but one or more SKU numbers on the master file. Sales history is arbitrarily maintained by the system. For example, a model airplane buyer made the last glue buy, so currently the system considers glue as part of his department. Suddenly the glue sales in wood crafts drop. Neither buyer has a clear picture of glue sales. This is a problem that should never occur, but it does. Two departments should never give one UPC (EAN) two different SKUs. Since forecasting must address all the bar-codes that share one SKU, it is impossible to identify the sales when one bar-code is reporting (randomly) to two SKUs.

Bonus Packs

Bonus packs have larger packages but often the same scan number as regular size. This is a difficult problem for forecasting since sales normally increase due to the bonus pack. However, the system is not able to recognize the bonus pack sales as separate from the normal sales.

Special Ads or Holiday Packaging

Sometimes, different packages share the same bar-code as regular product. This is just like the bonus pack problem, but with the additional difficulty that these holiday packs normally don't sell after the holiday and there is no way to distinguish them in the stores prior to season end. Assortment packaging (grouping mixed products into one sellable unit) makes forecasting extremely difficult. It robs sales from the normal single unit—often without the system support to track this relationship.

Set Sales (Table Linens, Bedding)

Consumers buy some products in units of more than one. These products are normally bought in sets, and in fact will not sell if there is not a set available. (CAO can create a self-fulfilling prophecy by reducing the product available in the store below a suitable minimum for the shoppers, and then reporting the product as a product that should be discontinued because it isn't selling.) A smoothed forecast may recommend that only one table napkin is necessary in a store, but the reality is that anything less than four or eight napkins will eliminate all sales. Clothing separates that combine to make a complete outfit present an even more difficult problem. Since people do not necessarily wear the same top and bottom size, the task of completing outfits is more difficult. Consumer impulse buys to complete a clothing combination are, of course, reduced if the combinations are not immediately available.

Catalytic Sales (Dish Sets and Accessories)

Some product is bought only with another product. Accessories to a main product normally won't be purchased at all if the main product is out of stock. Examples here include extra blades for food processors, serving utensils to flatware, and so on. Therefore, forecast is tied not only to the forecasted item, but also to the stock position of the base item. (The least desirable scenario is to have the catalyst in one store and the accessories in another.)

Sellable SKUs versus Orderable SKUs

Some products are ordered as a single SKU, but they are in fact made up of a nest or module of an assortment of UPCs (EANs) which are only reordered when a percentage of the total is sold. For example, this could be a nest of different sized baskets, or a free-standing module of different sizes and colors of hosiery. Often, this results in either out-of-stocks and low sales on the faster-moving SKUs within the assortment, or overstock on the slow movers.

Business Influences

Overall Business Climate

The overall business is usually declining or growing, regardless of what is happening to individual categories or items. Outside influences can have significant effects on several product lines at once.

Cyclical Economic Influences

Economic influences that affect disposable income are important but will not equally affect all product lines. For example, in tough times, people spend less on themselves. Men's and women's apparel sales are hurt when the economy suffers.

Legal Changes

Some product sales can be affected by laws restricting or expanding sales hours. An example might be a change in when liquor can or cannot be sold in supermarkets in certain states, or the hours of operation allowed for a type of retail outlet.

Store Influences

Competitive Store Openings and Closings

Individual stores' forecasted sales may jump or decline due to competition across all or some product lines. This can happen, for example, when a new category killer or club store opens in town.

Companion Store Openings and Closings

Individual stores' forecasted sales may jump or decline due to a companion retailer. Companion stores give weight and create a destination shopping experience. For example, when category killers group together, they increase their overall draw. All retail outlets have a basic driving radius from which their shoppers will arrive. Clusters normally increase this range.

Street Repairs

When access is blocked due to construction over a length of time, the forecast may be affected.

Impediments or Improvements to Transportation

Improved access, or changes in traffic flow that eliminate access, will have a long-term effect on forecast.

Weather

Weather that prevents or deters consumers from shopping can cause forecasting problems. Weather creates a desire for certain products. Bad weather years may need to be ignored when creating seasonal information for the future. A cold, wet spring will suppress the homeowner's desire to create a garden. A long, hot summer will encourage swimsuit and water sport sales.

Labor Unrest

Strikes, and other forms of unrest discourage consumers from shopping the affected store.

Competitive Store Labor Unrest

When the competitor's staff is on strike, sales can increase dramatically for the stores without labor problems.

Competitive Density

The general density of stores selling a particular product in a shopping area. Different types of stores have a different shopper radius, with club stores tending to have the largest. This must be considered when judging the influence of a new store opening.

Store Layout

Store Traffic Flow

Product that is set in a dead area of the store will create a low demand. The forecast will support this low demand. But bringing the product to a high-flow area, or eliminating the reason for the dead space, can completely change the actual demand.

Product Positioning

Products that are not in the right category group or the right location in the store will have a low demand and a low forecast. Some retailers still set shelves by supplier, rather than by consumer buying habits. This may work as a strategy in fashion, but it serves only to confuse the customer in other areas of retail.

Shelf Height

Products are normally displayed on shelves, pegboards, racks, or tables. Products that are placed at eye level are generally more visible to the consumer, and therefore have an advantage. Lighting can play a big role here—product on lower shelves may be less well-lit and truly not be visible to shoppers. Racks and tables mix products, and as a result sales are affected by the consumers' ability (or lack of ability) to locate desired sizes and colors.

Facings

Shelves and pegboards have specific facings for each product. For shelf product, a facing is each separate unit that can be "faced out." For example, if a box of detergent is given three spaces horizontally on the shelf and is stacked three high, the actual number of facings is nine. (Depth is the number of units behind each facing.) The more facings available for the product, the more the customer will notice it. Discounters often use this technique to give the impression of overwhelming supply.

Rack and Table Products

Rack and table products are displayed without definitive, separate locations for each item. Overcrowding makes it difficult for the consumer to locate the sizes and colors desired. Products arranged so that the consumer can readily distinguish sizes boosts sales. A store can enjoy a competitive advantage simply by arranging products so that consumers can easily find what they want.

Number of Locations within Store

Products—particularly those that are purchased on impulse to accompany other items—can be displayed in several locations within the store. Examples include batteries with toys or flashlights, scarves with blouses, crackers with soups, and dips with chips. We've noted earlier that it is difficult to address—solely through POS—what sales were generated from which location. It is also difficult to insure that put-away and audit counts are performed properly. This can be greatly helped by systems that provide not only planograms but also floor layouts. When these are integrated to the perpetual inventory system, it is possible to locate the product in all its locations. Customer cart and basket tracking systems, in combination with planograms and POS, reveal the "saturation" level of different store locations. Analyzing POS "market baskets" to determine the sales associated with catalyst items also can help evaluate the effect of marketing strategies and locations.

Corporate Influences

Marketing and Promotions

Featuring (or stopping to feature) selected product lines should have an overall effect on their sales. Overall corporate marketing strategies may emphasize or deemphasize selected lines.

Pro and Adverse Press about the Retailer

An increase or reduction of foot traffic should have an abrupt effect on demand.

Merchandising Strategies

Changes in merchandising strategies can have an ongoing effect on demand. Philosophical changes in store image can change customer draw. Even changes that enhance overall sales may detract from certain product lines that were previously more central to the image. For example, deciding to emphasize low price and deemphasize top brands may have an overall positive effect on profit, but certainly not on the sales of the top brands.

In the discussions of the forecasting formulas, the importance of these various sales influence will determine whether a formula will be successful in your environment.

FORECASTING COMPONENTS

Forecasting mathematics can be categorized as follows:

Sales Analysis

Sales analysis decides if the current data is usable, if a manual interface is required, or if a formula shift can be applied to realign the data to match appropriate stores, geography or time periods. This is a normal part of all forecasting systems. Examples of sales patterns to which usability edits are applied include:

- Unexpected and abrupt change in sales rate
- Sales not matching category (product group)
- Sales not matching geographic or demographic profiles

Sales analysis includes error checking and product edits for missing or incorrect products. In identifying all the influences on sales, we can see that sales analysis can result in changes to our math, but it can also result in changes to our merchandising.

Data Cleaning

Data cleaning edits for completeness, reasonability (is item movement "normal," "typical," or "expected?"), and data accuracy. In this phase, the data is measured against expected sales and known error rates. Where possible, the system researches the error and restores data to its correct values. Where the error cannot be identified through research, the data cleaning process may request manual audits. Data cleaning is offered by third-party vendors for a variety of different applications. This is an important function for suppliers and retailers. Forecasting well requires clean data.

Missing information is the reason most data is not usable. Usability edits often permit an automatic search to recover missing data. For example, unscheduled price changes may cause movement at the old price to be moved to an "exception" file and the movement counter to be reset to "0" in order to start counting sales at the new price. The edit system will notice that cumulative sales have been reset to "0" and will automatically look at the exception file to recover the missing unit movement.

Prediction

After the data quality has been assured, forecasting formulas are applied to create short- and/or long-range predictions of sales. This calculation may also include a volatility measure to determine safety stock. Most forecasts involve projection of previous sales trends using historical data, sometimes adjusted for planned promotions or price changes.

PREDICTION METHODS

Prediction forecasting can be categorized as:

- Naive
- Time series
- Statistical
- Artificial intelligence

In this section, we draw definitive lines between various forecasting techniques. This is done only to make it easier to understand each one. In reality, most systems combine these techniques, and the lines between them are not as definitive as depicted here.

Our goal here is to provide an overview, rather than an in-depth look at all forecasting methods. This discussion is not meant to be used for system design purposes and in no way attempts to provide complete mathematical information. This discussion is intended to help nontechnical readers understand various forecast methods so they can work more easily with software vendors and/or designers. For these reasons, the most simple versions of these formulas are presented. Often these formulas are implemented with mathematical modifiers not presented here.

For ease in writing, we use sales weeks to describe sales history in these examples. The discussions of forecasting could as easily refer to hours, days, months, periods, quarters, or years depending on the sales rate of the product and the forecasting goal. In deciding what length of time to use for forecasting, remember that forecasting too frequently can introduce unnecessary "noise," and forecasting too infrequently will mask important patterns.

In these examples, we use individual items as examples. The discussions of forecasting could as easily refer to geographic groupings such as stores or regions, or product groupings such as category or department. The level of the forecast depends upon its function. Using various levels of forecast in combination creates additional information as well as validation of the forecast.

PREDICTION METHODS

Naive

Naive forecasting is simply believing that what happened before will happen again. It is characterized by phrases such as:

"What was sold last quarter (month, period) is what we will sell next quarter (month, period)."

"What we sold last year during the winter season is what we will sell this year during the winter season."

"The average of the last two quarters (months, periods) is what we will sell next quarter (month, period)."

"What we sold the last time we promoted this item is what we will sell the next time we promote this item."

"Since this year our business is up 20%, we should plan that we will sell 20% more this quarter than we did this same quarter one year ago."

"This new item is enough like this old item that we will initially use the older item's forecast."

Naive forecasting is used when there really isn't enough history to do anything else. Naive forecasting can be used with long range forecasts such as merchandise planning, planograms, and production, as well as promotions and new items.

Advantages:

- Simple

- With limited data, it provides some information

Disadvantages:

- Cannot account for trends, business changes, current events

- Promotion history provides good information, but promotions can rarely be assumed to be identical

PREDICTION METHODS

Time Series

Simple Moving Average (SMA)

A simple moving average is the sum of the most recent weeks of product sales divided by the number of weeks used. This is the most simple and familiar of the formulas. A simple moving average uses only product sales. When the historical time frame is longer, there is more compensation for randomness—but the formula reacts slowly to changes in sales patterns. For example, if we use only two weeks, then what happened last week is going to have a much bigger effect on our forecast than if we use 20 weeks. The fewer factors used, the greater the effect that randomness will have on the calculation. Equal weight is given to each factor. Simple moving averages do not work well with fast-moving trends.

Advantages:
- A simple formula to understand
- The more factors used, the less the aberrations and errors in the data will affect the result
- Can handle extreme slow movers

Disadvantages:
- Uses only sales history, no other causal factors
- Cannot react to trends or seasons
- There is no error checking
- Cannot change forecast to react to outside influences
- Equal weight given to all factors

Explanation:

The most basic simple moving average formula is a two-week average:

(last week's sales + this week's sales) ÷ 2 = next week's forecast

Let's consider an example using instant ice tea. If 10 cases of ice tea sold last week and 20 cases sold this week, the average would be:

$$(10 + 20) \div 2 = 15$$

If the system used a two-week average, it would predict a need of 15 cases of ice tea for next week. This puts a lot of faith in the last two weeks of product movement. For example, let's say that normal movement on ice tea is about 15 cases per week. Then let's say there was an unusual heat wave last week, which just happened to coincide with the Little League playoffs in the store's neighborhood. As a result, last week's sales soared to 45 cases, instead of the usual 15. Now the two-week moving average would be:

$$(15 + 45) \div 2 = 30$$

The system now thinks that next week's demand will be 30 units. Using this method, the system will make a mistake not just this week but also next week, since this aberration will be included in our calculation next week too. (It's a separate question if you want to keep 50 cases around just in case there is another playoff tournament.) We know that the more factors used in the calculation, the greater the smoothing effect.

Let's look at the ice tea with a seven-week moving average:

(6 weeks ago) + (5 weeks ago) + (4 weeks ago) + (3 weeks ago)
+ (2 weeks ago) + (last week) + (this week)) ÷ 7 = forecast

or

$$(16 + 14 + 13 + 17 + 15 + 45 + 15) \div 7 = 19$$

So now we see that the effect of one week's aberration on the data is less disruptive. The system is now predicting that next week there will be sales of 19 cases of ice tea.

However, what happens when there is trend? Here's an example using our seven-week formula when the item is trending upward.

$$(5 + 10 + 15 + 20 + 25 + 30 + 35) \div 7 = 20$$

In this example, the forecast can't keep up with this rapid trend. Following this trend, we would believe that next week we would actually sell 40 cases of ice tea. Because this formula does not follow trend, it estimates sales of only 20 cases.

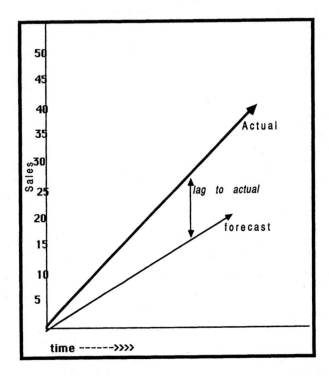

So what good is this simple formula? If we think about the product situations explained earlier, we see that perhaps this simple formula can have an important role in our calculations for very slow movers and new items. With new items, the number of weeks used depends on the rate of product movement or the number of weeks available. With slow movers, especially products that move less than one per week, we need to use many weeks, or months, to identify the sales rate (and perhaps several decimal places in our forecast).

It is important to remember that simplicity does not necessarily invalidate the usefulness of any formulas; nor, however, does it make the formula better.

PREDICTION METHODS

Time Series

Weighted Moving Average (WMA)

A weighted moving average uses the most recent weeks of sales more heavily than the prior weeks. The formula multiplies the recent weeks by weighted factors and then divides all the weeks by the number of weeks and weights used. This method has the same characteristics as simple moving average but relies more on recent history. As a result, it reacts more effectively to trend. However, invalid movement or randomness will have a more significant effect.

Advantages:

- Simple
- Reacts more to trends
- Reacts more to start of season

Disadvantages:

- Uses only sales history
- Does not get in front of trends or seasons
- Buys too heavily at season end
- No error checking
- Cannot change forecast to react to outside influences
- Oversensitive to data aberrations
- Weighting factor is a constant

Explanation:

There are many ways to weight a moving average. Obviously, the results vary by the weighting factor and the approach. For this discussion, we will use the same seven-week moving average. We use weighting factors that downplay sales from five and six weeks ago, and put emphasis on the more recent sales.

$$\text{Actual Sales: } 5 \quad 10 \quad 15 \quad 20 \quad 25 \quad 30 \quad 35$$

$$(.25(6 \text{ weeks ago}) + .50(5 \text{ weeks ago}) + .75(4 \text{ weeks ago})$$
$$+ 1.0(3 \text{ weeks ago}) + 1.25(2 \text{ weeks ago}) + 1.50(\text{last week})$$
$$+ 1.75(\text{this week})) \div 7 = \text{forecast}$$

$$(.25(5) + .50(10) + .75(15) + 1(20) + 1.25(25) + 1.50(30)$$
$$+ 1.75(35)) \div 7 = 25$$

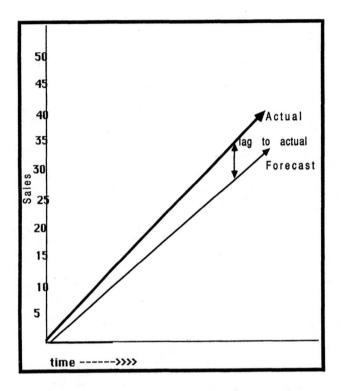

Those weights helped somewhat, but what if the weights were even stronger?

$$\text{Actual Sales: } 5 \quad 10 \quad 15 \quad 20 \quad 25 \quad 30 \quad 35$$

$$(.10(6 \text{ weeks ago}) + .25(5 \text{ weeks ago}) + .40(4 \text{ weeks ago})$$
$$+ 1.0(3 \text{ weeks ago}) + 1.25(2 \text{ weeks ago}) + 1.75(\text{last week})$$
$$+ 2.25(\text{this week})) \div 7 = \text{forecast}$$

$$(.10(5) + .25(10) + .40(15) + 1.0(20) + 1.25(25) + 1.75(30)$$
$$+ 2.25(35)) \div 7 = 27$$

The formula looks like it's not ahead of trend, but it does a better job keeping up than the simple moving average. No matter how much we weight the most recent past, we are always behind trend. If we went so far as to use a naive forecast approach and just say that because last week we sold 35, next week we will sell 35, we would still be wrong. With the existing trend, next week we are going to sell 40.

There are two big problems with this method. First, what if there isn't trend, but an aberration in the sales such as in the first example?

Actual Sales: 16   14   13   17   15   45   15

$$(.10(16) + .25(14) + .40(13) + 1.0(17) + 1.25(15) + 1.75(45)$$
$$+ 2.25(15)) \div 7 = 23$$

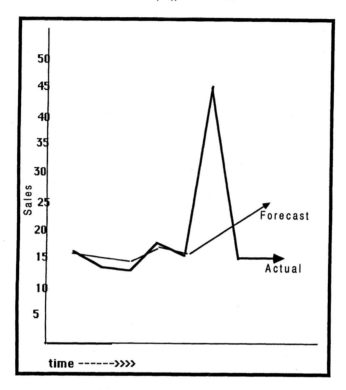

In this example, the weighted formula is reacting too much to the aberration. Furthermore, it will overreact to this aberration for three weeks (each of the weeks with the heavier weights). Without error checking, an aberration in data can cause a weighted moving average to swing too high or too low.

When there are seasons, particularly cliff seasons, the system also overreacts. In our earlier discussion of seasons, there was a picture of a cliff (holiday) season. In this diagram, we can see what will happen with these formulas. Going into the season, the forecast lags behind actual sales. Right before the season ends, the system will be using the height of the seasonal sales to make its projections. Even worse, it will be projecting accelerated sales into the future weeks—at precisely the time sales were about to stop.

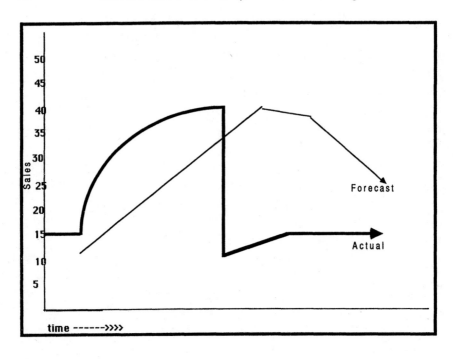

PREDICTION METHODS

Time Series

Double Moving Average (DMA)

The double moving average attempts to calculate the trend, rather than just chasing it as the weighted moving average does. First, double moving average calculates a simple moving average of actual sales to produce a forecast. Next, it calculates a moving average of the forecasts. Now we have both a moving average of our actual sales and a moving average of our calculated forecasts. The difference between these two is the "lag to trend." Therefore, if the forecast is consistently lagging behind actual sales by five packages a week, we can assume that if we add the difference to our simple moving average forecast, we will be closer to actual.

By computing the moving error, double moving average computes a trend factor which it then adds to the forecast for each progressive time period forecasted. The main advantage is that this formula doesn't just chase trend, but it gets ahead of trend. The danger here is that the calculation doesn't know the difference between a trend and a season. Double moving average, used alone, has no ability to manage seasons.

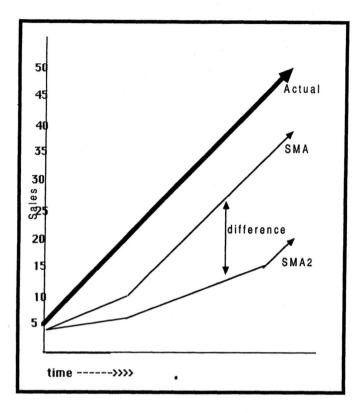

Advantages:

- Actually tries to get ahead of trend
- Reacts strongly to start of season

Disadvantages:

- Uses only sales history
- Cannot recognize difference between a trend and a season
- Buys too heavily at end of cliff-type seasons
- No error checking
- Cannot change forecast to react to outside influences
- Sensitive to data aberrations
- Users may have trouble understanding

Explanation:

Let's go back to our item that has been selling five per week, then starts trending upward at the rate of five more per week. All the previous weeks had sales of five items. We are using a six-week moving average. This chart shows ten weeks of calculations.

Actual is the actual sales each week.

SMA is the six-week simple moving average.

SMA2 is the simple moving average of the forecasts.

Diff is the difference between the average of actual sales (output of SMA) and the average of the forecasts (output of SMA2)

trend fcst is the addition of the diff (difference) to our calculated forecast (SMA)

Up trend:	1	2	3	4	5	6	7	8	9	10
Actual	5.0	10.0	15.0	20.0	25.0	30.0	35.0	40.0	45.0	50.0
SMA	5.0	6.7	7.5	10.0	13.3	17.5	22.5	27.5	32.5	37.5
SMA2	5.0	5.3	5.7	6.5	7.9	10.0	13.0	16.4	20.6	25.1
diff:	0.0	1.4	1.8	3.5	5.4	7.5	9.5	11.1	11.9	12.4
trend fcst:	5.0	8.1	9.6	13.5	18.7	25	32.0	38.6	44.4	49.9

In this sample, the trended forecast is still lagging slightly behind actual. By adjusting the number of sales weeks used and by using a weighted moving average rather than a simple moving average, the trended forecast would be closer to actual. A mathematical adjustment factor is usually calculated. This accelerates the trend even more. Eventually, the formula can actually get in front of trend and closer to actual.

Here is an example using a three-week moving average and a slowly down-trending item. If we added a mathematically calculated adjustment factor, we could actually go ahead of the trend.

Down trend:	1	2	3	4	5	6	7	8	9	10
Actual	30.0	28.0	26.0	24.0	22.0	20.0	18.0	16.0	14.0	12.0
SMA	30.0	29.3	28.0	26.0	24.0	22.0	20.0	18.0	16.0	14.0
SMA2	30.0	29.7	29.1	27.8	26.0	24.0	22.0	20.0	18.0	16.0
diff:	0.0	−.4	−1.1	−1.8	−2.0	−2.0	−2.0	−2.0	−2.0	−2.0
trend fcst:	30.0	28.9	26.9	24.2	22.0	20.0	18.0	16.0	14.0	12.0

The problems with a double moving average are the same as with weighted moving average. First, there is seasonality. Since these formulas can't recognize the difference between a trend and a season, they easily predict sales after the season has ended. The following sample is a holiday cliff season.

Season:	1	2	3	4	5	6	7	8	9	10
Actual	5.0	10.0	15.0	20.0	25.0	30.0	35.0	40.0	45.0	50.0
SMA	5.0	6.7	7.5	10.0	13.3	17.5	22.5	27.5	32.5	37.5
SMA2	5.0	5.3	5.7	6.5	7.9	10.0	13.0	16.4	20.6	25.1
diff:	0.0	1.4	1.8	3.5	5.4	7.5	9.5	11.1	11.9	12.4
trend fcst:	5.0	8.1	9.6	13.5	18.7	25.0	32.0	38.6	44.4	49.9

Season:	11.0	12.0	13.0	14.0	15.0
Actual	50.0	5.0	5.0	5.0	5.0
SMA	41.6	37.5	32.5	26.7	20.0
SMA2	29.8	19.9	34.9	34.7	32.6
diff:	11.8	17.6	−2.4	−8.0	−12.6
trend fcst:	53.4	55.1	30.1	10.7	7.4

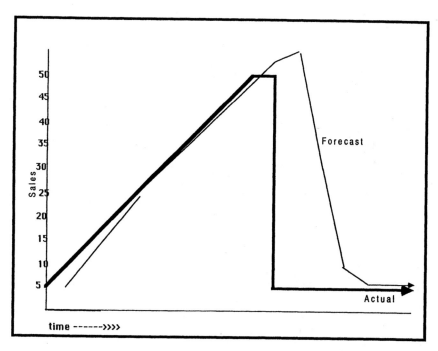

As you can see, the forecast continues to build product after the season has ended. This sample is using trend just one week out. Normally, once trend is calculated, it is assumed to continue. Therefore, if product is increasing its sales by five per week, we assume that next week we will sell five more than this week, the week after that we will sell 10 more, the next week 15 more, and so on. This is very good logic when we have actually determined a trend. Of course this sort of assumption at the crest of season would build disastrously high inventories.

The second problem is that when we combine this formula with a weighted moving average, there is no definitive way to establish the weights. Moreover, once the weights have been established, they are fixed with no automatic way to adjust them.

Third, there is no way to apply an abrupt change to the forecast due to a change in competition or business climate. What if our biggest competitor has decided to go out of business and we want to be sure we are the retailer that picks up the customers? We want to be in a good in-stock position to impress these new potential shoppers. However, there is no way to "jump" all the forecasts by 20% due to an expected sales increase, and maintain that jump thereafter. (Many people recommend "changing history" in order to change the ongoing forecast with moving average formulas. We feel that any distortion of this most precious business resource, your sales history, is a severe error.) Each time the system calculates the new forecast, it goes back through history and reuses the same data.

Fourth, double moving average requires the system to keep many different factors in order to make the calculation. The number depends on how many weeks are being used in the smoothing routine. Deciding on how many weeks are needed is based on the item sales rate.

Double moving average works very well with horizontal or trended sales, but runs into problems with seasons.

PREDICTION METHODS

Time Series

Exponential Smoothing

Exponential smoothing is mathematically similar to a weighted moving average, but it reduces the need to carry as many forecasting factors. It also creates a forecast that can be maintained into the future, and it is easier to error-check. The exponentially smoothed forecast is a percentage of the old forecast added to a percentage of actual to produce the new forecast. The percentages we use are similar to the weights selected for the weighted moving average. Normally these weights vary between 90% of old forecast + 10% of actual sales for items that are not showing signs of rapid changes in pattern. For items that are more volatile, weights are more commonly in the range of 70% of old forecast plus 30% of actual.

$$90\% \text{ (old forecast)} + 10\% \text{ (actual sales)} = \text{new forecast}$$

$$70\% \text{ (old forecast)} + 30\% \text{ (actual sales)} = \text{new forecast}$$

Advantages:
- Not difficult to understand
- Can change forecast manually to react to outside influences
- Can error-check with system and change forecast automatically
- Can error-check and react to aberrations in data

Disadvantages:
- Uses only sales history
- Reacts the same as weighted moving average to trends and seasons
- Weighting factor is a constant
- Buys too heavily at end of cliff-type seasons

Explanation:

Adding together what we thought was going to happen and a little of what actually happened is the basis for exponential smoothing. For example,

$$80\%(15) + 20\%(20) = 16$$

Balancing the percentages is identical to balancing the weights on the weighted moving average. There is always confusion with system users on how fast to smooth the calculation. For example, if there is product trending up at the rate of five cases per week, the temptation is to smooth faster and faster in order to "keep up with trend." If the product sold 45 last week, 50 this week, and will sell 55 next week, no matter how fast we smooth, the forecast will still be behind trend.

$$
\begin{aligned}
80\%(45) + 20\%(50) &= 46 \\
70\%(45) + 30\%(50) &= 46.5 \\
60\%(45) + 40\%(50) &= 47 \\
50\%(45) + 50\%(50) &= 47.5 \\
40\%(45) + 60\%(50) &= 48 \\
30\%(45) + 70\%(50) &= 48.5 \\
20\%(45) + 80\%(50) &= 49 \\
10\%(45) + 90\%(50) &= 49.5 \\
0\%(45) + 100\%(50) &= 50
\end{aligned}
$$

Even with 100% of the actual we are still behind trend, since next week we will sell 55. The only way to keep up with trend is to get ahead of it as with double moving average. Exponential smoothing works like a weighted moving average, not a double moving average.

Here is an example of how exponential smoothing works. We will use 80% of the old forecast and 20% of actual sales. The new forecast is what we think we will sell next week.

Actual: 5   10   15   20

Week 1:

Starting forecast is   5

Actual sales are   5

Calculation   80% (5) + 20% (5) = 5

New forecast   5

Week 2: |

Starting forecast is   5

Actual sales are   10

Calculation   80% (5) + 20% (10) = 6

New forecast   6

Week 3: |

Starting forecast is   6

Actual sales are   15

Calculation   80% (6) + 20% (15) = 7.8

New forecast   8

Week 4: |

Starting forecast   8

Actual sales are   20

Calculation   80% (8) + 20% (20) = 10.4

New forecast   10.4

As you can see, a trend factor would be needed to keep up with this steep trend. Trend can be combined with exponential smoothing—using what is called double exponential smoothing. This is identical logic to double weighted average, but uses the exponential smoothing logic. The disadvantage would be the same as we have seen with double moving average, since the formula cannot recognize the difference between a trend and a season.

One advantage of the exponential smoothing formula is that fewer factors need be stored than with moving averages or double moving averages. A second advantage is that since the old forecast is the basis of all further calculations, we can error-check and change this number to cause all future forecasts to be adjusted—without affecting sales history. For example, let's say we decide to cut back on variety and not carry one of two competing brands. We check our past sales of both brands combined, and take into consideration our customers' lack of brand loyalty. We figure we can expect a 50% hike in sales on our remaining brand. All we have to do is fill out the shelf sets and up the old forecast by 50% at the appropriate time, and our system has accounted for this sweeping merchandising adjustment.

Another advantage is that it is possible to analyze our forecast against actual sales to make a determination of the quality of the forecast. This allows us to produce warnings to inventory managers that a forecast is not reflecting actual sales. An item (item A) can average sales of 50 per week by selling 25 one week and 75 another week and continually bouncing back and forth between these extremes. Another item (item B) can average sales of 50 per week by selling 48 one week and 52 another week. By measuring this average error (the average amount the forecast misses each week) we see that item A has an error of 25 and item B has an error of only 2. So if Item A reports sales of 75 this week, these sales look reasonable since we know that this item is relatively "bouncy." On the other hand, if item B reports sales of 75, we would ask if this was due to an unreported promotion or if there were another reason.

Unusual sales movement, promotion periods, and sale spikes can be ignored by "freezing forecast" during the period when sales do not represent the base pattern.

As with weighted moving average, there is no definitive way to set the percentages (weights). Furthermore, once the percentages are set, they do not react automatically to changes in product situations.

Note: There are two different formulas that are mathematically identical for exponential smoothing. You may be familiar with this other formula.

$$\text{exponential smoothing} = \text{old forecast} + 20\%(\text{error})$$
$$\text{error} = \text{actual} - \text{old forecast}$$

$$= \text{old forecast} + 20\%(\text{actual} - \text{old forecast})$$
$$= 100\% \text{ old forecast} + 20\%\text{actual} - 20\%\text{old forecast}$$
$$= (100\% \text{ old forecast} - 20\%\text{old forecast}) + 20\%\text{actual}$$
$$= 80\%\text{old forecast} + 20\%\text{actual}$$

PREDICTION METHODS

Time Series

Adaptive Filtering/Variable Weight Smoothing

Variable rate smoothing is similar to exponential smoothing, but the weighting factor is calculated based on the system's knowledge of ongoing error, deviation from forecast, and product influences or situations. Variable rate smoothing attempts to resolve the problem of setting and maintaining the weighting factors. This difficult problem is incurred in both weighted moving average and exponential smoothing.

This is the first formula that attempts to introduce "judgment" into the equation. The previous formulas used history and mathematics, but all analysis was manual. This formula does try to analyze how reactive the weights need to be. A reactive formula uses more recent sales than a formula that is set to be less reactive.

Adaptive filtering is a mathematically defined technique using past observations to set the weights of future forecast periods. Adaptive filtering and variable rate smoothing are not identical but the advantages of both are similar. Variable rate smoothing does not have a precise mathematical definition and varies in definition with the software system. Adaptive filtering has a precise definition that is beyond the scope of this book.

Advantages:

- Forecast is reactive
- System error-checks and automatically adjusts forecast
- System error-checks and produces recommendations for manual intervention
- Weighting factor adjusts dynamically

Disadvantages:

- Some complexity to install and use
- Uses only sales history
- Reacts the same as weighted moving average to trends and seasons
- Buys too heavily at end of cliff-type seasons

Explanation:

Variable rate smoothing attempts to resolve the problem of setting the weighting factor that was incurred in both weighted moving average and exponential smoothing. The weighting factor is also referred to as the smoothing rate or the alpha. Depending on the software system using this formula, there are several different ways and reasons for adjusting the weights.

Weights may be adjusted by circumstances. The systems may be set to be more reactive after the end of a promotion or during a season. The weights may be set to be less reactive when a product is out of season or if the product is a slow mover.

Weights may be adjusted by analyzing error. Error is the deviation between forecast and actual sales. Later in this chapter we will discuss in detail some error measurement techniques. The basic assumption is that when the forecast is not tracking closely to actual sales, the formula must become more reactive.

When the forecast is doing a good job predicting actual sales, the weighting factors do not need to be overly reactive.

Weights may be adjusted by analyzing trends. When a sales trend is detected, the system may need to react more quickly to recent sales. Although this formula is flexible and reactive, it does have the same problem as the weighted moving average formula as far as not being able to differentiate a trend from a season. Promotions and unusual movement are ignored using the "freeze" forecast logic.

Exponential smoothing formulas are based on sales history. Although the formulas can be taught to be more reactive, unusual movement—whether caused by a promotion or an "aberration"—are limited to historical sales (or demand). When other factors such as seasons or weather are affecting forecast, new techniques must be introduced. There are two possibilities. One is to introduce an external overlay to de-seasonalize or de-weatherize the forecasts. The other is to try to incorporate other factors into the basic forecasting formulas.

PREDICTION METHODS

Time Series

Seasonal Indices and Decomposition Forecasting

These formulas attempt to separate the *baseline* or normal demand forecast from other factors such as seasonality, cycles, trends, promotions, or weather. (Note: we are using the term *baseline* in the generic sense, not in any software systems specific definition. The definition of baseline varies among various systems.) By decomposing the forecast, the various factors can be separated and managed with overlays and/or profiles. This allows the system to analyze the sales demand including its upward and downward trends without these outside influences.

There are several factors that affect forecasts. When the forecast is broken apart or decomposed into its various factors, we can talk about the forecast separately from its trend, promotion, weather, or seasonal factor.

Advantages:

- Can change forecast manually to react to outside influences
- Can error-check with system and change forecast automatically
- Can error-check and react to aberrations in data
- Can react to seasons
- Can implement trend calculations
- Can "stop" the system during promotion periods

- "Intuitive appeal of seasonal profiles presented in charts"

Disadvantages

- Does not consider all the factors affecting sales
- Data to create profiles may not be available
- Profiles at SKU store level may be difficult to maintain
- Requires concentrated up front work and ongoing maintenance

Explanation:

Seasonality. By using seasonal indices (profiles) it is possible to deseasonalize actual sales and analyze those sales without the seasonal influences. For example, the new line of private label men's neckties is growing steadily in popularity and trending upward. We expect at Father's Day to sell four times our normal number of these neckties. When we remove this expectation from the data, we see that the ties are trending upward before, during, and after Father's Day. Because we recognized the upward trend before the season began, we were in a good stock position for Father's Day.

Many retail items are seasonal. Seasonal indices (profiles) are used for basic items that have a seasonal component. Our first example is frozen orange juice. Frozen orange juice actually has two seasons. It has a rather long summer season which varies regionally, but is related to warm weather. It also has a lesser and shorter (but important) Christmas holiday season, when it is used as a mixer with holiday cocktails.

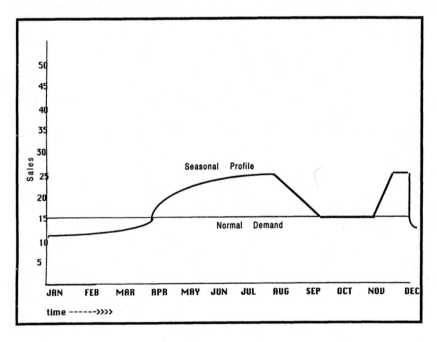

The seasonal indices (profiles) are created mathematically from two or more years of history of sales. After the system creates the indices, staff personnel who know the product line review the indices for accuracy. The indices are as good as the quality of the sales history the systems are using to create them. Normally, initially creating the seasonal indices is a time-consuming process. Graphic representations of seasonal profiles greatly aid the manual effort of reviewing seasonal profiles.

Seasonal profiles have "intuitive" appeal because it is easy to create visual representations of the seasonal curves. Once the time-consuming task of creating and modifying the seasonal profiles has been completed, inventory control personnel can maintain the seasonal profiles in successive years and for new items. The index profile can be created for a group of seasonally similar items. For example, a retailer may sell short leather jackets all year. All the short leather jackets will have increased sales starting in the fall as the weather cools down, and again at Christmas as gifts. All color, sizes, and styles have the same seasonal profile.

Normally, seasonal profiles provide one index for every forecast period. These indices can be created at the level of one item per store or in seasonally pure groups. These seasonally pure groups can be like items within a category, or across a geographic region. When systems attempt to "group" items into one profile, they must also be able to identify the items that don't fit the grouping—the "outliers." If we use the short leather jacket example, we find that the winter profile holds true for all this retailers' outlets except in San Francisco, where the lighter weight jackets sell all summer due to the cool summer nights there.

A nursery supply company has one spring fertilizer seasonal profile for all of its Midwestern and Eastern seaboard companies. The Florida division, however, has a winter planting season and a reverse profile to the rest of the company.

Inexpensive artist paints have a fairly flat profile when looked at as a group. But when we look at the individual paints, we find that the orange and black paints have a Halloween season, the red, green, gold, and silver have a Christmas season, and the pastel plants have an Easter season. Therefore, these paints cannot therefore be grouped into one seasonal profile.

Items with vastly different sales rates can be grouped under one seasonal profile as long as the rate at which sales increase in-season is the same (rate of change versus rate of sales). Since the indices are multiplied times the correct sales rate, it doesn't matter if the item is selling two or 20 per week. What matters is that we expect these grouped items to sell three times their non-seasonal rate during the height of in-season. We expect the slower item to sell $3 \times 2 = 6$ per week, and the faster item to sell $3 \times 20 = 60$ per week.

Think back on our children's book example from the slow mover section. There is a need for caution here. In general, children's books advance in sales during the Christmas season when they are given as gifts. But expensive gift books are exceedingly slow off-season, so their increase is considerably more than the increase of the books that are bought year-round. There are also books in the mix that are slow because they are not popular. They have no increase during the Christmas season.

Weather and Promotion Profiles. A similar logic applies for promotions and weather overlays. The differences are that promotions and weather are not identically repeatable year to year, and that the data to analyze promotions and weather may not be available. As we discussed in "Promotion Sales Influences," the data needed to predict the effect of a promotion may not be available.

With profiles, we are able to account for sales influences that we were not able to consider in previous formulas. But what if we want to consider the effect of individual pricing and promotion decisions? We would need to consider the relationship of these sales influences as they relate not independently to the sales rate, but as they influence the sales rate in compounded fashion. Influences like promotions and seasons are not additive, however. They have a relationship that we cannot define using simple profiles.

PREDICTION METHODS

Statistical

Multiple Regression

Multiple regression assumes that the causal relationship on sales trend is influenced by more factors than past sales. It allows the user to enter a series of other influences. Other factors to consider are changing seasons, weather, demographics, manufacturer-sponsored promotions, GNP and consumer confidence indices, business cycles, retail prices, competitors' actions, in-store product cannibalization, and health warnings. Multiple regression can be an extremely effective tool for forecasting if the other factors can be quantified, maintained, and electronically stored.

Perhaps the easiest way to think about multiple regression is to consider it as the ability to use multiple sales influences in different relative weights. Assigning and creating these weights is the task of implementing and designing the multiple regression formula.

Advantages:

- Accuracy can be evaluated statistically
- Factors used are relative
- Reacts well to trends

- Can consider any factors that can be quantified, maintained, and electronically stored.

Disadvantages:

- Difficult for users to understand
- Difficult to obtain necessary factors
- Relative weights of factors are fixed
- May be "too much" formula for some product

Explanation:

Using multiple regression, the correlation of the various factors and the significance of those factors can be calculated. Multiple regression can be used as the forecasting technique or as the basis for evaluating various factors (other than past sales) in other forecasting methods.

Selecting, obtaining, and quantifying variables is an extremely difficult and time-consuming task. Variables must be independent influences on future sales. For example, price increases or competitive product price increases might be seen to have a direct relationship to forecasted sales on highly price-sensitive products. It is important not to duplicate what is essentially the same piece of information. For example, coffee prices increase when there are weather problems in South America. In this case, the system wouldn't need both "weather problems in South America" and "price increases," since they are really one and the same issue.

Multiple regression is a method that allows the user to predict sales using prices, promotion activity, seasonal influences, and competitive activity. Each factor must be defined and correlated.

When would multiple regression be useful? One example would be a hosiery sale. Through our data we know that if we reduce the price by more than 20%, we can increase sales. But if we also set up a freestanding module, there is another significant increase. If we set the module in a high-traffic area near the cash registers, we increase sales even more. But if all brands go on sale at the same time, then this individual brand suffers because other brands are more popular.

Normally, on the Fourth of July, we sell enormous amounts of charcoal and barbecue utensils. We run a full-page ad with coupons. However, we also know that the forecasters are predicting an unusually cold and wet Fourth of July. As always, many factors influence our expected sales.

The challenges of multiple regression are obtaining, defining, and correlating the potential factors. Identifying a complete set of factors is difficult and time-consuming. Mathematics cannot tell us what data is missing—it can only tell us that the formula is not tracking as closely as we would like. Often, when we discover the data that is missing, we also discover that we do not have access to the data that we need.

Multiple regression is a lot of wasted formula if it is doing no more than what exponential smoothing or seasonal profiling would be doing because of lack of data.

Another problem is that this is a static model. The relative weights are set when the system is designed and implemented. The system can analyze itself as to the quality of the forecast, but it does not dynamically change or "learn." However, there are implementations of this method that have been coded to "learn." This is an important question to ask system providers.

PREDICTION METHODS

Statistical

Box-Jenkins and Focus Forecasting

Box-Jenkins and Focus Forecasting, although different mathematical models, both say that we don't know the best model up front, and that the system is where the model can be determined. In these approaches, the system analyzes the relevance of forecasting models or patterns and iteratively selects the best model.

Each of these methods begins with a static choice of several models. Over time, the models and weights are analyzed for the quality of the forecast to actual sales. Depending on the software installation, the system than selects the correct models and weights, or suggests the selection to the system manager who makes the final approval.

Advantages:
- Not all items should be using the same formula
- Same advantages as individual formulas that are used

Disadvantages:
- Difficult for users to understand
- Requires ongoing user interface
- Statistics do not recognize incomplete data

Explanation:

Where these approaches vary between software installations is the amount of human interface they require to make their decisions. For example, there is obviously a difference in the amount of time a manager can afford to spend reviewing individual forecasts when forecasting 100 very expensive jewelry settings or over 100,000 SKUs at the Hypermart. Generally in retail and especially for store level CAO, the idea of a self-evaluating system that doesn't use extensive personnel time is preferable.

The model types used in Box-Jenkins and Focus Forecasting are by definition quite different. However, the software systems using these methods do not necessarily adhere to these strict mathematical definitions.

There is a great appeal to a system that can vary the model depending on the product situation: slow mover, new, normal, or promotion. As explained earlier, one item can pass through each of these product situations at different times of the year or during the item life cycle. These systems use "judgment" in selecting the correct model. These systems essentially are still choosing between models with fixed relationships.

PREDICTION METHODS

Artificial Intelligence

Artificial intelligence (AI) systems are mathematical models of theorized brain activity, and offer a completely new approach to forecasting. They use many more factors than simple time series mathematics. AI is not static in the relative weights that are applied to the various factors or in the way the relationship between factors is defined. But AI requires the ability to collect and store a variety of forecasting factors in order to fully utilize AI's capabilities. AI uses history, models, and judgment, but AI can also learn from experience, and is therefore a dynamic approach.

(AI is also referred to as neural networks, connectionism, adaptive systems, adaptive networks, artificial neural networks, neurocomputers, and parallel distribution processors.)

Advantages:

- Relative weights of factors are dynamic
- AI can use any and all factors that can be quantified, maintained, and electronically stored
- The most dynamic of the formulas

Disadvantages:

- Difficult for users to understand
- Long-term implementation
- Necessary data may not be available or correct
- Requires ongoing user interface at a level that may not be available

Explanation:

Neural networks are normally used in retail for one-off analysis, but have the ability to be a central part of forecasting technology.

AI mimics human thinking and differs from traditional computer software in the following ways:

Non-sequential Logic. When people consider a problem, they consider all aspects of the problem simultaneously and analogously to other similar situations. Traditional computer programs think sequentially (what we old COBOL programmers remember as our nested if—then statements.) Even many "expert systems" still copy this strict, sequential, if—then logic. Sequential logic says that for every cause there is an effect; if A happens then B will happen. Why do we care about this when we are forecasting sales? Let's think in terms of the Fourth of July promotion that we discussed previously. What if we decide to advertise charcoal and other barbecue supplies? There is the effect of running a full-page color ad. Then, we decide to reduce price, and we also decide to build a colorful end-rack display in our "hottest" end aisle right near the registers. What can we expect to sell? We also have a long-term weather forecast of cold and rain this Fourth of July. Maybe this isn't the best merchandising strategy. As intelligent people, we consider all these combinations in combination, not one by one.

Additive Knowledge. Human knowledge grows. Computers replace information. When storage space in the computer is limited, we summarize detail information for storage and back older information out to tape storage. We humans maintain an amazing amount of learned and experiential information. Even information we would prefer to forget is permanently lodged. As humans, we consciously and unconsciously draw upon this mass of information. AI uses masses of information in its learning and decision-making processes. Of course, what is problematic for retailers is that they may not have electronically stored the pertinent information.

Flexible Connections. Humans not only change and increase their information base, but they change and reshape the connections of information. As humans, we change the way we relate pieces of information together. As we look back on past formulas, we see that not only are the strategies sequential, but also the way information is related is inflexible. This is not just a matter of changing weights, but of actually redefining the relationship. Not all AI installations are this flexible, but the possibility exists within this technology for the system to learn over time.

The following was provided by Global Management Technologies of Norcross, Georgia.

Neural networks use a methodology designed to capture, retain and distill patterns of information in a fashion similar to that of the neurons in the human brain. These networks are designed to emulate the brain's ability to identify patterns and arrive at a conclusion. This methodology is recognized to include the processes that give computers the ability to "learn."

The benefits of this approach results in a system that can accurately predict customer demand by detecting both prominent and subtle patterns in history. Much like a human gains knowledge through experience, a neural network's accuracy improves as more history is learned.

Each neural network is trained and used to solve a particular problem; to store and process a specific pattern. It may not yield the exact answer, but will give a very close one. More importantly the neural network takes all the inter-related and varying conditions into account. Overall, it is more accurate than statistical or expert system methods in cases where many variables must be considered. Much like a manager using what he has learned from past experiences to make future sales predictions, a neural network learns from collected history and makes its predictions. Problems with normal forecasting methods include limited data and/or lack of accurate information. Old data, graphs and charts must be located and combined with some form of regression analysis or moving average, with a twist of human instinct to produce usable satisfactory answer.

A typical neural network consists of three parts, the input layer, the output layer and the hidden nodes in the middle. The inputs are the conditions that affect your forecast (day of week, holidays, weather, etc.). The outputs are the answers, the forecast. They are connected by "hidden nodes."

Each neuron in one layer is connected to a neuron in the next layer. These connections represent weighted values which are applied to the values passed to the second (hidden) layer. Neurons in the hidden layer serve as feature detectors and enable the network to solve nonlinear problems. Neurons in the hidden layer "fire" or produce outputs by an activation function (also called the squashing function) and map the sum into the neuron's output value. The hidden layer passes values to the output layer in the same manner, the output layer produces the desired results (predictions).

The network "learns" by adjusting the interconnection weights. The results produced by the network are compared repeatedly with the correct answers and each time the connecting weights are adjusted slightly in the direction of the correct answers. A network is trained until this error reaches its minimum. Eventually, if the problem can be learned, a stable set of weights adaptively evolves and will produce reliable answers for all the sample decisions or predictions. The real power of neural networks is evident when the trained network is able to produce good results for data which the network has never "seen." This is the ability to generalize, something humans do with ease.

Once trained, a neural network can be used to predict results given by previously unseen inputs. (i.e., if you feed the neural network a combination of inputs, it will supply you with an answer, a prediction.)

The advantages of neural networks over rule-based systems or more primitive types of pattern recognition systems are:

- Neural networks are self-adapting. They will "see" the trends in your sales. As the patterns (or rules) change so will your neural network.

- Easy to maintain. If accuracy is falling, just retrain your network with more history/data.

- Easy to update. If you need to add a new condition or input, it's simple to add the new input then retrain the network. In a rule based system, you would have to rewrite the entire system.

- Increased accuracy.

	SMA	WMA	DMA	EXP	DECOMP	MULT REG	BOX JEN	AI
sales history	X	X	X	X	X	X	X	X
follows trend	X	X	X	X	X	X	X	X
maintenance				X	X	X	X	X
ahead of trend			X		O	O	O	O
seasons					X	O	O	X
mult factors						X	O	X
best model							X	X
dynamic fctrs						O		X
learns						O		X

where,

X indicates that this is a standard part of this model

(O) indicates an optional part of this model

EXCEPTION ANALYSIS

Almost all prediction methods depend on some level of manual intervention to maintain the forecasting system. When forecasting retail, we are really trying to forecast human behavior—which is no easy task. The difficulty in exception analysis is finding the balance between creating careful forecasting and yet avoiding a personnel-intensive audit control. The goal of exception analysis is not to eliminate all manual intervention, but to direct personnel to the most productive use of their time. Even if the forecasting and ordering system is so efficient that it can manage inventory without any out-of-stocks or overstocks and without any manual intervention, the system uses exception analysis to alert for merchandising opportunities and shelf space requirements.

Item-Based Exception Analysis

Exception analysis in forecasting occurs within all three of the forecasting components:

• Sales analysis
• Data cleaning
• Prediction

It is important to remember that forecasting or prediction is generally wrong. What is important is that the forecast is wrong within a reasonable tolerance, and that this tolerance has been correctly measured. The tolerance is one of the major factors in building safety stock. When the safety stock is sufficient, the service level objective can be met.

Time series models are not able to use all the pertinent factors that affect forecasting. Statistical and AI models can use many more factors, but these systems may not be set up correctly or may not be able to access all the necessary information. What is perceived to be product forecasting variability may actually be a lack of sufficient information. When the product variability is artificially high due to lack of information, the system and the store require excessive safety stock to cover for forecasting error.

As we saw with the various forecasting methods, error detection causes these systems to take different actions. Most of the static time series models can only report problems with forecasting to management. Variable rate smoothing uses the error rate to adjust its weights. Box-Jenkins and Focus Forecasting use error to select the correct model and adjust weights. When profiles are used, error may indicate that this item has an incorrect seasonal profile.

Error is the difference between what was expected and what actually happened. It is a simple subtraction. Exception routines smooth, square, square root, and take the absolute value of this error. By mathematically adjusting the error, the system is able to recognize spikes in the error, trends in the error, and overall product volatility. The goal is to find when the current error in measuring forecast or data is beyond reasonable expectation. This will vary considerably by product type and product situation.

Error terminology that you might hear when reviewing forecasting systems includes the following:

ERROR = Actual Sales − Forecast

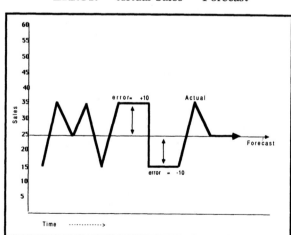

Sum of Errors (SOE)

The sum of errors is an ongoing addition of each period's error. This is an indication of trend. Error is summed with positive and negative errors. If the error is evenly divided between positive and negative, the SOE will be close to zero.

Smooth Sum of Errors (SSOE)

The smooth sum of errors is a weighted moving average of the sum of errors. Like SOE, if the error is both positive and negative, the SSOE is close to zero. If the error is consistently positive or negative, this would show that the forecast is not keeping up with the upward or downward trend.

Mean Absolute Deviation (MAD)

The mean absolute deviation sums all error—whether negative or positive—as positive (absolute). MAD is used as a measure of sales volatility, since MAD measures all the deviations. MAD, as a measure of sales volatility, is often used as a factor in safety stock. Unlike SSOE or SOE, MAD is not tracking to a trend but rather simply measuring how "bouncy" this item's sales rate is and how much off from actual sales is the forecast.

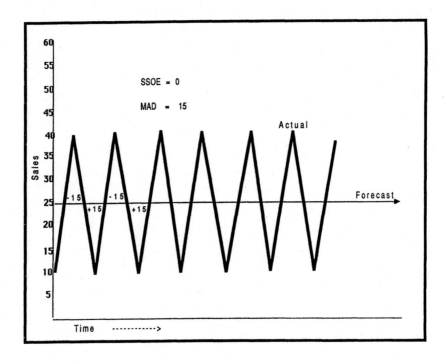

Mean Square Error (MSE)

The mean square error squares each error and then sums this error. This works the same as taking the absolute value, but it puts emphasis on the bigger errors as more important.

How does error detection work with each of the product situations? It is reasonable to expect that a *new item* will do the unexpected and require manual intervention. New items are affected by manufacturer promotions, retailer promotions, customer initial interest, competitors' reactions, inability of the supplier to deliver, and a myriad of other factors. A new item can potentially affect the sales of the entire category.

Promotion forecasts often lack sufficient data to be accurate. Promotions require careful attention since they are particularly important to consumers. The unexpected always is worth our attention with promotion product.

Slow movers are not appropriate for traditional forecast error detection techniques. The slower the sales, the more that noise or randomness plays a role. In some ways, all slow mover sales are an exception. Toning down the slow mover exception reporting and understanding the different types of slow movers is imperative in keeping the manual intervention reasonable.

Demand forecasting exception reporting must be able to determine:

• Is there a data problem?
• Is the forecast and tolerance calculation not matching actual sales?
• Is the item variability (tolerance) unreasonably large?
• Is this a situation that requires manual intervention?
• Is an automatic system adjustment needed?

Comparative-Based Exception Analysis

Comparing an item to its own history is not the only form of exception analysis. An item's movement, trend, and seasonality can be compared to the store's movement, trend, and seasonality. An item and a category can be compared demographically and geographically to other item and category performances. In this way, differences and problems are identified. For example, if an item is selling in all stores but one, this may indicate a problem in the store set or merchandising. When there are stocking problems, other stores or other items within the category in one store can be used to project the forecast.

OUTPUT AND BENEFITS

Demand and Promotion Forecasting provide input to:

Order Determination

Forecasting is not used by all order determination modules, but in some form it is used by all *dynamic* order determination modules. In the order determination function, the forecast can be compared to other similar stores to determine if sales are above or below the expected norm.

Labor Scheduling

In order to schedule store personnel, there must be a projection of both sales and receipts. Labor scheduling differs from other sales forecasting in its emphasis on time-of-day projections.

Promotion Planning

As discussed earlier, forecasting promotions is limited only by the ability of the retailer to retain and quantify promotion data. Promotion forecasting can provide input to the merchandise plan to support the development of the promotional markdown.

Category Management

Category management organizes groups of merchandise as business entities to be managed by an individual or group. Item forecasts and trends help the manager identify and control the items included in the category. The item forecasts provide sales estimates, projected turns, and ROI information.

Supplier Direct Deliveries

Suppliers use forecasts to control their production lines (MRP), delivery schedules, and retailer service level. They must depend heavily on good data cleaning and sales analysis formulas since they have no direct control of the retailers' in-store procedures. Suppliers use both long- and short-term forecasts.

DSD Audit

Although DSD is a supplier-controlled function, the forecasting algorithms can be used to audit the deliveries. The axiom in DSD—a theft is as good as a sale—is unfortunately true. The forecasting function gives the retailer the ability to control this often out-of-control area.

Planogram Setup and Audit

Planogram setup is initiated using item level forecasts. There is no reason for these forecasting routines to be different from the other store forecasting routines. The only difference is the length of time of the forecast, since obviously a planogram is set for several months into the future. The ongoing problem with planograms is maintenance. The forecast can determine when a planogram is working and when it is not. The forecast determines which items are overplanned, overpacked, and underplanned. Forecast/planogram exception routines can detect when a plan is no longer working or when a central plan is not working for an individual store.

Potential Out-of-Stock Audits

Forecasting can be used in conjunction with perpetual inventory to project potential out-of-stocks. Since the system knows the next possible delivery date of the product, expected sales are used to project potential problem areas.

Planning

The planning system requires forecasts at various levels and at various times in the planning cycle. Both pre-season and in-season forecasts can be considered.

Department, class, and category forecasts for basic categories can provide essential input to plan development. In fashion categories, projections at the department and class level are often used. Although new categories and items may be bought, the forecast for the department and major classes is very relevant and very useful.

The pre-season forecasting is also very important when derived at store level and built up. A forecast by class or department at store level with the local economic and logistic effects can be very helpful in developing the plan. Competitive and customer influences are most relevant at store level. If this store level forecasting is applied, weather forecasting can also be applied. This store level methodology provides the basis for the true bottom-up or micromarketing approach to planning.

Assortment planning uses the long-range item and group forecasts to develop a performance estimate. The assortment plan provides the product definition at store level, considering customer preference, in-store cannibalization, price points, trends, cannibalization, and so on. The performance estimates help translate the assortment plan into a sales estimate for reconciliation with the merchandise plan.

Allocation

The successful distribution of non-basic products is based on a sound allocation system. The allocation system uses planning and forecasting information to derive ratios for store distribution of product. For example, one methodology for allocation utilizes a forecast of the store receipt plan in units by week to derive relative open-to-ship parameters, which determine the allocation ratios. Sales forecasts by store are also helpful in the overall allocation process.

CHAPTER 6

Order Determination

OVERVIEW

Order determination replaces examining store shelves to determine product to order. It automatically decides how much product to order and when, and then processes the order. It also acts as an auditor on the product and order limits as well as supplier-managed and DSD product.

Order determination includes three basic functions;

1. *Product Need Determination.* Product need determination calculates how much product is required to meet a targeted service level, or a fixed or calculated order-up-to-level. This initial calculation uses basic, seasonal, and promotional forecasts. Based on the predictions of consumer demand, the product need is calculated.

Order determination does more than just analyze predicted consumer purchases. Season and fashion product are often sold down over a season from a full initial set, and distribution during season can be limited. Much seasonal and fashion product is produced in limited quantities specifically for the early, pre-book orders. Consumers expect to see a wide selection early in the season. Both the supplier and the retailer expect to reduce inventories to zero by season-end. These non-basic products must also be managed through order determination.

A percentage of basic product, especially for retailers carrying variety within categories, is in the store for presentation and store look. Depending on the corporate philosophy on planogram shelf depth that is needed to create the aesthetic minimum, the quantity of product in the stores above what is needed for immediate sale can be quite high.

The order determination calculation techniques presented at the end of this chapter enable you to insure that product need is fulfilled and that store look (presentation) and merchandise mix meets goals. Additional safety stock insures the service level expectations, and product need is adjusted by the product limits. These limits are based on the physical store layout, management strategies, orderable pack, presentation, and type of product.

Calculations for product need determination can be done more often than is necessary for simply generating orders. This is because the calculations are also used for evaluation and exception reporting. While the calculations for product need are, naturally, limited by the product and order limits, keep in mind that these calculations can also question these limits if they seem out of kilter.

For example, if the system calculates that four cases of frozen pizza will sell between now and the next time product is delivered, but the freezer case can only hold three cases, the system produces an exception audit. Either there is a forecast error, the planogram for frozen pizza needs to be reset, pizza deliveries need to be more frequent, or a larger freezer case needs to be purchased. This same type of thing can happen with fashion product. The plan may be to deliver an additional 100 winter coats to each store in the New Jersey area on November 1, but using a product need calculation, it is clear that the stores on the West side need 150, whereas the stores on the East side really don't need any or need new merchandising strategies. The product need calculation is an ongoing system audit to planograms and planning.

2. *Order Generation.* Order generation triggers the requests for product to the supplier. In this function, the decision is made on when to order and precisely how much. Order generation adjusts the product need quantity to conform to order limits. These are the limits which are set by retail management and suppliers to manage logistical considerations and product availability. For example, if the system determines the need for this product is 70 but the product is packed in orderable cases of 50, the system must decide to order 100 or cut the order back to only 50. (Eventually, the system may also complain about the size of the orderable case.)

In this chapter, we'll be looking at order generation as part of individual store order determination. Under these circumstances, the logistics system fulfills the specific store's orders as they relate to quantity and delivery time. The only thing that enters the picture is individual store orders.

However, in Chapter 7, we'll be viewing order generation as a part of logistics. In that environment, logistics can optimize across the entire retail need. When order determination occurs for one individual store, an order for hammers is filled by the supplier or distribution center. However, when the logistics system looks across all the stores it may see that this store has sufficient product to last through one more order cycle, and at that time all the stores will need hammers and saws. Since the same supplier provides both, the logistics system can make a simple full-truck, flow-through (cross-dock) order of hammers and saws.

3. *Order Management.* Order management issues the order, transmits it to the supplier (or the distribution center), ages the on-orders, matches receiving quantities and costs to the original order, and creates a history of supplier delivery lead times, lead time variances, and order fulfillment. Order management maintains the supplier and purchase order databases.

Order management performs functional requirements. It also audits, analyzes, and reports on-order factors and limitations. *There is no need to install an automated system in order to perpetuate existing inventory problems.* Automated order determination questions the product and order limits, the quality of the suppliers and carriers, and the initial planning and planogram functions. For example, let's say you are losing sales on Whimsy Poodle Dogs every week in the toy section because the planogram is under-planned for the delivery cycle. Current demand is running Whimsies down to zero by mid-week. Moreover, because of their high theft rate, Whimsies are never kept in the back room. The system can tell you that there is a problem. But if you don't use the system to warn you, then it is no better than the reorder clerk who refills the shelf each week and lets the product sell down to zero.

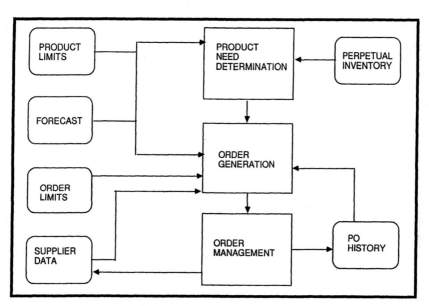

Order determination creates suggested orders, automatic orders, or audits on vendor deliveries. Not all categories, planograms, or product lines within one retailer need to be managed in the same way, but all should be managed under one system.

Suggested orders are reviewed and released by store personnel before fulfillment. They are transmitted to hard copy, RF (radio frequency) units, portable computers, or electronic shelf interfaces. If you want to process suggested orders effectively, it is helpful to:

• Show the orders in the same sequence as the shelf plan. If items are planogrammed, it is possible to display the suggested orders in the sequence of the plan. This is extremely helpful for store personnel processing the orders.

- Supply two-way communication at the shelf site. When suggested orders are printed and then processed by store personnel in the back office, there are delays and possibilities for errors.

- Provide easy access to the additional information the order clerk requires to investigate questionable orders. When the information is accessible not only can the order be communicated, but also investigative information, such as back room stock, is accessible.

Automated orders are not reviewed before placement, but are transmitted directly to the supplier or to headquarters. They may have hard copy or electronic review capability. Some retailers are afraid to allow the system to order without review. Unfortunately, when CAO orders correctly, store personnel may interfere with the system's ability to bring down overstock. It is human nature to correct the system when it seems the order is too small. There is less of a tendency to reduce an order than to inflate it.

Automated orders transmit directly to the supplier or distribution center, reducing the lead time. If the system is constantly monitoring itself for exceptions, retailers should not be worried about automating the ordering process. If automated orders are not ordering correctly, the emphasis is on fixing the inputs to ordering rather than correcting the orders.

Audit measures the accuracy of a supplier's delivery when the product is DSD or supplier-managed. In these cases, stores do not order product, since it is mutually agreed that the product is better managed by the suppliers, third-party logistics managers, or the distribution center. This is particularly true when product freshness or velocity is a concern. This practice can be audited by the system to evaluate the quality of deliveries managed from outside the store.

A note on available product versus requested product: The most dynamic calculations assume that when the retailer wants to order the product, the supplier will be able to fill the order in full and on time. But not all product is available product. Highly promotional, seasonal, fashion, and commodity-based products may require early purchasing to insure availability at time of need. This product is referred to as requested product. The order determination system can work with both available and requested product. Order determination performs more functions than simply calculating an order quantity. Its functions can be interfaced with plannable categories and their support systems.

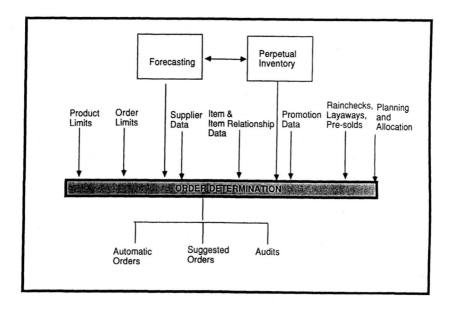

The functions required to achieve order determination are consistent across all the methods. Each method, however, may not perform each function in the same sequence. Functions may be automated or manual, implicit or explicit. Individual formulas, and how they perform each function, are discussed at the end of this chapter. Functions include:

- Calculating the available product considering the perpetual inventory, presold, and on-order
- Establishing the product necessary to satisfy consumer need
- Establishing the product necessary to fulfill upcoming promotions
- Adjusting raw need by the product and order limits
- Deciding when to order
- Deciding the final quantity to order
- Generating and managing the order
- Exception reporting problems

In the pages ahead, we will discuss the data used by these functions, the management of the order and supplier information (which provides the basis for the ordering functions), and the calculations used to calculate orders. The formulas are explained sequentially, with the first formula defining most of the variables into one constant and the last formula defining the variables individually.

A note on store ordering and distribution center ordering: In Chapter 7 we will discuss why distribution center ordering and store ordering should be considered as part of the same pull process into the stores. However, as we discussed earlier, there is a difference between when the stores ask for product and when the consumer is ready to buy it. There are several valid reasons for these differences.

- Initial sets of planograms or categories which must fill the store shelf.
- Holiday sets frequently go up early enough to suggest to consumers that when they are ready to buy product, this is the store they should come to. These sets purposely go up prior to actual customer desire, as a form of advertisement.
- Weather sets go up at the earliest part of the season for two reasons. The first is that without good weather forecasting, the store must gamble on the season start being the earliest possible. The second is that like the holiday sets, early weather sets tell the customer that when the rain starts, this is where the umbrella selection is waiting for you.
- Personnel management at the store during the high season or a promotion activity will sometimes require that product be delivered in staggered fashion in order to afford the stores the time to receive and slot the product.

LIMITS

Limits set boundaries beyond the calculation of forecasted consumer sales. The following limits relate to sales, but are not necessarily sales-based. Product need is the quantity required to supply demand and is based on forecasted promotion or normal sales. Product limits are related to the size and content of the selling space and the merchandising philosophies. Order limits are related to the product size and content of the delivery.

Product Limits

The following limits are applied in determining the product need.

Presentation Stock

Presentation stock is the minimum acceptable stock level of this product for the "look" of the store. It may be expressed as units per facing or units per category, and is one of several factors that make up the minimum store set.

Presentation stock is related to actual product need only through the planogram, which uses product sales forecast to recommend required facings. There is an assumption that the facings in the planogram represent product need, but this can be false. Depending on the product pack, product size, and shelf dimensions, excess facings can exist for slow-moving products.

Planogram systems are constrained by variations in supplier pack, order cycle, shelf dimensions, corporate philosophy for minimum week supply of product, and the product dimensions. The default minimums have a substantial effect on slow movers. The minimum is stipulated as a percentage of pack, number of facings, and/or weeks supply.

One factor that plays a major role in creating excess facings is pack size of slow movers. A case of canned pears, for example, may be so big that a single case which requires at least two facings is in itself overstock. Most planogram systems provide the necessary analysis tools to consider such factors, but many retailers don't have sufficient staff time available to allow someone to do the full analysis. There are other complicating factors, too. For example, extra facings for slow-moving products can result when merchandisers try to create a "ribbon" effect with product color, sizes, or packaging to produce an aesthetically pleasing result. Extra facings are also created as a part of an overall presentation/merchandising strategy.

Given all the factors that can spoil "the perfect set," it's important to keep a key point in mind: "product presentation can often far exceed product need."

In the distribution center, the ideal order arrives just as the last unit of product is picked or, even better, just as the next order arrives. But the philosophy breaks down in a store where shelves with only one or two units are considered unappealing to the consumer. A basic difference between store orders and warehouse orders is that stores have both minimum and maximum shelf restrictions.

Store Physical Maximum

Store physical maximum for planogram product is facings times depth, unless this product is to be placed into reserve locations. For non-planogram product, the store physical maximum is a logical setting that can be derived from the planning system and is based on category rather than individual product. All products should have a store physical maximum. One benefit of automating orders is reducing the amount of product that is kept at in-store reserve locations. Store reserve locations are difficult to manage and product is frequently "lost" in them. Ideally, these reserve locations should be used primarily for promotions and fast movers.

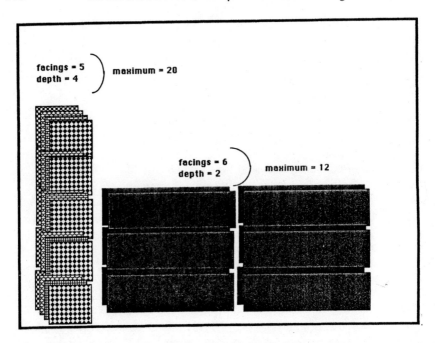

Store physical maximum refers to true physical capacity—it's not to be confused with model stock or the max in the min/max formula. The actual desired product might be much less. For some product lines, such as frozen foods, the system cannot order product, no matter how much the system thinks the store should carry, if the product won't fit in the freezer. When the system calculations indicate the stores should have more product than will logically fit, it is time to change the planogram layout or rethink delivery cycles.

Reserve Storage In-Store

This indicator determines if this product can be stored in the back room, top shelf, or other location reserve storage. Controlling the product that can be put in reserve storage is an important first step in managing store inventories. Under manual systems, clerks often do not know they have available product in uncontrolled reserve storage locations. They just go ahead and order more product for the shelf. As the back room becomes more crowded and more out of control, more product is misplaced. The problem fuels itself.

The quantity of product that must be placed in reserve depends on store layout size, order cycle, and delivery pack. When many products are destined for reserve, a reserve management system is required.

The more back room (basement) storage resembles a warehouse, the more the reserve storage support system must resemble warehouse management.

When ordering is automated, scheduled reviews are not subject to variables such as how many clerks/managers are available on a given day. There are other advantages, too. The ordering system is monitoring order/delivery cycles, product need, and shelf sets—all at the same time. Happily, this means you are less likely to wind up with as much product in additional storage areas. Moreover, when shelf size restraints do in fact require back room storage, the order determination system using a perpetual inventory knows enough not to order additional product until everything is cleaned out of the back room.

Product Shelf Life

Product shelf life is the maximum number of days that the product can safely be displayed for sale. Supplier shelf life is the time between production and ultimate use by the consumer. As a retailer concerned with your own definition of shelf life, you have to know how fast products turn in order to gauge order cycles. No sense taking delivery of two weeks' worth of product if it spoils in 10 days—so calculating accurate turn rates is essential. Retail shelf life is a subset of supplier shelf life.

Order Limits

Here are the limits applied during order generation to create the final order amount.

Product Order Minimum

Product order minimum is the minimum quantity for this product allowed on one purchase order. The orderable unit for this store is determined by logistics considerations set either by the supplier or the retail distribution center. By setting the order minimum, the distribution center can eliminate excess trips down the slow-mover aisle. Logistics considers both store and delivery costs. There is a balance between the cost of picking and delivering small orders and the cost of storing overstock on the shelf. Product order minimum is expressed as a sellable unit, inner sleeve, pack, case, pallet layer, or pallet. Infrequently, product has its own dollar order minimum separate from the supplier order minimum. That is, a supplier who delivers direct to the stores and requires both a minimum quantity and a minimum dollar amount to make the trip cost justifiable. Product order minimum controls the ordering function, not the store physical set.

Product Order Maximum

Product order maximum is the largest quantity for this product allowed on one purchase order (PO), expressed as sellable units, inner sleeves (inner packs), packs (orderable units), cases, pallet layers, pallets, or dollars. It is normally set as a management or supplier control to insure even product distribution. In a sense, this is a short cut to allocation and may be put into effect during promotions and high seasons (particularly where there is manual ordering or manual override to suggested orders). Suppliers use the product order maximum to contain or stop purchases that the supplier thinks are being diverted, or to distribute limited supplies.

Supplier Order Minimum

Supplier order minimum is the smallest total amount allowed on a single supplier order (shipment minimum). This amount may be expressed in dollars, units, weight, layers, pallets, cases, and/or cube. This figure may represent a truckload quantity or other minimum shipment amount. It is determined by suppliers as part of their overall logistics considerations, and may or may not relate to the realities of the retailer environment. Retailers and suppliers can work together to create optimized logistics including order cycles, ordering minimums, delivery methods, and payment terms.

Supplier Order Maximum

It is the largest amount of the overall supplier purchase order (shipment maximum). This amount may be expressed in dollars, units, pounds, pallets, cases, and/or cube. When there is a one-for-one relationship to the PO, the supplier order maximum represents the maximum size of the delivery vehicle.

Annual Limit

Suppliers can also set limits to individual stores or chains in order to distribute limited product evenly or prevent diversion. Typically, the limits are cumulative for orders over a period of time, such as a season or a year. Retailers circumvent this restriction, which is usually based on the previous year's sales, by building up their purchase history through even more extensive diversion.

INPUTS

Following are the inputs used by order determination to establish the time and quantity of the order. Each calculation uses the information slightly differently. The applicability of these inputs varies by product and retail outlet. The most important thing to remember is that the quality of the order determination function is dependent on the quality of the inputs that follow.

Perpetual Inventory

Perpetual inventory is the basis for all but the sales-only order determination method. Perpetual inventory, on-order, and pre-sold are the components of available stock. The quality of the perpetual inventory will determine the quality of the product need calculation.

On-Order

The on-order amount considers both the on-order quantity and the on-order arrival date. Order management includes the management and aging of the on-order quantities.

Forecasting

Forecasting and forecasting variability are used in the dynamic order determination formulas. Forecasting is used implicitly in the static calculations. That is, forecast is part of the thought process used when setting the min, max, and order point. The dynamic models explicitly use the forecast in their formulas.

Incomplete forecasts—ones that do not manage seasons, events, and other sales influences—create a need for increased inventory and safety stock at the stores, the distribution center, and at supplier production. Incomplete forecasts make the forecast appear volatile in relation to actual sales. The forecast variability is the basis for safety stock. The quality of the forecast and the size of forecast variability are fundamental in the excess quantity of inventory at all levels of the supply pipeline.

Promotions

Promotion forecasting and the overall effect of promotions on a product category should not be ignored. This includes the actual promotion sales, promotion cannibalization, promotion companion marketing, and post-promotion acceleration and slumps. However, as discussed in Chapter 5, there are many other factors to consider in promotion forecasting. If promotions are not forecasted, there must be a systems or manual override. When there are push and pull systems that don't effectively communicate with each other, order determination will not be able to effectively manage inventories. (Push product is sent to the stores from central without store orders; Pull product is ordered by the stores.) Where there is incoming product from a promotion push or expected sales from promotion sales, this information must be communicated to the order determination system.

Rain Checks, Layaways, Pre-Sold

Order determination modules calculate both available stock and sell-down based on expected normal sales. When there is pre-sold merchandise, some portion of the inventory must be considered reserved. For each retailer the percentage of rain checks, layaways, and pre-sold considered as reserved varies. Not all consumers who take rain checks redeem them. Many retailers do not keep all this information in a systematized fashion. This data should be documented with scanning functions or with other in-store systems and used by order determination modules. Getting a handle on the percentage of redeemed rain checks requires tracking the issuance and redemption.

Lead Time, Order Cycle, and Supplier Delivery Information

This information is normally stored as supplier to central distribution center. In today's environment, little of this information is kept at the supplier-to-store level. This is not a particular problem for slow-turn products; but for high-turn products using dynamic logistics decisions, supplier-to-store and distribution-to-store information is imperative.

Supplier-to-store order and delivery databases are necessary for order determination to calculate safety stock and product sell-down. Data comes from the management of the suppliers and purchase orders. When order generation is calculated as a stand-alone function within store order determination, this information is fixed and inflexible. When order generation is a part of logistics, it is possible to treat this information as variable.

Item Information

Basic item information includes the SKU to UPC (EAN) relationship, category and group assignments, and other factors used by the system to adjust the order determination settings such as in/out season, item rank, and regular/alternate suppliers. This information is normally derived from the headquarters item master database, and it must be complete and accurate.

Planning

The inputs from planning to order determination include:

- The "basic item" plan provides the basis for the items being replenished. The order determination module can use various parameters from the "basic item" plan such as WOS (weeks-of-supply) or stock to sales ratio. Order quantities are thereby kept "in-synch" with the overall merchandise plan.
- The OTB (open-to-buy) controls that are based upon the inventory and receipt plan provide the guidelines for order determination (e.g., the OTB established for "basic items" provides limits for order quantity calculation).

Some order determination methods pull their original estimates from planning systems. First, if the merchandise hierarchy has delineated basic and non-basic merchandise, then the plan can provide an overall guideline for the ordering process. If planning is performed down to store level, then the initial forecasts by store can be a very good control over the order process. Also, the planning system uses concepts like WOS (weeks-of-supply) and inventory turn, which control the amount of inventory maintained each month or week. The order determination systems also use these concepts. (Note that there may not be a consistent definition of the elements that constitute weeks-of-supply. This becomes a problem when both planning and order determination are using weeks-of-supply in very specific but different ways.) The automated ordering function should buy to both forecast and plan, and report when plan no longer matches actual.

Allocation

Order determination can be used when undistributed flow-through product arrives at the distribution center. Undistributed flow through product is pre-ordered due to long lead times or other factors and arrives at the distribution center without a store assignment. When the advance ship notice arrives, order determination algorithms are used to distribute the store ship quantities based on the latest forecasts of performance and store need (open-to-ship, etc.). When the product arrives at the distribution center, it is cross-docked based on the pre-distribution quantities developed in the allocation system.

Item Relationship

The item relationships discussed in Chapter 5 play a role in setting limits in order determination. These include catalytic items, set items, and mixed order items.

Catalytic items do not need to be carried by a store that is not carrying the catalyst. For example, flatware serving utensils are sold when the flatware is available. The worst scenario is to have the flatware in one store and the accessories in another.

Set items are not as straightforward as catalytic items. Set items are normally purchased in multiples, such as with table linens. Table napkins can be both catalytic and set, since they sell with the tablecloth and in sets of four or eight. When there is a limited supply, management must determine if it is better to have eight napkins in one store or one napkin in eight stores. Most reorder systems would place one napkin in eight stores.

Displays, modules, and nests are packaged or ordered in mixes of sellable products. Displays may include different speeds of film, prepackaged in a special Christmas exhibition. Modules include freestanding assortments of panty hose. Nests such as various sizes of baskets are shipped "nested" inside one another to reduce handling and possible damage. Management must make a decision about the percentage of sales of the total needed to place the order.

ORDER MANAGEMENT

Order management is a key component of order determination. It includes generating the initial order, managing the order through its life cycle, and reviewing the order history for communication and delivery problems. There is no way for order determination to function effectively if the incoming orders to the stores are not managed.

Order Generation

Order generation builds a supplier order from individual product need. Order minimums cause the system to build individual product orders. However, store limitations can prevent this build-up even when there is calculated product need. For example, the system may be limited by preset planogram or planning maximums. The system must be able to inform the retailer of potential out-of-stock or low service level conditions caused by the limits. Unit pricing, unit discounts, and all purchase order size discounts are applied when the purchase order is generated. This requires a level of communication from the supplier to the retailer's headquarters and stores that may be lacking. If there is an approval process at the store, the order must also be "staged" or aged as it awaits approval or rejection.

Order Communication

Electronic data interchange (EDI), eliminates not only the paper order generation, but the lag that otherwise exists between the time an order is written and when it is received. Perhaps equally important, it reduces the errors of manual handling by eliminating the need to print, transmit mechanically, and key enter information into the supplier's system. Payments and invoice matching, as well as the communication of price and promotion information, is also standardized and automated. The quality of supplier data and the level of detail is improved due to standardized communication. Third-party suppliers of interchange software and EDI management make this task relatively painless. For suppliers that are not prepared to use EDI, fax communication at least eliminates the transmission time of mail.

Incoming Order Management and Aging

After the order is communicated, the items on the order go into on-order status. At this point, they must be aged and analyzed for exceptions. Depending on the product lines, orders are received as:

- One-time receipts, where all items not delivered on the purchase order are considered shorted.
- Automatic backorders, where all or some of the items on the purchase order are considered back-ordered. In this case, an additional order is generated at the product cost listed on the original order.

- Multiple shipments, where the purchase order is held open for a stated period of time and all products not received are considered on-order.

- A canceled order, due to its passing the latest possible receive date.

Supplier Communication

Advance ship notices from the supplier tell the store about expected arrival time and quantities. This allows the store to manage staffing levels and seek alternate methods of maintaining service levels if necessary. This transaction, as well as the purchase order status change transaction, updates the on-order quantities used in the order determination models. Accurate, timely on-order quantities are imperative for successful automated order determination.

Order management requires scheduling back door deliveries. Automating this function, and integrating it into the order determination system, allows management to tell suppliers to advance or delay shipments based on actual need. The scheduling activity feeds labor management. Labor management at the store level is especially important where product is time-consuming to receive and where there is flexibility in the logistics function. *When product remains for too long a time in the receiving function, it always finds its way to the consumer whether or not it has been officially counted and received into the system. (And there goes your perpetual inventory system!)*

Order Receipt

When product arrives at the store's backdoor, RF units and mobile computers should be used to improve speed and accuracy. Retailer distribution center deliveries to the stores are often less accurate than the deliveries from suppliers. There are steps to help resolve this.

First, the retailer distribution center deliveries to the store should be considered received at the time of arrival, not at time of shipment. Second, distribution center deliveries should be periodically audited for accuracy at the center or store. Problems must be addressed at once.

Sophisticated, automated distribution center pick and outbound systems reduce the percentage of mis-picks. *The inability of a distribution center to ship the correct product to its own stores will destroy even the most sophisticated CAO system.*

Sometimes you can speed up the receiving process by eliminating the need to count in all supplier product. If supplier partnerships, supplier managed lines, and distribution center deliveries have built up a track record for consistent accuracy, ease up on the checking process. Advance ship notices inform the stores of the quantities of incoming products, and the cases are scanned in at the backdoor. Periodic audit counts insure continued accuracy.

Logistics Analysis/Supplier Analysis

Order systems continually analyze themselves. Even without full integration into the logistics system, a store order system should be able to recognize when lead time variance is unreasonable and when supplier mis-picks or shorts are unacceptable. (Lead time variability is the difference between the expected time to deliver product and the actual time.) The system reports product cost discrepancies and problems with damage and theft.

SUPPLIER MANAGEMENT

Accurate supplier/store information is imperative to determine product need, generate orders, and manage logistics. Many retailers have only headquarters supplier information. The following discussion addresses the issue of supplier/store information.

What Is a Supplier?

The problem with supplier data is that few systems provide the level of detail needed to manage a CAO system. Suppliers are manufacturers, vendors, brokers, wholesalers, distributors, and third-party logistics providers. Some products have multiple suppliers for the same store. Some software systems define supplier differently under different systems, and fail to maintain an accurate cross-reference of the suppliers.

All of the following may vary for one retailer by store or region. Individual suppliers can be thought of in a hierarchy of information. The supplier hierarchy includes:

Accounting

The accounting supplier is the office that issues invoices and to whom payments are made. Normally, this is also the office with whom terms, product cost, discounts, and promotions are negotiated. However, it is possible that additional discounts, terms, and promotions are negotiated on a local level.

Order

The order supplier is the office that receives and manages purchase orders. If there are multiple production or staging points for the product, this is the office that determines where the product will be sourced. This office or representatives of this office negotiate additional discounts, promotions or terms.

Delivery Source

This is the production plant, regional warehouse, or logistics staging location. This location may vary with the order size from the customer. One product from one order source can have multiple delivery sources and, consequently, multiple lead times.

What Is a Destination?

A destination is the point to which the product is delivered from the supplier. These delivery destinations include:

Distribution Center

Product managed by retailers in their own facility is delivered from the supplier to the retail distribution center.

Store

Product delivered directly to the store. Suppliers fill orders from head-quarters, from the stores, or resupply the product based on supplier-controlled product need calculations.

Flow-through (Cross-dock)

Product that is delivered for individual stores to the retail distribution center. This product is staged by the docks and is processed directly to the stores without going through the distribution center put away and selection process.

What Is Lead Time?

Lead time is the time it takes from order generation until the product is ready for customer purchase on the shelf. Accurate lead times to the store shelf are important in order determination. *There is no reason to implement complex calculations based on lead time if there are no accurate lead times.* When reviewing the list that follows, it will be clear that many of these time factors should not exist and could be eliminated with enhanced automation. Since all changes cannot be undertaken at once, it may be necessary to run CAO for awhile with problem lead times. It accomplishes nothing to pretend that lead time problems do not exist, especially if using formulas that depend on lead time. Multiple lead times are another problem. When a product has multiple suppliers or multiple sources within a supplier, it will have multiple lead times.

Lead time is best maintained in an hierarchical fashion. Maintaining lead times only at the item/store level is a maintenance nightmare. When lead time is defined by its components, it is easier to maintain as individual factors change.

Lead time includes:

Data Collection

This is the time it takes to collect and transmit the raw. data used for order determination. If the retailer's system is making the calculation real time, this would be zero. If the retailer system is transmitting the data to a central location the delay time could be 24 hours. If a supplier or other third party is making the calculation, the delay time could be 24 to 48 hours.

Order Generation

This is the time the system takes to issue the recommended order, for orders to be reviewed (if these are suggested orders) and for these orders to be approved. Obviously, orders issued that do not require approval will process more quickly.

Transmit Time

This is the time it takes to send the order into the supplier's system. EDI eliminates the need to print the order, then fax or mail it, and wait for the supplier to enter the order into the system. It also eliminates manual errors. Third-party communication software suppliers can manage this data for retailers who do not wish to manage their own communications.

Supplier Production and Order Process Time

Supplier production time is for product lines that are manufactured only after the orders are placed. Suppliers also have their own order process time. Orders communicated as hard copy must be received and entered into the supplier system. For product that is sent by a third-party delivery service such as the mail or UPS, the product must be properly packaged. Some suppliers have an extended pull time due to poor automation.

Supplier Staging Time

Supplier staging time is used when product must be staged at a pool truck staging location or other fixed delivery site. One problem in lead time calculation is that some products are "staged" with other orders when the order quantity is small—but there is no staging time when the order quantity is large enough to use one delivery vehicle (full truck load). A second problem is that pool truck staging is often not a number of days, but rather a fixed day of the week or month. If the system considers a lead time as a number of days, this variability can throw it off.

Transport Time

Transport time is the time it takes to move the product from the supplier's staging site to the retailer's store. If there are various delivery sources, there are various transport times. If the stores are spread across a large geographic range, there will be various transport times to the various locations.

Receive Time

Ideally, receive time does not exist, but ignoring this can be foolish if the reality is otherwise. If it takes excessive time to free a backdoor for the delivery (which can be especially important during high season) or to "count in" the product, then there is a receive time factor. Labor management systems working with advance shipment notification can help insure necessary staff to manage receiving. It can be considered an axiom of retailing that all product that takes more than one day to receive into a store will eventually be sold before it is received.

Distribution Center Production Time

If the distribution center must stamp, process, license, card, or construct the product, there is a distribution center production time.

Cross-dock Time

Cross-dock time affects product that is ordered for a store but sent from the supplier to the distribution center, where it is staged and reloaded into the delivery vehicles.

Transport Time (2)

Transport time (2) is for product that is delivered and staged to a preliminary location, and then transported a second time. All cross-dock (flow-through) product has a second transport time.

Receive Time (2)

Receive time (2) is for product that is delivered and staged to a preliminary location, and then transported and received to the final destination. All cross-dock (flow-through) product has a second receive time.

Retail Production Time

There is some product that must be stamped, processed, carded, licensed, or constructed before it can be sold. When this process takes place at the retail location, there is a retail production time after product receipt.

Retail Slotting Time

This is the time it takes to display the product on the retailer's sales floor. This lag time shouldn't exist, but it does for some product—such as small items that must be pegged, especially during high season. In these circumstances, slotting time can be several days. Slotting time can be different from the store's receive time (receive time (2)), which is the time it takes to enter the product into the perpetual inventory system.

What Is Lead Time Variance?

Lead time variance is a calculated average of the variance—negative or positive—between expected lead time and the actual lead time. It can be a factor in the safety stock calculation. Lead time variance is always used to analyze the quality of suppliers, carriers, and delivery services.

Do one or two days of difference between a general corporate lead time and a specific supplier-to-store lead time really make any difference? The answer depends entirely on the delivery cycle and product turn. For product that is ordered once a week, multiple times per week, or even daily, a lead time variance of a few days can have significant effect on the quantity of product ordered. For slower turn product that is ordered infrequently, a few days will probably make no difference.

What Causes Lead Time Variance?

- Product may be shipped from various delivery sources.
- Product may be shipped using various delivery methods, often depending on the order size.
- There is a substantial difference between the delivery time of a smaller order which is staged and delivered via a pool truck versus a product sent in full-truck quantities.
- Within one product line there may be a difference in lead times among the different items, depending on production locations and demand.
- Imported product often has a two-phase delivery cycle, moving the product into the United States and then staging and shipping from the initial delivery point.
- Sometimes lead time variance is not a variance at all, but simply a matter of a retailer computer system treating lead time as a flexible number of days when the reality is that shipments and orders are made only on fixed days of the week or month.
- Problem transportation includes bad weather, road construction, or other transport delays—delivery times may vary between summer and winter.
- Lead time variance can also be caused by the retailer's own system when there is a need to expedite or delay deliveries due to accelerated need or problem delivery cycle.
- Work calendar: Does the supplier ship on Saturday or Sunday? Does the store receive on Saturday or Sunday?
- The ability of the supplier to meet the shipping schedule can be impaired by internal supplier problems, such as materials acquisition and/or unusually large demand.
- Lead times are often impacted by the retailer's ability to meet a receiving schedule. Both at the distribution center and especially at the stores, there is a limitation of doors and personnel.

Controlling and understanding lead time variance is imperative when using order determination. All order determination models contain either calculations based on actual lead times or user-assigned constants based on assumed lead times. Safety stock—whether calculated by the system or assigned through user experience—considers the effect of lead time variance. Even when the formal calculation does not explicitly use lead time variance, a knowledgeable buyer or planner will build this information into the basic need calculation.

MODELS

These models are described as uniquely different from each other so that you can more easily understand each of them. The reality is that software systems use an amalgamation and variance of several formulas or techniques. By understanding each technique separately, you will be able to understand what is accomplished by combining several techniques.

As with forecasting, there is no one correct method. Depending on product type and data availability, one model may be more appropriate than another. When data is limited or its quality is questionable, a formula not requiring that data is the only viable option. Different product lines may require different formulas. CAO must always be considered in the light of what can be done now, and what initial steps can be used to build to the "ideal" solution.

We're presenting the formulas in sequence. That's because new concepts are introduced in each formula. The third formula, for example, uses concepts presented in the second, and so on. If you try to leapfrog your way through the formulas, you will likely be missing some of the necessary concepts. We'll explain each one as we go along. The first formulas define most of the possible variables as fixed within one or two constants. As the formulas become more dynamic the variables are treated as separate entities.

It is important to remember that order determination is not forecasting. Instead, it uses the output from forecasting.

In the following methods, there is a balance between automated and manual intervention. If the systems are set up requiring continual manual intervention, they will be ignored at the store. *Store personnel will not use an order determination system that requires more work to maintain than was needed to order manually.* On the other hand, some auditing and intervention is necessary and profitable. None of us would feel comfortable with an airline pilot who walked to the back of the plane with a martini and a pillow, assuring the passengers that everything was on auto pilot. None of these systems should be left to auto pilot, either. Finding the balance is the work of the implementation process.

Product limits, item relationships, and sales forecasting are key to determining product need. Order limits and logistics constraints (order cycle, order day, lead time) are key to generating orders. In the first formulas in this presentation, these variables are used by retailer personnel when they create the formula constants such as order-up-to-levels, min/max, weeks-of-supply, and model stock. In the dynamic versions of these formulas, the system uses the same rules the system user employed manually. For the dynamic systems to work right, all the same information that was available under the manual process must be available to the electronic system.

When reviewing order determination, the system user should remember the following:

- The static systems are only as good as the people who set the constants and the data that is available to them.
- The dynamic systems are only as good as the data the system can access. For example, if the user knows that the presentation minimum is always three units per facing, then the dynamic system must also access the planograms and facings, to determine the presentation minimum before setting the formula constants.

Is the last model in this presentation the best? The last model considers the most variables when they are actually available to the system. This formula cannot function better than the availability and quality of the data. The most sophisticated model assumes that if it waits for the optimal time to order, the product will be available. It is impossible to use this type of formula with requested product which is only available in limited quantities during limited time periods.

The order determination models don't always explicitly use the limits. But implicitly, they all use the limits in the manual settings of model stock, min/ max, and weeks-of-supply. The problem is that there is rarely a clear definition of which are implicitly used and which are explicitly used during system implementation. *The merchandisers are often asked to set these constraints without a clear understanding of which limitations the system is handling and which limitations are contained within the definition of the constraint.* Consequently, the merchandisers do not have the necessary information to successfully set up the system.

Terminology

Lead Time: The length of time until the product is available on the shelf for consumer purchase.

Lead Time Variance: The difference between expected lead time and actual lead time.

Review Time: The scheduled order review days. If a line is reviewed every Monday, the review time is seven days. If a line is reviewed every four weeks, the review time is 28 days. If there is no fixed order day for logistic considerations, an order can be reviewed daily with a review time of one day.

Order Cycle: The average length of time between orders. If an order is not placed every time a line is reviewed, the order cycle will be different from the review time. If review time is seven days but an order is needed only once every two weeks, the order cycle is 14 days. The advantage of the system is that it is not necessary to limit product reviews. Need determination can be more frequent than order generation.

Product lines can be reviewed for need-to-order more frequently than purchase orders are generated. The product need calculation tells us when product is overstocked, when there is a need for an emergency order or product transfer, and when an order cycle or planogram setting is wrong. These types of problems happen all the time. For example, the planogram for a new line of auto accessories was set last December. We had a supplier direct delivery every two weeks. All through the winter we were in a good in-stock position with a reasonable sales rate. As soon as the weather warmed up in the spring, however, it seemed everyone started to buy the special car wash and wax— just two items out of the assortment. The planogram no longer is sufficient with a two-week order cycle. These are the hottest products in our auto line, and we want to be in stock. By running the product need calculation, the system warns us that we will have a problem if we wait to order and if we don't change the planogram or start storing the product in the back room.

When the order cycle is fixed, the order size and delivery dates are also fixed. When the order cycle is dynamic, the logistics are more fluid. Dynamic order cycles can only be used with available product, since requested product requires a fixed order time. If the supplier only delivers via a pool truck on the third Tuesday of the month, we either have to find another means of product acquisition or we need to order for a monthly order cycle. If our distribution center delivers daily and they have not restricted our ordering, we can order this product anytime. The system can order for the optimum inventory position because it can wait to order to the last possible moment. Of course, the system assumes the product will be delivered when ordered.

Service Level: The target service level set by management is required for the formulas that calculate safety stock. Service level is the percentage of time this product will be available when the customer wants to buy it. It is important to remember that this is the percentage of sales that management will tolerate as lost sales. A lost sale is when the consumer wants the product but it is not available.

The calculation for service level is ((actual sales) ÷ (actual sales + lost sales)) × 100. At the distribution center, lost sales are relatively easy to calculate. When the stores order but do not receive product, this is considered a lost sale. At the store, the lost sale must be assumed. Using a daily perpetual inventory, assume that when the inventory is zero and the sales are less than expected, the difference is the lost sale amount. Of course, unless the customer actually says something to the store personnel, we don't know how many sales were lost. We also don't know if the customer became annoyed and not only didn't buy this product, but walked out of our store without buying anything.

Safety Stock: The extra product available to insure the target service level.

Safety stock is the extra product required because of volatility in sales and lead time.

Sales Volatility: The average number of units by which the expected sales (forecast) do not match the actual sales.

Forecast: Forecast is the prediction of future sales including seasons, trends, and promotions.

Weeks-of-Supply (Days-of-Supply): Weeks-of-supply (days-of-supply) settings are required by the formulas that create dynamic min/max, model stock and order-up-to-levels. This is management's attempt to control the order cycle and order quantity for a particular product, product line or category. Weeks-of-supply is a single constant that encompasses several purposes at one time. Weeks-of-supply is also used in planning calculations.

Model 1: Replace Sales

Definition:	Sell one; Buy one
	This is the most basic of all reorder formulas. The idea is that if the retailer sells one, the system replaces one.
Formula:	unadjusted product need = accumulated sales Adjust product need to the order limits.
where	
Accumulated Sales	Accumulated sales are the total POS sales transactions since the last purchase order was placed.

Explanation:

Even this most simple of all formulas has variations.

1. The simplest version is with product that is pack equal to one. In this version every recorded sale is replaced immediately.

2. The next level of complexity is pack not equal to one. The system counts recorded sales and stores the count. When the count equals a pack (or a percentage of a pack), a pack is replaced and the count is reset. If there is a preset order date, the system accumulates sales until the order date.

The *replace sales method may work for a small percentage of retailers as a final solution, particularly where the product is pack one with little seasonality or mathematically predictable trend.* This may include certain types of video, books, magazines, or other selected categories within a retailer's total selection.

Replace sales works as a backup and audit for a retailer implementing a full-CAO system and still using manual orders. This method can be used when a contingency plan requires creating an order with the system due to an absent employee or communication problems. It can also be used for manual order reasonability checks.

Seasonality and trend are not considered, since replace sales doesn't use forecast. The store will be understocked at season-start and overstocked at season-end.

Since replace sales does not use perpetual inventory, it will preserve whatever problems already exist. If the store has 100 units on hand and sells 10 per week, the system replaces 10 units per week. If the store sells only 10 per week because every Wednesday it runs out of stock, the system replaces only 10 and continues to run out of stock.

For example, the last order was placed two weeks ago. Today is the order date. Sales since the last order were nine. The pack is 12. The system either doesn't order or orders 12. With replace sales, the decision is difficult. The system must either restart at a negative three or not order until a full pack is reached. If there is no order, the system must know that no order was issued and next time the accumulated sales will be nine, plus the future sales. If there is no order there may be customer out-of-stocks. If, on the other hand, 12 are ordered, overstock is created. And if there is an order of 12 and every week, the system builds overstock.

If the replace sales method is used, it is necessary to consider the following:

1. These methods do not use an actual perpetual inventory. This eliminates the many difficulties of establishing a clean perpetual inventory but eliminates all of the many benefits of actual perpetual inventory.

2. There is an enormous dependency on the accuracy of the POS sales data. The POS sales data is the only basis for identifying store problems and creating orders. This elevates the need for POS data cleaning and analysis.

3. Replace sales preserves all existing inventory problems. Where there is shrink or other cause for the product to disappear other than sales, replace sales will not replenish the shelf.

4. If replace sales continually rounds up to pack, it will build up inventory over time unless there are controls to reduce inventory.

Replace sales is useful for selected types of products when there is no perpetual inventory. It can also be used as a contingency order.

Model 2: Static Model Stock (Order-up-to-Level)

Definition:	Static model stock is set for in-season and out-of-season. The system attempts to keep the store inventory at this fixed level. Model stock is the desired level of inventory at the time of purchase order calculation.
Formula:	(1) unadjusted product need = static model stock − available inventory (2) Set the unadjusted product need within the limits

where

Static Model Stock   A Static model stock is usually developed by the mer-
                                  chandisers using past sales history or the planning sys-
                                  tem. There may be two model stocks: in-season and
                                  out-of-season. Static model stocks are expressed as
                                  units of product.

Available Inventory   (perpetual inventory) + (on-order) − (pre-sold)

Explanation:

Static Model Stock. Static model stock depends on the merchandiser to
manually set the target product level, possibly with the help of a one-off system analysis. This target can be derived from planning, the planogram, sales
history, or a combination of systems. It can be based on forecasts and lead
times. It is often derived by asking the merchants to provide the information
with little or no assistance or guidance. Model stock varies during in- and out-
of-season.

The static model stock is one constant that attempts to provide for expected
sales, presentation stock, order cycle and lead time. Whether this is calculated
by the system or by the merchandiser, this is a one-time best guess. Unfortunately, there is often an unclear definition of what system limits are being
used and what the merchandiser must consider when creating this model
stock. The static model stock is only as good as the people who set the model
stock and the information available to them.

For non-basic products that are in plannable categories, the merchandiser
can use much the same information that was used to create the plan. Model
stock represents the highest inventory amount desired (the inventory amount
at time of order calculation). The category (class) weeks-of-supply from the
plan multiplied by current sales average is an approximation of the static
model stock.

*Static model stocks are used with basic and non-basic products when either
the POS data is not available or is problematic.* In this way, this method is a
"stepping stone" which will be replaced after the quality of POS data and
forecasting can be improved. If this static formula is used as a stepping stone,
it can be used to "debug" forecasting methods and POS quality. Initially, the
information can be used as an exception audit against the static method. In
time, more dynamic methods can be implemented.

Available Inventory. The concept of available inventory is deceptively simple. It is the perpetual inventory plus the on-orders minus the pre-sold. The
perpetual inventory must be complete, timely, and accurate. All decrements
and increments must have been applied prior to this calculation. (See the note
at the end of this section on shadow perpetual inventory.)

If stores have previously not managed orders, there may be no mechanism in place to manage the on-order status. Even when there is a rudimentary method of managing incoming orders, the system may not be sophisticated enough to manage open orders and partial receipts. Aging orders is the only means of eliminating outstanding orders that may no longer be valid.

Available inventory must recognize not only product on-order, but also product that is considered sold when it arrives. Pre-solds are products that are promised to consumers upon arrival. Not all pre-solds will actually be taken by the consumers—many more rain checks are distributed than are collected. There must be a system in place that tracks the number of pre-solds issued and the percentage collected.

Formula

(1) unadjusted product need = static model stock − available inventory

After the system calculates the available inventory, the mathematics is simple. The available inventory is subtracted from the static model stock. A positive difference is the unadjusted product need.

Static model stock systems use fixed order dates. That is, a static model stock order is placed every Wednesday, or every four weeks. This formula does not calculate when to order, only how much to order.

(2) Set unadjusted product need within the limits

The static model stock is compared to the limits after the product need is calculated. Order and product limits that affect the ability of the system to supply the store with the required product are reported as exceptions. Order determination compares the unadjusted product need to the limits. (No matter how much chocolate ice cream the system thinks a store needs, if there is no freezer space, either the planogram or the order cycle must be revised.)

No matter how much seasonal product order determination thinks necessary, the order cannot exceed supplier limits. Rather than ordering, store transfers are investigated, alternate sourcing of the product located, or the supplier is contacted. For example, a beach ball manufacturer may not have made enough beach balls to supply an unusually hot and long summer season. Consequently, they have put an allocation limit to evenly distribute their product to their customers. The San Diego store needs more beach balls. The Orange County store has an excess. A transfer is made rather than an order.

No matter how little product the system thinks should be on the shelf for a slow mover, the presentation stock insures the required store look. Order determination must both create orders and advise store and headquarters personnel about potential problems.

This ability to analyze the limits is one of the most important features of order determination, and separates it from manual ordering.

For example,

When to Order?	Order on a fixed order date.
How much to Order?	This product line is ordered every 7 days. The model stock is 25. The available inventory is 10. The unadjusted product need $(25 - 10) = 15$. Set the product need within the limits.

Static model stock is a useful formula when the ongoing forecast quality is questionable and, therefore, the model stock must be reviewed. It's also helpful when the product type requires a fixed order date, such as with requested product.

A note on Shadow Perpetual Inventory: When suppliers are managing inventories for retailers, they often do not have the actual store perpetual inventories. They are able to obtain the perpetual inventory for the distribution center only. Suppliers trying to manage store inventories—or headquarters systems attempting to automate store supply without actual store perpetual inventories—use a shadow perpetual inventory.

The shadow perpetual inventory adds in all shipments and subtracts out all sales. There must be an initial count for a starting point. The shadow perpetual inventory can be periodically reviewed by a physical inventory count.

Shadow perpetual inventories make these important assumptions:

1. Product sent to fill an order is the correct product in the correct quantity and arrives at the retailer undamaged. For supplier-managed categories there is an auxiliary assumption that all the product is delivered by supplier-controlled sources, and not from any other source. Diversion buys or regional transfers of product are out of the supplier's control.

2. Where the shadow perpetual inventory is controlled by the orders "booked" rather than by the orders "filled," there is a very large assumption that when an order is placed it is either filled or held in an on-order status until it is filled. Many systems are ill-equipped to recognize what actually happens to an order after it is transmitted.

3. Product departs the shelf only when there are sales. Returns, supplies, and transfers continually create the need to restart the shadow perpetual inventory.

Model 3: Dynamic Model Stock (Order-up-to-Level)

Definition:	The system calculates a target or model stock level on a scheduled basis. Orders are placed to keep stocks at this level.
Formula:	(1) Calculate dynamic model stock: weeks-of-supply × forecast (2) unadjusted product need = dynamic model stock − available inventory (3) Set the unadjusted product need within the limits
where	
Available Inventory	(perpetual inventory) + (on-order) − (pre-sold)
Dynamic Model Stock	The system considers the product forecast and continually resets the model stock to insure product availability. Dynamic model stock usually is reviewed manually.
Weeks-of-Supply	A preset number of weeks of product supply desired at time of order generation.
Forecast	Product or category forecast

Explanation:

1. Calculate Dynamic Model Stock (weeks-of-supply × forecast)

Dynamic Model Stock. The dynamic model stock uses product (or category) forecasts to derive the current inventory target. Rather than asking the merchandisers to create a model stock, the system creates it using current sales and predictive forecasting. Dynamic model stock is continually recreated as the forecast changes. As with the static model stock, this method uses a fixed order date and does not determine when to order.

Weeks-of-Supply. This dynamic method uses forecast, but bundles all other variables into one static component—weeks-of-supply. Weeks-of-supply is expressed as a fixed number that encompasses lead time, order cycle, and safety stock. Model stock is the maximum desired product on the shelf. Using the forecast the system determines how much product is required to meet targets for weeks-of-supply. For non-basic products that are in plannable categories, the plan weeks-of-supply can be used.

For example, if management wants a three-week supply, and the system is forecasting 10 sales per week, the model stock is 30. If the available product is 10, the order amount is 20. Dynamic model stock differs from a calculated but static model stock, in that it continues to calculate the inventory target as the forecast changes and uses a sales forecasting method.

Although the model stock calculation is shown as weeks-of-supply forecast, this is only true when the forecast is unaffected by promotions, seasonality, or trend. When the forecast is more sophisticated, the calculations are actually an accumulation, and represent the forecasted future sales over time. (We use the multiplication as a shorthand.) For example, let's say an item that has been selling 10 items per week suddenly starts trending up at the rate of three extra units incrementally per week. The item is ordered every three weeks, so using multiplication the model stock would be $10 \times 3 = 30$. But with recent trending up, the model stock will actually be $10 + 13 + 16 = 39$.

Forecast. The forecast was explained in the previous chapter. Forecast volatility is considered in the model stock. Forecast should encompass promotions, seasons and other sales factors. When forecast is incomplete, the manual review process is used to adjust the model stock for incomplete data.

2. Unadjusted Product Need = Model Stock − Available Inventory

This is the same calculation as with the static model stock.

3. Set the Unadjusted Product Need within the Limits

Since this method is dynamic, the results of the product need calculation must be continually measured against the limits. Where the limits prevent the system from keeping the store at the desired supply level, exception reporting is necessary.

The ability of order determination to audit and report supply chain problems to store and headquarters management is as important as its ability to reorder. There is no reason to create a dynamic automated system in order to maintain the status quo of problem situations.

For example,

When to order?	This method uses a fixed order date.
How much to order?	Weeks-of-supply is three weeks.
	Forecast is seven units per week.
	The model stock is $3 \times 7 = 21$ units.
	Available inventory is 10.

Unadjusted product need is $21 - 10 = 11$.
Set unadjusted product need within the limits.
The dynamic model stock is used primarily with requested product and fixed order dates.

Model 4: Static Min/Max

Definition:	Preset minimums and maximums for in- and out-of-season. When the available product is at minimum or less, it is time to reorder this product. Order up to the max.
Formula:	(1) When to order? Order when the available inventory is less than or equal to the min. (2) How much to order? Calculate (max − available inventory) (3) Set the unadjusted product need within the limits
where	
Available Inventory	(perpetual inventory) + (on-order) − (pre-sold)
Static Min	This is the minimum product acceptable on the shelf *at time of ordering.* This is created manually by the merchandiser. There may be an in- and out-of-season min.
Static Max	This is the maximum product allowed on the shelf *at time of ordering.* This is created manually be the merchandiser. There may be an in- and out-of-season max.

Note: min and max should be at least one orderable pack different.

Explanation:

The static min and static max, like the static model stock, are used when there is not sufficient data or data quality to create more dynamic ordering systems. This formula is also used with extreme slow movers. The difference between static min/max and static model stock is that the system waits to order until it reaches the minimum rather than when it is down one pack from the model stock or on a fixed order date. By setting a minimum for ordering the system avoids issuing unreasonably small order quantities.

As with static model stock, the system may be used to create "suggested" minimums and maximums, which are then reviewed by the merchandisers. As with model stock, at the time these minimums and maximums are created they are compared to the product limits.

Static min/max can be used as a stepping stone when logistics, forecasting, supplier information, and/or POS data are not yet in place. As with the static model stock, more dynamic formulas can replace this method by first being used as an exception technique.

1. When to Order?

Order when the available inventory is less than or equal to min.

Static min/max decides when to order. Order time is when the available inventory falls below min. Min is created by manually considering order cycle, lead times, presentation stock, item sets, and sales rate. Store and order limits are built into the min.

Min is the minimum acceptable product *at time of ordering*. This level must last a lead time and order cycle until the order arrives. Sales and delivery volatility must also be considered.

2. How Much to Order?

Calculate (max − available inventory)

Max is the store inventory at time of order receipt and is built considering order cycle, order size, order frequency, lead time, and sales rate. The store and order limits are built into max. Since forecast is not used, problems with in-store quantities are retained. For example, the max is set at 48 bottles of Mother's Cough and Cold Remedy based on its popularity in winter. The new private label Cough and Cold remedy was introduced at half the cost, and Mother's sales dropped off rapidly. Since the min/max formula doesn't use forecast it retains the setting at 48 even though Mother's is now selling only five per week.

For non-basic products, the weeks-of-supply from planning can be applied in creating the max. (weeks-of-supply × forecast = max)

3. Set the Unadjusted Product Need within the Limits

If the limits were not built into the min/max, the unadjusted product need is compared to the limits.

For example,	Available inventory is 10. Min is 15. Max is 30.
When to order?	Order when available inventory is less than or equal to min.
	10 < 15, order now!
How much to order?	Order: (Max − available inventory)
	30 − 10 = 20
	unadjusted product need is 20.

Set the unadjusted product need within the limits

Static min/max can be used as a stepping stone when logistics, forecasting, vendor information and/or POS data are not yet in place. Also, as with the static model stock, more dynamic formulas can replace this method by first being used as an exception technique.

Static min/max is used successfully with extreme slow movers. These products sell less than is cost justifiable but are carried to fulfill customer expectations. Many slow movers sell in sets (two or four at a time). The min/max method allows the merchandiser to set the minimum to provide enough product to satisfy the consumer. For example, table linens sell in sets of four or eight. A few romantic souls buy in sets of two, and a few whimsical souls buy only one at a time. The problem is that when the consumer wants to entertain, he or she wants to buy at least four. In this case the min would be set to four and the max to 12.

Even with system help, static min/max is difficult to manage across all products. All exceptions must be managed manually. *Static min/max is labor intensive.*

Model 5: Refill Shelf for Product Arrival

Definition:

Calculate available inventory at estimated product arrival.

Use either mix/max or model stock to calculate order quantity based on the need at the time product arrives.

This formula uses the previous models but instead of using them at the time of ordering, it attempts to make the calculations at the time of product arrival.

Formula:

(1) Estimate product arrival date based on lead time

(2) Calculate available inventory at product arrival

(3) Calculate order quantity

(4) Set the unadjusted product need within the limits

where

Available Inventory

(perpetual inventory) + (on-order) − (pre-sold)

Forecast

Product and category forecasts

Lead Time

The time until the product is available on the shelf for customer purchasing.

Available Inventory at Product Arrival

Estimates of future available product consider not only the forecast sales between today and the estimated arrival date, but also the estimated arrival of the current on-orders.

Explanation:

This is the first formula that uses lead time to determine the store order quantity. This method still depends on predetermined model stocks or min/max to decide how much to order. But now, the system is ordering *for time of arrival rather than for time of order.* Particularly where the buyers or merchandisers are being asked to create the shelf amount, it is easier if they can think of their stock position in terms of time of arrival rather than time of purchase.

1. Estimate Product Arrival Date Based on Lead Time

The lead time is considered to be fixed in this formula, without variability. But there are variations of this formula, since lead time represents total days and receive dates may be restricted to weekdays. In this case, the calculated arrival date may be a Saturday or a holiday, and therefore the actual arrival date will be a Monday.

2. Calculate Available Inventory at Product Arrival

The system calculates what the stock position will be at the time the product arrives if it is ordered now. At its simplest, this can be thought of as the available inventory today minus the forecasted sales before the arrival date. This is the available inventory at product arrival.

Of course, in the real world, it is never that straightforward. Since product cannot be sold before it arrives, the on-order arrival dates must be considered. Let's say there are 10 widgets on-hand today, 25 widgets on order, and normal sales are five widgets a day. If the product arrival from this order is in seven days, you could estimate that the product on hand in seven days will be zero: $((10 + 25) - (7 \times 5))$. But if the on-order quantity isn't arriving for six days, there will be lost sales (and perhaps rain checks and angry customers) and 20 widgets on hand in seven days. This situation occurs when the lead time is greater than the order review cycle. (It is important to remember all the components that make up a lead time.)

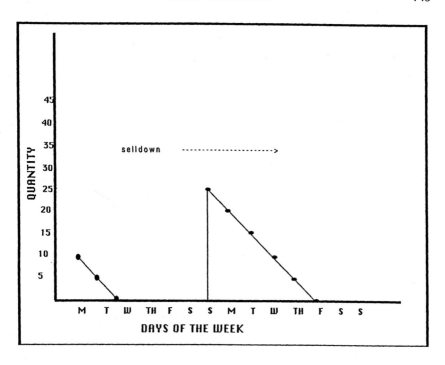

3. Calculate Order Quantity

When the stock position is established at time of arrival, the system uses one of the previously explained methods to create the order quantity.

4. Set the Unadjusted Product Need within the Limits

As explained previously, the calculated need is compared and reset to stay within these limits. The system reports problems with the limits to management.

For example: Here are some widget sales again. We have a two-week lead time and a fairly large outstanding on-order, and we are in a pretty bad inventory position today. Typical of widgets, the bulk of our sales are on the weekend, when people have time to make their home repairs.

> Perpetual inventory is 3.
>
> Lead time is 14 days / 2 weeks.
>
> On-order is 24.
>
> On-order is due on Wednesday, May 7.
>
> Forecasted sales are 11 per week.

50% of the sales are on Saturday and Sunday

The daily sales are one per day, Monday-Friday

Saturday and Sunday sales are 3 per day.

Today is Thursday, May 1.

Min is 24.

Max is 48.

	1	2	3	4	5	6	7	8	9	10	11	12	13	14	15	16	17
May	T	F	S	S	M	T	**W**	T	F	S	S	M	T	**W**	T	F	S
	order day						arrival							arrival			
expected sales	1	1	3	3	1	1	1	1	1	3	3	1	1	**1**	1	1	3
inventory after day's sale (start 3)	2	1	0	0	0	0	23	22	21	18	15	14	13	**12**	11	10	7
actual sales	1	1	1	0	0	0	1	1	1	3	3	1	1	**1**	1	1	1

$$\text{Maximum} - \text{available inventory} = \text{unadjusted product need}$$
$$48 - 12 = 36$$

Notice that we assume that we have lost sales on May 4, 5, and 6. Since we are not the only widget supplier in town, we assume that demand won't be pent-up, and that our customer just went to our competitor. Then the product arrives on May 7 (and is set out in time to sell one) and we're actually overstocked. (We hope there is enough room on the shelf, because we know that if the product goes into the back room it will be lost forever.)

This formula is useful when there is enough POS data to create a useful, very short-term forecast, but not enough history to account for seasonality and create the target store quantities. This method is a stepping stone used when the POS data is usable, but there is no sales history that is usable and consequently no valid forecasting.

Model 6: Dynamic Min/Max (Order Point/Order-up-to-Level)

Definition: The system calculates the order point and the order-up-to-level (dynamic min/max) based on lead time, sales forecast, service level, and review time. When inventory reaches order point, the system orders enough product to reach the order-up-to-level. This is the first formula that calculates safety stock and order minimum based on lead time and review time. The order-up-to-level is still controlled by weeks-of-supply.

Formula:

(1) Calculate order point = (lead time + ½ review time) × (forecast) + safety stock

(2) Calculate order-up-to-level = (order point) + (weeks-of-supply × forecast)

(3) When to order? When available inventory is less than or equal to order point

(4) How much to order?

unadjusted order need=

(order-up-to-level- available inventory)

(5) Set the unadjusted product need within the limits

where

Available Inventory	(perpetual inventory) + (on-order) − (pre-sold)
Forecast	Product or category forecasts
Review Time	Review time is the days between product reviews. Since order point could be reached any time during the review time, half the review time is the reasonable compromise.
Order Point	The minimum inventory position at the time of ordering.
Safety Stock	The calculations for safety stock vary considerably. Some safety stock calculations consider only sales volatility. Others consider both sales volatility and lead time volatility. Using the forecast error measurement (see Chapter 5), the system determines the quantity of extra product required if the sales are greater than expected. The same logic is used to incorporate lead time variability.
Weeks-of-Supply	Pre-set weeks-of-supply
Order-up-to-Level	Order-up-to-level (max) is the desired inventory level at time of order receipt. The order-up-to-level is calculated using a fixed constant of weeks-of-supply and the dynamic forecast.

Explanation:

Order point/order-up-to-level uses a dynamic method to decide when to order. The order point determines when the system will order. The system does not order before the available inventory has fallen to order point. Once the system has determined when to order, it must determine how much to order.

1. Calculate Order Point =

(lead time + ½ review time) × (forecast) + (safety stock)

Order point calculates the product required to last until this order arrives. This formula uses a fixed lead time and one half of the review time. The assumption is that the order point can be reached at any time during the fixed review period, and that half a review period is a reasonable average estimate. This is a sophisticated version of the previous formula's estimate of product needed for sell down from today until this order's arrival.

Safety stock is discussed in detail at the end of this section.

2. Calculate Order-up-to-Level =

(order point) + (weeks of supply × forecast)

The order-up-to-level is a combination of a static factor and a dynamic (reacting to forecast, etc.) one. The weeks-of-supply quantity is management's attempt to set order size. If the system always orders a three-week supply, it should need to order only once every three weeks. Management considers the on-order quantity, store labor, supplier minimums, and delivery methods in deciding weeks-of-supply.

During both the planning and ordering processes, it is important to know which factors were considered part of weeks-of-supply, and which factors the system considered separately. Non-basic product that is requested product may be able to use the weeks-of-supply from the merchandise plan in the calculations. The order-up-to-level (forecast X weeks-of-supply) adds to the calculated order point. If this amount was already considered in the weeks-of-supply for the plan, the order-up-to-level would be too big. This highly dynamic system insures that there is enough product on hand both for expected sales and for volatility.

For example, at our nutrition store, we were selling an elixir for perpetual youth from China at a faster rate than we could get it from the supplier. Our forecast was very high and trending up. We set our weeks-of-supply based on our supplier's very reliable delivery schedule (two weeks), but we kept an extra week on-hand for safety stock and to cover that upward trend. Last month *60 minutes* ran a special which debunked the elixir. Our sales aren't zero, but they fell by half almost overnight.

We have a pretty reactive forecast method so the next time our supplier called for an order this was our calculation:

Our old forecast was 100 bottles of elixir per week.

Our order point was one week or 100 bottles.

We were always targeting 4 weeks at a time:

(weeks-of-supply(3) × 100) + (order point(1) × 100) = 400.

Since we were selling so much and the trend was so high, we usually only had 100 or less on-hand and we ordered 300 or more each time. This time, when our supplier called, we still had 275 bottles on hand. Our forecast is down to 50 per week and falling. By our calculations, our need is down to 200 and falling. Since we have 250 on-hand and the product is rapidly down-trending, we basically told the supplier, "don't call us, we'll call you."

In this calculation, weeks-of-supply is used differently than it was for previous order-up-to calculations. This is because the order point is added into the order-up-to-level. Previously the order-up-to-levels included the time between order placement and order arrival (order point). Since many companies with planning use several of these models in conjunction, remember that weeks-of-supply does not always carry the same definition.

3. When to Order?

When available inventory is less than or equal to order point.

As with the static min/max formula, ordering does not take place until available inventory is at a level below the order point. This avoids creating nuisance orders.

4. How Much to Order?

Unadjusted order need = (order-up-to-level − available inventory)

As with the static min/max formula, the system orders the difference between available inventory and the order-up-to-level.

5. Set the Unadjusted Product Need within the Limits

After the product need is calculated, it is adjusted to conform to the limits. Ordering problems created by the limits are reported.

For example,

available inventory = 10

forecast = 5

weeks-of-supply = 4 weeks
review cycle = 1 week
safety stock is 3 units
lead time is 2 weeks

When to order?

order point =
(lead time + ½ review time) × (forecast) + safety stock
15.5 = (2 + ½(1)) × (5) + 3
Is available inventory < order point?
10 < 15.5 Yes

How much to order?

order-up-to-level =
(weeks-of-supply × forecast) + (order point)
4 × 5 + 15.5 = 35.5

unadjusted product need = order-up-to-level − available inventory
25.5 = 35.5 − 10

These formulas are useful when there is accurate data but order or receive dates are limited. These formulas are useful with requested product, which is product that must be ordered on a limited schedule. If the system waits for the ideal inventory level, the product may not be available to order. This formula cannot be implemented if the forecast, vendor data and/or POS data is inaccurate or incomplete.

A note on safety stock: We've already discussed the reasons for lead time variability. If those reasons can be identified and solved, it is far better to do so than to build excess inventory to cover for volatility. If the lead time varies between 10 and 15 days, the inventory position must provide for an extra five days. If management targets service level near 100% (not uncommon at store level) and the lead time volatility is high, excess inventory and costs are dramatically increased.

Demand volatility was discussed in Chapter 5. Even when considering some form of seasonality, most time series formulas are only using past sales history to determine future sales. If weather, price, promotions or other factors are playing a large role in future sales patterns, these must be built into the formulas. Otherwise there will be a high demand volatility and consequently a high safety stock.

In this sample, both items have an even forecast of 50. One item averages 50 sales a week by selling 40 one week and 60 the next week. This item has a sales volatility of 10 units. The other item sells 20 one week and 80 the next and also averages 50. The second item has a sales volatility of 30 units. This second item may just be randomly bouncing. On the other hand, there may be a direct relationship to pricing or welfare checks that the forecasting system is not considering. If the volatility is high, the necessary safety stock to insure the service level is also high.

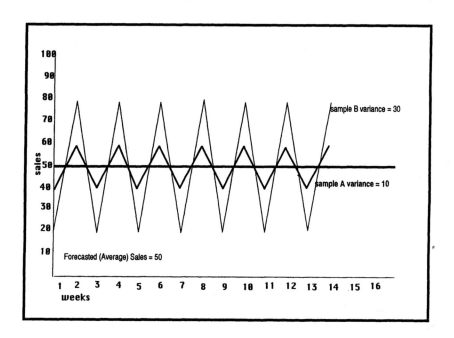

Safety stock is based on the concept of MAD (mean absolute deviation), which measures an item's average variability between actual sales and forecasted sales. This was discussed in Chapter 5. Safety stock is an insurance for the short term that there will be sufficient product on-hand to cover consumer desire for the product. For long-term projections, the randomness over time begins to average out (a little high one week, a little low the next). There isn't a need to continue to carrying as much weekly safety stock week after week as the projection continues into the future.

An item with a very low MAD, demand volatility, will require much less safety stock than an item with a very high MAD to achieve an identical service level. This is simply because if I don't know if an item is going to sell 25 or 50 next week, and I want to insure 100% service level, I need to have at least 50 units on-hand. If I don't know if I will sell 25 or 28 of another item and I want 100% service level, I only need to carry around 28 to insure that I have enough product. If you remember the MAD calculation from the forecasting section, two items can average the same amount but have vastly different MADs and sales patterns.

This is extremely important to us at store level, especially with high-variety retailers. Do you remember the discussion about items that own their history versus items that share a sales history with several other items because of in-store cannibalization? We have also talked about whether service level was always for one item, or if it was sometimes for a group of items. Items can have extremely bouncy demand patterns (i.e., high MADs) when there is on-shelf cannibalization due to price sensitivity. If each item is treated separately, each item will require a high safety stock to insure a high service level. But the reality is that these items are bouncy because sales are lost to other items within the category. If we do not consider price in our forecasting, the lowest price items will probably be understocked and the higher priced items will probably be overstocked at any point in time. At the distribution center we traditionally built up safety stock on bouncy items without asking the question, "why is this item's demand so volatile?" At the store, we cannot afford to be so cavalier.

In the retail store, service level is different than it was in the distribution centers. This has significant consequences.

- Lowering safety stock at the distribution center—when we know the stores are always ordering with a cushion of product on-hand—will not necessarily translate into an unhappy consumer.
- Increasing safety stock at the distribution centers increases safety stock product in one to a dozen or so distribution center locations. However, increasing safety stock at the store level increases product at dozens if not hundreds of retail outlets. It also uses shelf space that may be needed for other products. Therefore, it is worthwhile in store forecasting to trap the reasons for volatility and factor them into our thinking rather than just adding more product to cover for volatility.

Model 7: Statistical

Definition:	Use sales forecast and service level to calculate the sales need and necessary safety stock. The quantity to order is calculated from the lead time, order cycle, order minimum, and sales forecast rather than from using the fixed weeks-of-supply. This formula calculates when to order and how much to order with much greater flexibility than the previous formulas.
Formula:	(1) Calculate available inventory at time of this order's arrival
	(2) Calculate the expected sales from the time of this order's arrival until the next order after this one arrives (the period of time that this order is supplying)

(3) Calculate unadjusted product need

(4) Set unadjusted product need within the limits

where

Available Inventory	(perpetual inventory)+(on-order)−(pre-sold)
Forecast	Product forecast or category forecast
Service Level	Service level is a goal of percentage in stock to the consumer.
Lead Time	The time from order calculation until the product is available for customer purchasing
Available Inventory at Product Arrival	Estimates of future available product at the time this order arrives.
Review Time	The days between product reviews.
Order Cycle	Order cycle is the average time between orders.
Safety Stock	The amount of product ordered in addition to product need, providing a cushion for variability in sales or lead time.

Explanation:

This is the most dynamic of the formulas presented. Rather than fixing the order-up-to-level by a targeted weeks-of-supply, this formula calculates the product need based on lead time, order cycle, and forecast. This formula assumes the product it is ordering is available product. Available product can be shipped on an as-needed basis. This is the first formula that looks beyond this order. It actually considers the times between this order's arrival and the next possible order thereafter.

1. Calculate Available Inventory at Time of This Order's Arrival

This formula is identical to the calculation used for "refill shelf for product arrival." The system calculates the available inventory at the time that this order will arrive

2. Calculate the Expected Sales from the Time of This Order's Arrival until the Next Order after This One Arrives

The system uses its forecast to calculate what the sales will be between product arrival and the next logical arrival of the order after this one. This is the first formula that asks the question, "Is it possible to wait to order without running out of stock?" It is looking to the inventory level at the time of the next possible order. Previous formulas assumed that if it was time to order, they should order up to a fixed level.

This formula considers the quantity of product that can *logically be sold* between the day this order arrives and the delivery of the order after this order (next-next delivery). As explained in the previous method, this is not straightforward, since this is not the forecasted demand between product arrival and next-next delivery. This is the logical sales between product arrival and next-next delivery. Since product that has not arrived cannot be sold, the delivery dates of the on-order product must be considered. The system calculates the minimum product that must be delivered on this order to satisfy *product need.*

For example: There are currently (May 1) no widgets in the store and there are two on-order quantities. The first on-order (A) is for 20 widgets. The second on-order (B) is for 45 widgets. The store sells 5 widgets per day. On-order quantity A is scheduled to arrive tomorrow (May 2). On-order quantity B is not scheduled to arrive until one week from tomorrow (May 9). The lead time is ten days and the order cycle is once a week, always on Mondays.

Today is Monday (May 1) and the inventory position is zero. Since none are available, today's sales are zero.

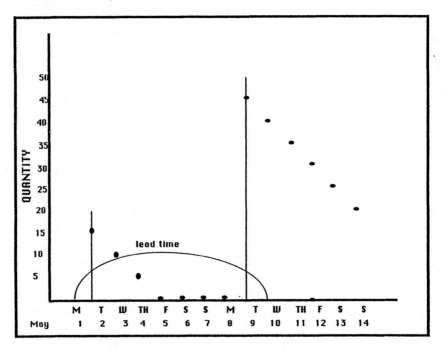

On May 2, our first on-order arrives and receiving personnel put the product on the shelf; five sell. If things go as expected, five widgets sell on Tuesday, Wednesday, and Thursday but by Friday widgets are out of stock again. There won't be another widget sold until next Tuesday (May 9) (and that's providing receiving keeps up the good work).

On Tuesday (May 9), the second shipment arrives and selling begins again.

The order we are calculating wouldn't arrive until the next Wednesday (May 10). The next order after that won't arrive until the following Wednesday (May 17).

We need to order enough product to last until the shipment that arrives Wednesday (May 17). (The idea is that we are ordering enough to last between logical orders, but no more than what we need.) When the order that we are currently calculating arrives, there will still be 40 widgets in inventory (since we just received a big order the day before). There is no need to order widgets on this order. It is possible to wait and order at the next order cycle.

The actual sales (actual POS transactions) are 60, but the estimated demand (consumer desire) was 80. There were 20 lost sales of widgets. It is hoped that no customers stormed out of the store without buying the rest of their shopping list!

A note on sales patterns: The reality is that nothing sells five every day because that's not the way people shop. In this example, most customers come in on Saturday and Sunday. Fully 75% of the total weekly purchases are on the weekend.

Now let's look at the same widget scenario again. This time, instead of selling five widgets per day, the store sells 26 widgets on the weekend and only nine widgets during the other five days of the week. If there is out-of-stock on the weekend, lost sales are 26. The system must know not only how much sells during the period, but how much is projected to sell each day. It also needs to know how much other product is arriving during the period and when.

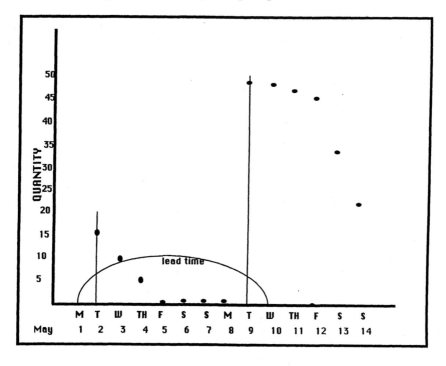

3. Calculate Unadjusted Product Need

The system has calculated how much product is required if there is no volatility. Safety stock based on lead time volatility and forecast volatility (forecast error rate) must be added into the equation. This is the same safety stock that was used in dynamic min/max (order point/ order-up-to-level).

When to order? Is there enough product to cover for the expected sales between today and the next-next arrival date (today is May 1 and next-next arrival date is May 17)? The product needed during this period includes both forecasted sales and safety stock. The available inventory is decreased as previously explained. If the remaining available inventory exceeds all the limits, it is not time to order.

How much to order? If the available inventory is below any of the limits, it is time to order. The system calculates the minimum product needed to cover the expected sales (forecast + safety stock), subtracting out the available inventory appropriately.

This creates the lowest possible inventory level—possibly too low for many retailers. Order cycle controls the frequency of the order and their size. The order size is determined by the supplier order minimum in our order limits. Product can be reviewed daily. However, by setting the supplier order minimum to a reasonable logistical level, the orders would be less frequent than the reviews. This formula pushes order control into logistical considerations. With the exception of grocers and very high-turn retailers, it is a rare situation that a store would order as frequently (daily) as desired, and in the smallest quantities. This would be the situation with daily orders.

4. Set Order Need within the Limits

Finally, when all the factors, product need, and safety stock are considered, the order determination model must still return to the limits. When product need is cut back due to limits, discrepancies are reported. For example,

Sample 1

> Available inventory is 40.
>
> Zero product is on-order.
>
> Forecast is 20 widgets per week.
>
> Safety stock is 7.
>
> Service level is very important on this product.
>
> Today (Monday) is the order day.
>
> Lead time is one week.
>
> Order cycle is weekly.

The available inventory on the day this product arrives at the store is $40 - 20 = 20$.

If we order today, the product will arrive in one week. The next chance to order is one week from today, and that order would arrive two weeks from today. The sell-down between today. and the next-next order arrival would reduce our inventory to zero. That is, if we order nothing at all today and wait to order until next week, we should sell our last widget just as the truck is backing up to the receiving dock with a new widget delivery. That sounds pretty good from the point of view of low inventory and high turns.

Technically zero is ideal, except there is a need for safety stock or there won't be enough product to cover for the volatility of the item sales. In other words, if we wait to order, we have absolutely no margin for error, no presentation stock, and possibly no job next week. The problem is that our home repair buyers need widgets to construct most of their projects, and they will walk out the door and buy nothing if there are no widgets. Therefore, we lose not only our widget sales, but we lose sales of lumber, nails, or other products. Our customers don't bother to buy anything until they are sure they have their widgets.

The product is pack 20, and since we want to be sure we have enough product to cover for volatility, the order quantity will be one pack of 20.

Sample 2

> Available inventory is 40.
>
> Zero product is on-order.
>
> Forecast is 20 per week.
>
> Safety stock is zero.
>
> Today is the order day.
>
> Lead time is one week.
>
> Order cycle is weekly.
>
> Presentation stock is three units per facing.
>
> This product has two facings.

If we follow the above scenario, the system falls below the presentation goal midway through the week. Forecasted product need does not necessitate an order, but management philosophy does. Order 20.

In this example, the presentation stock is 3 units × 2 facings = 6 units. In two weeks we will have sold all 40 of what we currently have on hand. We don't keep a very high service level on any particular brand, since our customers have no brand loyalty on this product. The problem is, midway through the second week we will go below the recommended presentation stock. Management prides itself on a full shelf look and the impression this makes on the customers. A hole on the shelf—any hole—is seen as destroying the retail image. For this reason, we will order this week, even though there is no possibility of lost sales.

The system, however, also reports that it is forced into an overstock position because of the presentation stock or the pack size. The category manager or merchandiser can decide to reduce the pack size, reduce the number of competing brands, or live with the overstock since this product is not very expensive and customers expect to see a lot of it on the shelves.

Sample 3

Available inventory is 40.

Zero product is on-order.

Forecast is 20 per week.

Safety stock is zero.

Today is the order day.

Lead time is one week.

Order cycle is weekly.

Presentation stock is 3 units per facing.

This product has 2 facings.

Shelf maximum is 50 and there is no back room reserve.

Following the above scenario, it is necessary to order 20 for the same reasons as explained in sample 2. However, when these 20 arrive, they won't fit on the shelf (shelf maximum is 50). It is necessary to rethink the limits. The many limits of store ordering are more difficult to work with than distribution center ordering. Store ordering must consider and audit many more factors. Many of these factors are traditionally "combined" into one concept, and the problem is thrown at the merchandisers like the proverbial rubber chicken.

In the distribution center, modern inventory control systems have dynamic bin allocation. That is, they assign bins (slots) to products on an as-needed basis. When there is more product than fits into what is called the picking slot, the excess product is put into a reserve location. The system assigns the reserve location slot. There is a daily routine at the distribution center that does let-downs. Let-downs move the product from reserve to the picking slot by sending distribution center personnel to the reserve location, telling them exactly how much product to move, and then telling them exactly where to move the product. At all times the system knows the exact location of the product.

The store is a whole other matter. We purposely did not want these widgets in the back room because it is small and we need the space for high-turn and promotion product. Widgets are small and inevitably get lost in the back room. Normally, they are put on a shelf in the back room and after some time, another product is put in front of them on the same shelf. Even conscientious clerks can't find them hidden behind several other larger products.

Sometimes the clerks try to keep the widgets out on the floor by putting them onto a top shelf, stacking them on the shelf just a little higher than fits comfortably, or setting them in a space nearby. What happens next is that the widgets age in the nearby space since the customer doesn't see them.

If the widget section is manually ordered, the reorder clerk doesn't order the nearby product because the space is full of our widget overstock. If there is automatic ordering, the system correctly orders the nearby product and when it arrives, the clerk shoves our excess product to the back of the shelf (in the wrong area). We lose sales because the system orders no more product. In fact, we have sufficient supply in inventory, but it is hidden behind another product and the customer can't find it!

Limits that make sense and work together are fundamental to successful CAO. When order methods are dynamic they must be self-auditing, have complete information, and work with available product.

Summary

	static mod stk	dynamic mod stk	static min max	refill at arrival	ordr pt ordr up	statistic
lead time	fixed	fixed	fixed	dyn	dyn	dyn
lead time variability	fixed	fixed	fixed	dyn	dyn	dyn
order cycle	fixed	fixed	fixed	fixed	fixed	dyn
forecast	fixed	dyn	fixed	fix / dyn	dyn	dyn
sales volatility	fixed	fixed	fixed	fixed	dyn	dyn
minimum order size	-----	-----	fixed	fixed	fixed	fix / dyn
delivery time/method	-----	-----	-----	-----	fixed	dyn
seasonality	on or off	dyn	on or off	dyn	on or off	dyn

Fixed indicates that this formula uses this information, but the information is part of a constant that cannot be changed to reflect actual.

Dynamic indicates that this formula uses this information and can use actual information at the time of the calculation.

On or off is used with seasonality, since most of the formulas that do not use a forecast usually have an in-season and out-of-season setting. That seasonality is dynamic in the other models assumes that the forecast has a seasonal component.

AUDITS

Here are samples of the types of audits that can be made by order determination. *Automated systems have the advantage over manual ordering in their ability to constantly review and analyze the current situation. Order determination can run more frequently than order generation and continually audit the store.*

Planogram

Order determination questions the current planogram as insufficient or too large. When the orders do not make sense with the set, the ordering system can recommend a reset. Planogram maintenance is currently a difficult problem. Since many planograms are created centrally, individual stores may not fit the core planogram and require individual attention. *Order determination can report when a store planogram is not appropriate because the initial set did not fit this store's demographics, sales volumes have changed over time, or the introduction of new products have resulted in new buying patterns.*

Perpetual Inventory

Order determination compares sales to product on hand. It can compare this store's past history as well as other store sales within this store's demographic and/or geographic group. Inventory levels reflect the planograms, presentation stock, and normal and promotion ordering. *When order determination reviews available inventory for placing an order, it can at the same moment suggest that the current stock position is too high.* This excess inventory amount is useful for central buyers making buy decisions midway through seasons or on non-basic product.

Planning

Order determination compares the actual allocation or distribution of product to the stores (store inventory levels) to the planned store level inventory quantities developed in the merchandise plan. Deviations can be explained by analyzing store level plan versus actual sales, inventory, markdowns, receipts, shipments, and so on.

Limits

Order and product limits may make it impossible to keep the store in stock efficiently and in a cost effective manner. Problems are detected and reported by order determination. Management philosophies on weeks-of-supply, presentation stock, reserve stock, and so on are created at a moment in time but the actual situation changes over time. *Order determination constantly reviews these limits to analyze if they are still appropriate for the current situation.*

Order Cycle

The scheduled order cycle may not be adequate to keep the product in stock and within limits. Order cycle is used to control frequent ordering. However, this must balance with space available and sales rate. When any one of these three factors changes, the balance is lost.

Supplier and Carrier Analysis

Order determination provides the information needed by the analysis systems to evaluate:

• Supplier delivery shorts, shrink, on-time record
• Invoice cost matches between retailer and supplier
• Lead time problems and variability

Unreliable suppliers and carriers create the need to carry large inventories. *Rather than simply enlarging the inventories to cover the problem, order determination analyzes and reports on ongoing problems.*

Order determination also reviews supplier order minimums and maximums. The order minimum prevents the most dynamic system from producing an abundance of small orders. However, as with order cycle, there must be a balance between sales, space, and ordering limits. When any factor changes, the balance is lost.

OUTPUT AND BENEFITS

The benefits of order determination include consistent ordering, orders based on consumer forecasted need, and not ordering when the product is in the store but not on the shelf. As explained previously, these benefits are dependent on the quality of data from the interface systems.

Automated Orders

The most efficient method of processing computer-generated orders is directly to the manufacturer or retail distribution center without in-store manual review. Most retailers will have some product lines that bypass manual review and some that don't. The problem is to understand this difference during the install. You also need to keep from getting discouraged with the concept of automatic ordering simply because not all sections are appropriate for its use.

Manual review always adds to the lead time by at least one day. Retailers want to wait to generate perfect orders before they generate an automated order. (You wouldn't wait to order until you found the perfect order clerk.) Having a system that constantly audits itself is the way to make automated orders work. Automated orders reduce lead time and reduce inventory.

Suggested Orders

Suggested orders must be processed efficiently and easily at the store. There are three keys to accomplishing this:

- Having two-way electronic communication
- Providing the exception information needed to decide if an order should be changed
- Reviewing the suggested orders in the sequence that matches the planogram

Changing a suggested order is not a simple matter of overriding the order presented. When this is the policy, store personnel will not search for back room stock or misplaced stock. The majority of the changed orders will be order increases, many of them unnecessary. Order personnel need information on outstanding orders, promotion plans, forecast, and forecast volatility, as well as supplier information.

Too many stores are measured on the in-stock position and not on their turns or overstock. Store bonuses are paid on increased sales with no concern for inventory. It is difficult to find product in back rooms, which are often out of control. Time constraints prohibit a thorough search before every order. By management philosophy, the stores are always punished for lost sales or understock and never for overstock. Learned behavior is to err on the side of ordering more. Suggested orders reduce manual effort and continue to order when new or temporary personnel have taken over.

Order Audits

Not all order determination functions need to generate orders. Order determination can be used as an audit function for:

- Supplier-manage, DSD, and other supplier controlled areas
- Stepping stone functions that are being replaced
- Reviewing product and order limits

Order audits prevent suppliers from delivering too much or too little product. In product lines where it is logical for the supplier to manage the line directly, the order determination system is used to audit the reasonability of the deliveries.

The audit function is used to test the quality of the order determination system that is replacing a manual or more rudimentary system. Before actual implementation, the self-auditing system is run in parallel with the manual system.

Order determination continually reviews the limits, as explained previously.

CHAPTER 7

Logistics

OVERVIEW

Logistics is the global optimization of product delivery for multiple stores, suppliers, products, and delivery methods. The more variables this global optimization has to work with, the better the opportunity of finding the best solution. Logistics attempts to satisfy the requirements of stores, headquarters, and supplier. Often the ideal solution for one is a disaster for the other. It might be said that logistics is the moment when theory meets reality.

This chapter is not meant to explain the science of logistics—that is obviously several books of information—but to concentrate on logistics as it relates to CAO.

Logistics within CAO includes the optimization and cost reduction of:

- handling
- transportation
- storage
- inventory
- labor

at the

- store
- distribution center
- supplier

The fundamental changes with CAO are the redefinition of the warehouse as distribution center, the use of consumer information to drive logistics decision making and a view of product delivery as a continuous pipeline from manufacturing to consumer—sheep to closet.

The distribution center is no longer merely an intermediate storage location for store product. The distribution center is the heart of logistical decision making. Products may or may not pass through the distribution center on their way to the store. Product may or may not pass through the store on their way to the consumer. The distribution center traditionally depended on store orders to forecast. Orders to suppliers were based primarily on these incoming store orders. There was a logical break where the stores were filling their shelves and the warehouse was filling its slots. The store carried safety stock to satisfy service level expectations for the consumer. The warehouse carried safety stock to satisfy service level expectations of the stores. The supplier carried safety stock to satisfy service level expectations of the retailer. When the retailer organized the staff, data processing departments, and computer systems, there was a division between store and warehouse/central. The division between supplier and retailer could often be described as an insurmountable hurdle. When retailers kept a true perpetual inventory for stores, it tended to be for planning-type products that sell through every season.

CAO changed all this. The distribution pipeline is now one unbroken chain—supplier to consumer. Inventory is total inventory—all the product that exists at the stores, warehouse, and supplier. Service level is service level to the consumer, which means safety stock needs to be considered in the context of what is necessary to support the consumer. The long-range forecasts traditionally used in planning need to be applied to basic products. The short-range forecasts traditionally used in replenishment need to be applied for non-basic products.

In the future, the same system that manages delivery of the product may be bypassing the warehouse or the stores on its route to the consumer. What is important is that the systems are sufficiently robust to be able to locate product anywhere in the supply pipeline and route it to the correct location.

EVOLVING THE FUTURE

CAO opens up new possibilities for logistics. Throughout this book, we discuss reaching goals by taking small, achievable steps. We are taking this same approach with logistics, but there are a few wild cards in the development of the new logistics.

- The logistical support systems needed to accomplish our goals are numerous and complex. Unfortunately, warehousing, replenishment, store systems, and transportation systems are not always as well integrated as they need to be. Depending on the software design, this can create an enormous stumbling block.

- The warehouse design itself may be a limiting factor. Physically redesigning the warehouse to accommodate the future may be a necessity. For example, the dock area in the current warehouse configuration may not efficiently accommodate flow-through.

- The role of the suppliers may hinder or accelerate the process. What is interesting is that some retailers are being lulled to sleep by helpful suppliers. A supplier/retailer partnership does not replace the need for intelligent retailer systems. There is a good deal of internal work retailers must do to define their own internal product flows and to stay ahead of the game.

• Third-party logistics suppliers and the "new wholesalers" can help retailers leap-frog over the step-by-step approach. As with suppliers, there is a limit to what they can do based on the quality of the retailer's internal information.

We will look next at a variety of steps. Although third-party logistics suppliers are placed last on our list, that is not an indication of the order of their potential participation.

Current Logistics

Store orders provide the distribution center with the quantity and expected arrival date, and the DC is expected to comply exactly. This is an extremely important point. Whether the stores are ordering automatically or manually, the DC has no flexibility in filling the orders. When there is limited product in the warehouse, most systems allocate this product either on a first come-first serve basis, or by store rank. The actual store need, based on its current stock position, is not considered by the DC in filling the order. The reality is that most retail warehouses act no differently than wholesale warehouses, and use exactly the same replenishment systems.

Current systems carry enough safety stock to fulfill orders based on a targeted distribution center-to-store service level. Warehouse-to-store service level ignores actual consumer service level. In fact, many retailers have no idea what their actual consumer service level is. If the store has adequate product on hand to fulfill the consumer demand at the time of ordering, the distribution center's service level is based on the store order, not on the customer need.

The distribution center orders product based on a history of store orders. Supplier-managed lines provide product based on a history of the store orders. Order cycle, review time, order minimum, delivery method, lead time, and product source are often considered constants rather than variables. There is little possibility for optimization because all the factors are fixed. Cost is reduced primarily by increasing the buy quantity or buying excess product during a manufacturer reduced cost offer.

Manufacturers encourage excessive buys with bracket and full-truck discounts in addition to temporary cost reductions. Payment terms are rarely negotiable and even more rarely tied to mutually advantageous logistics agreements. Product pack is created for the retailer by the supplier or selected by the retailer from a supplier choice. The retailer selection of pack size is frequently based on their "A" (highest volume) stores, even when there are multiple pack sizes. Retailers will often demand "volume incentives" when taking the larger pack sizes. Few retail systems can manage multiple packs on the same product from the same supplier. Some antiquated systems have separate databases depending on how the product is delivered—direct store product on one file and warehouse product on another. This completely eliminates any possibility of logistical options on delivery methods. The most difficult problems are created by push/pull systems where product is alternately pushed by central to the stores, and pulled via store orders. These push/pull systems may actually have no interface—literally a case of the left hand not knowing what the right hand is doing.

Although the science of logistics is well developed and extremely flexible, it is often hamstrung by inadequate data and support systems. For example, many retail systems cannot measure the net landed cost (the cost including handling, transportation, and discounts to supply the product to the store) with the retail price, and relate this to return on investment. Although it is impossible to imagine hiring computer experts and then expecting them to work with an abacus, it is not unusual to hire logistics experts and then expect them to work with a set of blueprints and limited data.

Flexible Store Orders to the Distribution Center

The first step you may want to consider is adding flexibility to individual store orders to the distribution center (DC). This is done by providing the distribution center with more information than merely the quantity and expected date of arrival in the store order. If the stores provide early and late arrival dates and quantities, the logistics system can treat these factors as variables. In order to provide this level of information, the store orders would need to be generated via a CAO type system. In this step, the store CAO is still making all the delivery quantity and timing calculations, but it is giving the supplier some leeway in the timing of filling the order.

When the order has built-in flexibility, the logistics system is able to optimize more factors. Normally, at the time a store orders product that is shipped in full cases, the store actually has a healthy cushion of product to fulfill customer service level. Orders are often produced to supply presentation stock or because the order cycle requires the production of the order on a certain day.

The optimization for one store includes the following:

Improved Load Building

Particularly where full truck loads are an objective, the DC logistics system would be able to make the decision of when it could order and what quantity. This logic includes the ability to delay or split orders. The cost of store receiving, if affected adversely, would be factored into the decision. In all cases, the more flexibility the DC has in adjusting the order delivery date and the order quantity, the more important would be the interfaces to labor management, perpetual inventory, and receiving costs.

Consolidation of Slow Movers

Distribution center efficiency is improved by reducing the number of picks of exceptionally slow items. If the slow items can be limited to certain days and/or double picked with another store's orders, distribution center efficiency is improved. (Of course, this depends on the DC automation.) If the distribution center knows these parameters, it can establish the optimal time to pick and ship the product.

Expedite/Delay of Incoming Distribution Center Orders

There are times when the distribution center can control the scheduling of deliveries from suppliers, generally based on its current inventory position. The inventory positions of the ordering stores and the overall inventory position of the retailer is a more valid reason to expedite or delay an incoming order.

Pack Review

Store level forecasting interfaced to planograms and perpetual inventory gives us new insight into the extent of overstock in the stores created by overpacked product. When this problem is identified, several courses of action can be determined. If the supplier offers a smaller pack or can provide a smaller pack, this is of course the first choice. If the retailer can handle multiple pack sizes of the same product or even desires to do so would be considered in this decision. Establishing this product in the repack area or buying it as repack through third-party providers is another choice. However, when the slower moving product represents a completion to the supplier line, there is a merchandising trade-off involved in setting the shelf. It is difficult to set a product line in an attractive fashion to actual sales when the line has slow movers as well as fast movers. The overall look can be quite uneven.

Optimization across Stores

The stores can provide the DC logistics system with an overall inventory picture that includes all product available within the entire chain—not only in the DC itself but in all the stores. This is particularly important at the end of a promotion or near the end of a season sell-down.

Decisions are based on the overall inventory position of the retailer and the current store product need. Now, service level is considered a consumer goal. Safety stock is seen not as belonging separately to the DC and to the stores, but as a single safety net for the entire company. When thought of in this context, less safety stock may be required.

The following examples do not necessarily involve suppliers. Of course, if the supplier loads or palletizes for cross-dock, there is an overall handling savings. But incremental steps do not require the immediate participation of all suppliers (although, of course, it is extremely helpful).

The optimization across several stores includes the following:

Consolidation of Orders

The distribution center logistics system can achieve benefits by looking further ahead of the stores' normal order time. This is especially true when the system has knowledge of the overall inventory position of the chain. For example, the system can vary the quantities and mode of transportation of product flowing in and out of the DC. One variation is bypassing the distribution center and sending selected product directly to the stores. The cost of this mode of delivery is measured against the cost of double handling at the DC. When the DC has flexibility in the load-building quantities and times, there are obvious advantages in planning outbound loads. The cost of this flexibility on store receiving and put-away must always be a part of the final determination.

Cross-dock

Product that need not be put away in warehouse slots (bins) can be ordered directly for the store and crossed from one delivery vehicle to another through a warehouse staging area. This may be done on a case-by-case basis without involving the supplier, or on mixed pallets with the supplier's cooperation. Even when there is product already in the DC, the possibility exists for cross-dock either by planning to use existing product for other orders or by consolidating a part of the DC product with the incoming cross-dock order. Where full pallets of products are moved through the dock—such as at high season or for promotions—this not only reduces the cost of warehousing, but may be the only way to turn the product rapidly enough to fill need.

Cross-dock offers the opportunity to eliminate the need to keep certain products in the DC. These are the products that have dependable lead times and sufficient safety stock at store level. (Once again, not all store sets are bare bones. If we must overset for merchandising, we can at least take advantage of that in-store safety stock in our ordering.) This elimination of selected products in the DC combined with the reduction of excess safety stock on stored products obviously reduces our overall inventories. An additional benefit is the freeing of space within the DC for other products. (For some warehouses, just the freeing up of space in which to operate efficiently can create an economic advantage.)

Unallocated Flow-through

Requested product traditionally is distributed as flow-through. These products can arrive at the dock pre-allocated or post-allocated. This rather common practice for non-basic product is coming to be better understood by retailers with basic products. Unallocated flow-through product is ordered early through long-range forecasting and then distributed at the time of arrival at the distribution center through short-range forecasts. Post-allocated flow-through can benefit many product and order types.

Requested products such as fashion and imports normally must be ordered quite early, as these products are often manufactured to the specific order. The actual store distribution can, however, be made based on current store data and need. Basic products that are highly seasonal at times also must be booked early long before actual store need is established. This is true of large-scale promotions that require a commitment to supply on the manufacturer's part. These truckloads of product may be pre-ordered but they do not necessarily need to be pre-allocated.

Purchasing Decisions

Traditionally, DC buyers make new buying decisions without complete knowledge of the current inventory position of the retail chain. Most retailers have already decided that transfers of products are unprofitable.

However, there are times when transfers are not only justifiable but necessary. Decisions on transfers therefore must be made on the basis of their logistical costs, availability and cost of additional product, and the overstock level in the chain as a whole. Times when transfers may be justifiable include near-end of season, promotion or high-season product imbalance, or severe overstock at the store.

Central buyers (and buying systems) should know the overall retail stock position. After a promotion has completed, it may appear at first glance that sales were terrific. But they may have been no match for the quantity of product shipped to the stores. When this happens, the buyers should be made aware of the current store need for product (especially if there will be post promotion slump) before purchasing additional product. If all the factors are known, decisions can be quantified and made on whether it is better to bring in additional product, transfer, and/or wait to buy.

Allocation of Limited Product

When the distribution center doesn't have enough product for the incoming orders, the logistics system can use the current weeks' supply position of each store, plus the distribution center's on-orders to determine how to distribute limited products. The first-come-first-served or biggest-stores-first approach to allocation makes no sense when it is possible to allocate product according to actual consumer service level.

Order Generation and Optimization of Sources

This is the most complex—and possibly the most profitable—of the evolving components of logistics. For much product, there are multiple sources, lead times, and costs as well as delivery methods. Store locations vary across a wide geographic area. Supplier production and staging locations vary. With supplier cooperation, costs and payment terms can reflect overall transportation and inventory cost reductions. Accomplishing this step requires that the retailer has accurate supplier to DC lead times and supplier to store lead times. And this is not just the general supplier but each of the suppliers' shipping points to this retailer. Currently systems do not adequately measure these factors, nor could most retailer systems manage multiple lead times from one supplier. Very few systems—even those that support CAO—have actual store lead time information.

As previously explained, the calculation of product need and the generation of a purchase order do not need to be tied into one function or even one system. They were presented together in the order determination chapter simply for ease of understanding. The following look into the future is through conversations with Marvin Woods, the founder of Marwood Distribution Systems, Inc. and the current president of Woods Associates, Old Bethpage, New York.

Logistics. A formidable word. It conjures up visions of military precision, complex scientific concepts, people lifting cases of goods, trucks rolling over the roads, and lots of sweat. It is all of that and lots, lot more. Let's start our peek into the future of logistics with a simple definition. Logistics is getting the right product to the right place, at the right time, and at the least possible total cost. The key operative phrase here is *least possible total cost.*

As we look out into the future of inventory management it is here, in the domain of logistics, that we can take a wide-ranging, all-encompassing view of the many pieces that have to be considered in order to truly achieve a least possible total cost. This view must consider the entire spectrum from the point of manufacture all the way through to getting the product into the hands of the consumer.

The problem in the past was our unwillingness (or inability) to deal with the full scope of the problem, and to cross political domains or company boundaries. So, in the 80's and even into the 90's, we pretty much limited ourselves to minimizing landed cost, and to controlling scheduling to the point that the product could be relied on to show up when and where it was expected. Landed cost is the cost of product to the initial delivery point (usually the warehouse), and is often limited to the price we paid the supplier for the product plus the transportation cost.

Unfortunately, achieving the least possible total cost is not a simple and straightforward matter. Lowering one component of cost often raises another. For example, let's say we have an item that we sell exactly one a day (I know we are ignoring presentation stock, movement variability, and safety stock, but it won't change this example). We can reduce our inventory cost to the minimum by bringing in exactly one unit each day, but of course we all know this approach doesn't usually make any sense. It will raise our transportation and handling costs. For reasons like this we must look at logistics as an optimization problem. The real goal is to balance the tradeoffs to achieve a minimum total cost. We must accept that some of the components will be higher than their absolute minimum in order to achieve this optimal mix. This may sound simple, but in practice we often try to minimize only a few of the costs (such as the price of the product and the transportation cost) and ignore many of the other expenses (such as storage and handling, and inventory carrying costs). We must consider these costs in our ever-more competitive world of retailing if we want to stay on top and be world class.

Flexibility. Optimization is only possible when there are choices. The more flexibility, the greater potential to improve results. Let's say we order a case of a particular item for a particular day using a traditional store system. Whether that ordering system is automated or manual, we have limited choices—especially when the demand is not known until the last moment. Our new view of advanced automated store ordering offers us wide new possibilities. One future strategy is to split forecasting and need determination from order generation and logistics.

The architecture of having the store system be responsible for forecasting and need determination, coupled with a centralized integrated logistic system that performs the actual order generation function, offers us wide latitude for optimization possibilities. The key to this approach is the longer time horizon provided by the forecasting system. Now we can look further out and, for example, consider drop shipping from the primary or secondary supplier direct to the store, thereby bypassing the warehouse (and all its costs) altogether. Another possibility that presents itself is far greater use of cross-docking.

To make this really work, we want the greatest possible freedom in how much to deliver to the store, and when. One exciting approach to providing this flexibility is for the automated store ordering system to provide the central logistics system with a range of needs. This can be in the form of earliest and latest need information. Given current inventory level, shelf capacity, forecast, and management philosophies, it is pretty easy to figure out the maximum quantity you can deliver to the store on its next scheduled delivery date. More realistically, what you really want to know is the earliest date you can deliver a store ordering unit (don't forget to consider the movement variability over the period). On the other hand, given the same data coupled with desired shelf minimums (including safety stock), it is possible to figure how long you can wait before you must ship to the store, as well as the maximum amount you can ship at that point. You also need enough information to figure out all the possibilities in between. However, shelf capacities and store ordering units often don't leave too wide a range of choices. For most shelf sets the maximum ordering amount and the minimum ordering amount are the same—one shipping unit—so the only choice is *when* to deliver that ordering unit. But if you remember that the role of these systems is both to perform operational functions and to audit the rules, the system can begin to question the size of shelf sets and orderable packs.

To be clear, we are discussing pushing the entire order generation process into the logistics function. In the first steps, we just passed a date range for the logistics system to work with. Here the logistics system can have access to the store database combined with the product need calculation. The logistics system actually determines when and how much to order, and how the product is to be delivered. Now, with order generation in the central logistics system, we have some real flexibility.

Eliminating Waste. Let's start our optimization trek with a look at a few small improvements that can yield some interesting results. Although our examples use truck load sizes and daily deliveries particularly appropriate to the grocery industry, it is not difficult to stretch out the time frames and realize the same successes in other industries. By having flexibility in when and how much we deliver to the store, we can make some significant changes. With sales often skewed toward the weekend, we normally experience very high demand to replenish the stock early in the week. However, we often won't need that stock until later in the week or until sales peek again next weekend. By changing when we ship this stock, we can lower inventory levels at both stores and the warehouse.

Another major area of savings is transportation. We can reduce the number of partial trucks and multi-stop trucks that are sent out. We can do a better job of truck loading by making informed decisions on what to add to fill a truck or what safely can be left off to avoid sending an additional truck. For example, instead of sending one and one-third trucks on Monday, Wednesday, and Friday, we can use newfound flexibility to send one truck on two of the days and two trucks on the third day. This obviously improves use of truck space (by sending fuller trucks), and reduces the number of multistop loads (or reduces the number of stops). Clearly, it will lower our trucking costs.

We can also improve warehouse productivity in the area of slow movers. Depending on the warehouse technology used, productivity is directly correlated with density of pick. The store system has no idea of where a particular item is being stored in the warehouse and can do nothing to affect this. However, our integrated logistics system could take into account warehouse location to possibly eliminate selecting from some aisles or sections unless absolutely necessary. Since we have flexibility in when we fill line items, the logistics system groups everything possible from that section into one pick.

True Cost. The crucial element in implementing an optimization strategy is actually making the cost trade-offs. You can do this in a simple but rough fashion by using basic rules-of-thumb. Using this approach, basic assumptions are made that a particular strategy is always better than an alternative, which therefore doesn't have to be considered. Unfortunately, in our ever-more complex and dynamic world, things just don't stay steady enough for this kind of approach. A common example of this is transfers. Many retailers abide by an unwritten rule of never making transfers and have burdened the transfer transaction with many general costs. However, when the system is able to analyze actual costs on an ongoing basis, it finds not only cost justifiable transfers, but necessary transfers.

Another approach is to fully understand all of the possible cost components in enough detail so that true optimization is possible. This is true cost. It parallels the kind of thinking that has led many retailers to adopt Direct Product Cost (DPC), a part of Direct Product Profitability (DPP), in some of their merchandising decisions, such as shelf layout and retail pricing. This approach will require that many parts of our systems have access to this true cost data in order to make a wide variety of decisions. True cost is related to activity-based costing. Activity-based costing says that we must know all the costs of procuring and selling product and choose between activities based on those costs. If we take this concept a step further, cost determination and, potentially, best price can be based on supplier logistics alternatives.

This approach requires the elemental cost factors that many advanced labor management systems use to calculate "fair work times." Another example of the use of elemental data used to calculate costs in order to maximize ROI can be found in advanced forward buying systems. This elemental approach provides both extremely accurate and flexible calculation of costs for "real time" evaluation of alternative strategies. However, what is needed to support integrated logistics is a modular strategy that makes even more extensive cost information available across the spectrum of supply chain functions. Such an approach will allow us to react easily in a dynamic world. Few if any decisions will be "hard coded" into our systems, where they would have delivered far less than optimal results when circumstances changed from the "steady state" environment these older approaches assumed.

Time Horizon. The next thing to consider if we are to minimize total costs is to optimize over a reasonable time period. Looking out one full quarter (13 weeks) may be fine in a fast-moving environment. A longer period of six months or even a full year might be required in lower-turn situations. Traditionally, most replenishment systems and procedures have tried to optimize only the current decision (the order we are creating now). Newer systems are looking out over the next order after this one. Ideally you want to make sure that what you are doing now won't create some problem that will cause your costs to increase down the road. For example, let's say we have a supplier from whom we normally buy once a week and normally carry a two-week supply. Now let's suppose we have a forward buy opportunity that works out to be a good return on investment at a 10-week forward buy. So we buy an extra truck or two of this one item and everything looks great. Unfortunately, our analysis didn't include that because this one item represents half our one truck per week, the next time we order from this supplier we will have to fill the truck with slower moving items (or perhaps have a system that is smart enough to adjust and buy only the one-half truck next time, albeit at a higher transportation cost). If we buy a full truck the next time we may well be buying a four- or six-week supply of these slow-moving items. All in all, our costs of these slower-moving other items will have gone up. That still doesn't mean that the forward buy was unprofitable, only that considering all the costs it wasn't as profitable as we'd expected.

Summary. An integrated approach to logistics views the entire supply chain as a single spectrum of opportunity. It starts out at one end of this spectrum—at the store. Armed with the product need for each and every store (with the widest possible latitude in when and how much is delivered), it leaps to the other end of the spectrum—supply alternatives. Armed with inventory availability (and cost) for every point in our supply chain (primary supplier, alternate sources, outside warehouses, store overstock positions, primary warehouse), it has the widest possible latitude in meeting store needs. It continues through all the pieces in between, including transportation, storage, and handling costs. Continuously and dynamically reacting to our ever-changing world in search of optimized solutions. Keeping the twenty-first century retailer ahead of the pack in reduced costs and improved service.

EVOLVING THE FUTURE

Third-Party Logistics Providers

Third-party logistics providers have grown rapidly in recent years, redefining roles within the distribution pipeline and providing a wide variety of value-added services. Rich Sherman, Director of Supply Chain Research at Advanced Manufacturing Research in Boston, Massachusetts, has excellent insights into the growth of this segment and where it is heading. The remainder of this section is an interview with Rich about the future of third-party logistics.

Cross-dock and flow-through are frequently cited as key to efficient replenishment. But it seems there is far more talk than action on this front in the retail industry. Many people in the industry never actually get started because they think the task is too complex and time-consuming.

Third-party logistics providers, of course, know otherwise. Their willingness to walk in where others fear to tread has served them well. Some have developed a sufficient track record to be able to suggest a total reconfiguration of the industry's distribution infrastructure. Not surprisingly, that reconfiguration puts third-party logistics providers at the center of the action.

Manufacturers are increasingly teaming up with third-party logistics providers to bring measurable benefits in service levels and profitability. For example, one major juice company called upon a third-party provider to help balance store inventories and use cross-docking to create a strategic advantage not only for itself but for its retailer partners.

The juice firm was designed to find that the actual sales rate among 140 stores in a particular chain varied 61 percent between the lowest and the highest store. Analysis showed that chain-wide shelf sets were a key culprit. Some stores were running out of stock, while others were carrying too much inventory for too long and were sending regular shipments of out-dated juice to reclamation centers. After the juice company studied the chain's promotion patterns and demographics, store by store, it was able to make corrections.

Working with its third-party provider, the manufacturer then calculated demand back through the pipeline to determine what shipments should be made to coincide with demand at each point. Using demand planning to establish what would leave the distribution center and when, the manufacturer and logistics provider coordinated shipments to arrive at the distribution center just as product was needed to satisfy store demand. Loads and shipments were built to optimize the amount of product that could be cross-docked.

The ultimate result was reduced inventory and higher service levels. Sales opportunities and distribution efficiencies were maximized for all parties. The success was based on two factors:

1. Accessibility, accuracy and intelligent use of necessary information. The number of product locations for which distribution must be planned has grown so greatly that use of technology has become mandatory. But sometimes systems share "data" and not "information." Trading partners need to understand the difference, and set ground rules they can use together.

2. Willingness to overcome a legacy of adversarial relationships. This applies to all parties in the chain—retailers, manufacturers, wholesalers, and so on. Without an open-minded understanding of how widespread use of cross-docking, parties tend to avoid it. Cross-docking is not a single process. It is, rather, only one components of a holistic, fluid system that requires trading partners to understand both the challenges and the benefits, both upstream and downstream.

What if my physical warehouse design prohibits these new concepts?

Any facility can be economically redesigned to accommodate flow-through operations. However, until you eliminate the practices causing non-flow-through design, there isn't any point. Warehouse design (or redesign) begins with specific forecasts for specific products. You can't design a warehouse without product and movement information.

What's next for third-party providers?

Third-party growth will likely evolve by category, and eventually involve the whole store. Volume economics will determines whether you go third-party, wholesaler, or in-house. It's already clear that labor issues associated with pick-and-pack operations make the outsourcing of warehouse distribution attractive to the lower-volume retailer such as C-stores, grocery or chains with low square footage.

Is third-party logistics just for the grocery industry?

I see third-party logistics playing a larger role than ever across all industries and all products—not just grocery, and definitely beyond consumer goods. As more companies embrace time-based competitive and service strategies, the requirements to consolidate, postpone, and break bulk among many manufacturers becomes critical. The likelihood of cooperative management among potentially competing manufacturers is minimal; therefore, the usefulness of a third party increases. The lines of differentiation between the third-party logistics provider and the wholesaler are graying. The wholesaler's advantage is taking title to the inventory, thereby increasing manufacturer turn and assuming inventory risk. Wholesalers must transcend the traditional buyer seller relationship and begin selling their suppliers the value-added services they provide.

Is third-party logistics just for high-turn products?

Third-party logistics is even more important in slow-turn products. They have the capability of consolidating requirements for multiple retailers, thereby making pick-and-pack operations economical. The items can be picked at the inner pack level to specific store shelf slot quantities, placed in store- or route-specific totes or containers, and then delivered to the retail distribution center for cross-docking to individual stores.

What about pallet cross-docking?

Pallet cross-docking may be a pipe dream without third-party or wholesaler intervention. It is unlikely, especially in grocery, that any individual store will move a pallet of any given product within shelf slot or turn requirements except during a promotion for warehouse type stores. At the store level, pallets will have to be mixed product by layer or even case. Very few manufacturer product lines and store turns support a single vendor mixed pallet. Therefore, multi-vendor mixed product pallet will have to be built. This could be done by a third party or wholesaler.

What about more store directs?

As third-party and wholesaler services expand and the value-added is recognized by the retailer, a larger volume of third-party product will go store direct. As more product flows through the third-party facility, the economies of store direct will be realized. I think that home shoppers will facilitate this growth even further. However, there is still a question as to who will actually own and manage the home shopping and delivery operations.

LOGISTICS SYSTEM REQUIREMENTS

Electronic Communication

Using EDI to transmit purchase orders from the supplier to the retailer is faster and more accurate. Data is received instantaneously, and the typing errors that are an inherent part of manually transcribing information are eliminated. The advance ship notice interfaces with the on-order function and labor management. This interface allows the retailer to make contingency decisions and to plan on alternate sourcing and/or merchandising. This interface also provides the retailer with the necessary information for labor scheduling. Advance ship notices and information on current store need provide the basis for decisions on which products can be delayed, expedited, or redirected before arrival at original destination.

Sharing Real-Time Information

There are many benefits when the retailer, headquarters (DC), and supplier all have the same information available simultaneously in real time, rather than in sequential mode. Sequential information forces sequential decision-making—nobody can act to maximize advantage until all necessary data has moved from Point A to Point B to Point C. Database information must be shared and easily accessible to maximize the options for the supplier (one such option, as we noted earlier, is moving the order generation function into logistics). There is, however, a philosophical problem for the retailer. Retailers need to share data, but they also need to leverage their competitive advantage. How much data to share is an individual decision—especially concerning individual customers. Certainly most retailers set limits on how much data will be shared, and insist on signed confidentiality agreements.

Lower Level Information Sharing

A new level of information is needed for global decision making. This information includes the planogram, planning, product need limitation, consumer/demographic data, and elemental cost information by store/product as well as supplier-to-store specific information, such as lead times and interfaces.

Accurate Forecasting and Perpetual Inventory

As we noted previously, the more volatility in the forecast, the more safety stock needed. The safety stock grows exponentially from stores to DC to supplier. Some volatility is a function of the difficulty of attempting to predict the future. However, some volatility results directly from insufficient data available to the forecasting method or inadequate forecasting. Inaccurate forecasting exponentially expands the safety stock through the distribution pipeline. As we discussed in Chapter 5, volatility is made worse by formulas that don't take all the sales influences into consideration. Another problem is inherent in systems that do not capture these influences. More accurate forecasting at store level reduces safety stock not only at the store but throughout the distribution pipeline. Suppliers and third-party information sources can supply the information that retailers are missing, particularly about promotions.

Basic product retailers can take lessons in long-range forecasting from retailers who use planning. Although specialists in short-range forecasts, these retailers have often overlooked the importance of projecting supply needs. Flexible logistics requires the ability to look long range at the supply chain to maximize efficiencies in delivery methods and schedules.

Accurate perpetual inventory is the key to viewing the corporation as a whole, with service level keyed on the consumer instead of the distribution center. The perpetual inventory and the forecast are the basis for all logistics decisions.

Accurate and Reduced Lead Times

Dependable lead times are needed to process orders dynamically while maintaining high service levels and low inventories. Understanding the components of lead time is needed to identify the problem areas. It is difficult for our current systems to establish the various lead times for multiple sources delivering to multiple destinations. If we want to provide logistics managers with maximum flexibility, we must remove the handcuffs of "one corporate lead time" per supplier.

Move Purchase Order Generation to Logistics

As we discussed in Chapter 6, product need and order generation are two separate steps. There is an expanse of time when it is acceptable to deliver product to a store without causing consumer out-of-stocks. This should facilitate the following:

- Distribution center deliveries that are "logistically" beneficial
- Cross-dock opportunities
- Supplier direct opportunities

Although the concept of procurement as a part of logistics rather than a part of merchandising seems to be straightforward and logical, the reality is that most systems define procurement as part of merchandising and included within the merchandiser's job description.

Labor Management

As we build greater flexibility into the systems through logistically sensitive delivery schedules, pick-and-pack warehouses, and direct store deliveries, the ability to schedule and manage store receiving personnel is imperative. Yet, most labor management systems concentrate their efforts on the selling space, not the backdoor. Unlike the warehouse, stores have more sensitive use of parking lot space, potentially restricted travel times, and certainly no ability to "stack up" trucks during unload. The systems providing product to the stores cannot be more sensitive to the product than they are to the personnel who must receive and put away the product.

Here's an example to consider from the grocery industry. Certainly the high-variety retailer can reduce the slow-mover pack size of canned soups, puddings and gelatins, and jams and jellies. Why not go to eaches (individual units)? It's possible through pick-and-pack, but this must be balanced against the difficulty of putting away lookalike products and the general look of an uneven set.

As more information migrates into other systems, simple enhancements will be possible. When headquarters knows each product's planogram and planogram location, deliveries can be pre-tagged for the proper location. When headquarters knows the perpetual inventory in a store, promotion product can be tagged for a special promotion setup. One final note. In all this talk of dynamic systems and flexibility, it's important to keep one basic fact in mind: everything we do ultimately funnels to a single backdoor, to a very human receiving clerk.

BENEFITS

Reduced Inventory

Reduced inventories are created by reducing lead times, improved forecasting and order determination routines, more efficient delivery methods, and third-party pick-and-pack centers.

Reduced Workload

When we increase logistics flexibility, it is necessary to actively manage store receiving. Store deliveries are scheduled so that they make sense from a personnel and door availability standpoint. Advance ship notices are used for store direct deliveries. Store labor management systems control receiving in addition to the sales floor. Advance ship notices feed the store perpetual inventory system. Where there is confidence in the shipment accuracy, only occassional audits are required. For basic product, use the planogram information on the outside of the case to direct store personnel to the put-away location. For product picked in eaches or break pack, box by planogram.

Decreased Transportation Costs

The more variables that logistics can work with, the more opportunities there are to optimize delivery methods and loads. Manufacturers and third-party logistics providers can optimize across multiple products and multiple retailers. By moving the actual order generation function into logistics, the timing and quantity of multiple orders can be analyzed together.

Reduced Product Obsolescence

The ability to vary delivery modes, eliminate excess storage points, and base actual orders on individual store needs and space availability can reduce product excess.

Improved Customer Service (fewer shelf stock-outs)

Individual stores function differently and require different stocking levels. By basing the store orders on actual in-store inventory and forecasts and supplier-to-store lead times, the logistics system can insure the target service level.

Reduced Warehouse Costs

When retailers' warehouses function autonomously, the warehouse carries safety stock over and above the safety stock already available on the store shelves. When cross-dock and flow-through cannot be used on an as-needed basis, product is slotted that does not need to be slotted. Warehouses keep excess product and move product from reserve to pick much more often than necessary.

CHAPTER 8

Conclusion

The CAO benefits we have discussed tell only part of the story. In this book, we have made the case that CAO is not an off-the-shelf system but is an ongoing project, with each phase having its own unique set of benefits and cost justification. We have also explained that CAO is part of a bigger vision of retail that will be not only more responsive to individual consumers, but also more directly in touch with them.

Let's look again at our future paradigms.

- Functional integration
- Dynamic rather than static decision making
- Consumer based, real-time systems
- Global optimization of logistics
- Top-down strategies, bottom-up information
- New levels of data

Retail systems must support a vision where product may bypass the store on the way to the consumer, or bypass the distribution center on the way to the stores. Since consumers have a broad spectrum of choices in not only where they obtain product but how, shopping will need to be a satisfactory experience. This will mean providing an even greater level of service. This future vision requires systems such as CAO that use store-specific and consumer data to insure correct product is available at the store, locate product throughout the supply chain, and move it easily from any location to the consumer. Since no single store for the mass retailer operates in a vacuum, top-down management strategies implement retail philosophies, while bottom-up information impact the implementation. All levels of operation will work with real-time information, using decision-making tools that react and learn from new information.

Is CAO a crazy dream? We don't think so. Now, we're not suggesting that this is all possible tomorrow morning. But we are suggesting that whoever doesn't take the time to get there will not be able to address the needs of the future. However, getting there shouldn't be all cost without reward. Retailers must design their own series of steps to achieve their goals, but each step should have its own benefits. The importance of this future vision is to avoid spending time and money on solutions that camouflage problems rather than solving them. If money must be spent on systems or hardware that provide only stopgap solutions, then the retailer must understand and budget accordingly. It's easy to be lulled to sleep by the myriad of solution providers who solve immediate problems but fail to address long-term objectives. Implementing CAO correctly is difficult to do right and easy to do wrong—but implementing CAO correctly is the path to the future.

Let's take a look at a sample CAO implementation. Stan's Supersports is implementing CAO. The majority of their products are planogrammed and currently they are using a planning system on 45% of the products. There are 60 stores, and a single distribution center supplies most product. Stan's has expanded these past few years by buying other retail outlets, and consequently has many different store formats. Their product line has also expanded and changed these past few years. With the popularity of in-line skating they are now selling several different brands of skates as well as accessories and clothing. Stan's holds many in-store events featuring local sports celebrities. These are always a big draw and increase sales overall. Various manufacturers also sponsor events that are always popular. These manufacturer-sponsored events increase purchases primarily on the manufacturer's products.

Stan's began their CAO project by producing an RFP (request for proposal). In their RFP they asked extensive questions about forecasting and ordering. Finally they chose and installed the very popular Order-it! software product. Order-it! provides forecasting and order determination models.

The installation went smoothly, and Stan's began a trial run of one store and three departments. A full-time analyst spent all of her time at the store and corrected problems as quickly as they occurred. The pilot was such a success that Stan's decided to roll it out to all the stores in all departments immediately.

That's when the surprises started. The first problem was the forecasts. The forecasting portion of the system that seemed to work so well in the pilot didn't forecast correctly anymore. Each promotion event required the forecast to be overridden. Discussions started with Order-it! about why the forecasts didn't work. In-line skating data was incomplete, and the system didn't have enough information to handle the rapid trends and the seasonal surges. In-line skating needed better seasonal profiles and trend analysis. This was not available from the data. The in-store events had not been considered ahead of time. The forecasting expert assured Stan's that the forecast could handle these promotion events. Management was pleased because they knew they had a very effective ad system. However, the IS (Information Services) department explained that the ad system was used only by the ad department.

All the information was entered manually into another platform and used for creating print ads and flyers. At no time did the ad system communicate to the mainframe.

Second, some departments had several lookalike items, and there were problems with the multiple key. Management sent an edict to the stores to stop using the multiple key. The stores complied initially, but by the Fourth of July, when the customers fill the stores and lines start to form at the registers, the multiple key was back in use. The stores themselves never used the POS data and were less interested than central management in insuring POS quality. There were more problems with POS data than just the multiple key. The stores were resetting the POS equipment during the day, changing prices, and adding items. The stores were never consulted on the CAO project, and basically were untrained or undertrained. Edicts from central were generally ignored in order to keep the customers happy. During the pilot the full-time analyst was fixing all the problems manually and there was so much attention to the three sections in the pilot that there were never any real errors. Well, *everyone knew that management was watching!*

Third, there was a problem with fashion accessories on the planning system. These items were requested not available. The Order It! system is designed to function as JIT (Just-In-Time). Order It! is the most dynamic of all formulas. Sportswear which accounts for 60% of dollar sales is bought through planning and depends on post-allocation of pre-booked deliveries. The Order It! software had to be reconfigured to distribute a fixed amount to the stores rather than calculate a needed amount to purchase.

Fourth, there were problems keeping the POS data accurate. The mainframe item master file is unable to manage multiple UPCs for the same product or to link products. POS maintenance is a secondary concern of the mainframe system. In fact, there is no real POS delete capability or linkage between SKUs. Store order history always drove inventory levels, never the POS data. POS data was used to account for department and store dollar sales—not individual item movement. Then IS dropped the bombshell. They estimated it would take at least one year to replace the item master file with a database that could support the new requirements. They explained that for the last five years they had been using band aids and patches to hold all the new projects together. They were feeding so many one-off systems including planograms, category management, planning, labor scheduling, and now CAO that staff members were specialists who rarely understood the full impact of any change. Then someone got out the chart that showed all the interfaces and systems. It wrapped around two sides of the conference room.

If all these problems were not serious enough, the stores were complaining. Even in the departments where the sales data and forecasts were acceptable, the order quantities didn't make sense. All the stores were planogrammed but the orders weren't fitting on the shelves. Sure the system was keeping them in stock, but the back room was overflowing! "I thought this thing was supposed to talk with planograms?" "We have store level planograms, why isn't it working?" "Because all of the planograms are out of date!" The store managers were called in. "Why are the planograms out of date?" The store managers answered simply, "How do we know when to update them and who has time to do it? You guys at central are always changing lines—we can't run around fixing planograms every day!"

Discouraged? Of course! This is the moment that CAO projects come to screeching halt. CAO is like a big picture puzzle. CAO benefits depend on all the puzzle pieces properly fitting together. And if they don't, there are no benefits. The headaches seem far worse than leaving "well enough alone." CAO can be a bit like picking up a rock and finding all the bugs underneath. For Stan's, it's time to structure a project that includes all the variables. Stan's must concentrate on achieving the immediate benefits while working on other aspects that accomplish long-term objectives. There is no real problem with the Order It! software—there is a problem with the original RFP and project definition.

Almost all CAO project pilots succeed, but not nearly as many project implementations. When each piece of the puzzle was defined the benefits were also defined. Although Stan's found the project to be much bigger than they initially planned, they also found that the benefits were much more substantial. The real potentials and possibilities that result from CAO were initially as hidden as the extent of the project. By taking a more global view of CAO, Stan's is moving forward and enjoying the incremental benefits of a step-by-step approach.

APPENDIX A

Glossary

Adaptive Filtering: A forecasting technique similar to exponential smoothing. The difference is that the weighting factor is calculated based on the system's knowledge of ongoing error, deviation from forecast, and product influences.

Aesthetic Minimum: The minimum amount of product required on the shelf to establish the store look. It is independent of product need.

Allocation: Calculation of store distribution amounts from a fixed quantity of product.

Artificial Intelligence: Mathematical models of theorized brain activity.

Automated Orders: Orders not reviewed before placement.

Available Inventory: Product that is normally available from the supplier when it is needed by the retailer.

Basic Products: Individual items that are carried every year, have history that may be affected by trends, business cycles, seasons, and promotions, and have a measurable sales history.

Box-Jenkins: A forecasting method which basically says that we may not know the best model and that the system is where the model should be determined.

Business Cycles: Business cycles normally exceed one year in duration.

Cannibalization: Sales that are lost to other products within the same store are said to be cannibalized.

CAO: Computer Assisted Ordering. In its most basic definition, this is automatic re-order calculation for retail at store level. In the global sense, CAO includes the entire product flow to the retailer, including distribution.

Category (classification) (Class, sub-category, subclass): Items sharing a selling space in the store, and which are promoted and merchandised together.

Category Depth: Multiple choices of brands, sizes, colors, fragrances, flavors.

Cluster: A group of demographically similar stores.

Companion Marketing: Refers to when a product gains sales simply because another item is advertised or promoted. Examples include scarves with dresses, paint brushes with paint, and dips with chips.

Customer Returns: Products returned by the customer to the store. These products may be returned to the shelf (to a sellable status), returned to the supplier, or discarded. The customer may be given a refund, credit, rain check, or replacement product.

Demand Forecasting: This method uses formulas and history to predict future sales of product that has accumulated history and little promotion activity.

Department: Sections of the store that often have their own managers, P&L, personnel, and even support systems.

Double Exponential Smoothing: A forecasting method that uses a trend factor to forecast downward and upward sales movement.

Double Moving Average: A forecasting method that computes the moving error (trend factor), which it then multiplies by the forecast for each progressive time period forecasted; similar to double exponential smoothing.

DSD: Direct Store Delivery; products delivered to the stores by the suppliers without the necessity of store orders.

DSP: Direct Store Purchases. Products delivered to the stores directly from the supplier with a store purchase order (Supplier Direct).

EAN: European Article Number.

ECR: Efficient Consumer Response.

Exponential Smoothing: A forecasting method that uses a percentage of the old forecast plus a percentage of the error against actual sales.

Facing: One product dimension at the front of the shelf.

Forecasting: A mathematical means of analyzing the past and the present in order to predict the future. There are three major components of forecasting: history, math, and judgment.

High-Variety Retailer: Refers to retailers who carry depth of assortment within a category, not retailers who carry a high variety of product categories but with little depth within the categories.

In-store Cannibalization: What happens when products fight for a single customer purchase.

Item: An item may be the same as an SKU; or it may represent the overall product such as jeans with several sizes and colors of SKUs.

Item Group: Items grouped by like attributes such as color, fragrance, brand, flavor, size, style, supplier delivery route. Item groups are any linkage that brings information to the analysis process.

JIT: Just In Time. The ability to produce and distribute product on an as-needed basis without excess costs or inventory.

Lead Time: The length of time from order generation until the product is available for consumer purchase.

Lead Time Variance: The difference between expected lead time and actual lead time.

Logistics: The global optimization of multiple sources, multiple destinations, multiple costs, and multiple methods of delivery. Logistics is the ability to deliver product at the right time in the right quantity to the right place at the most effective cost for both the supplier and the retailer.

Merchandise Mix: Sets the tone for the retailer, and forms the basis for the minimum set and selection of forecasting options. It is key to setting the rules for service level.

Merchandising Philosophies: These include the store look, the merchandise mix, and the expected consumer service level.

MIS: Management Information Systems.

Multiple Regression: A forecasting method that assumes that the causal relationship or sales factors includes more than sales and sales history.

Non-basic Products: Items within product categories carried year after year but which have different individual items every year. Non-basic products are controlled in plannable categories via merchandise planning system. Plannable categories have trends, seasons, and measurable sales history at the category level. For example, fashion is primarily non-basic product.

On-orders: On-orders are products that have been ordered and are scheduled to arrive at the store. This includes distribution center backorders, partial receipts, and late purchase orders.

One-time Only Products: Merchandising in and outs that are sold to take advantage of a current consumer interest or a special supplier offer.

Order Cycle: The average length of time between orders.

Order Determination: Replaces the manual practice of examining store shelves to determine the quantity of product to order. Order determination decides how much product to order and when, then processes the order.

Order Generation: In this function, the decision to order is made. The system changes product need to conform to purchase order limits.

Order Management: A function that issues the purchase order, transmits the order to the supplier (or the distribution center), ages the on-orders, matches receiving quantities and costs to the original order, and creates a history of vendor delivery quality and timing.

Out-of-Season: Products that may be carried year-round but sell well only during their season.

Out-of-Stock: A condition that exists when available product is not sufficient to satisfy demand.

P&L: Profit and loss statement.

Pack: The shipment units from the supplier or retail distribution center to the stores. (cases, master case, eaches, pallets, etc.)

Perpetual Inventory: An accurate picture of a store's stock position. It can represent both a quantitative and financial picture of a store.

Planning: A mathematical approach to estimate future sales and profits, usually for one category, class, or subclass.

Planogram: A mathematical approach optimizing the use of space based on projected sales for one category, class, or subclass.

PLU: Price look-up. Store assigned, manually keyed bar-codes.

POS: Point of Sale. POS data refers to the transactions from the register. POS marketing refers to promotions at the location where the consumer picks out the product.

Presentation Stock: The minimum amount of product that is considered presentable for the look of the store.

Price Sensitivity: Refers to how consumers react to products, based on price. An item that is highly price-sensitive will easily lose sales to a competing item that is offered at a lower price. Products that are viewed as commodities are generally considered price sensitive. Branded prestige items targeted to upscale consumers—who will purchase a particular item with little regard to shelf price—are less price sensitive.

Private Label: A brand of product created uniquely for a particular retailer.

Product Characteristics: The attributes of the various products. These vary by retailer and category of product.

Product Need Determination: The calculation of the quantity of product required, based on meeting a target level or a calculated supply of product over time.

Promotion: Any merchandising activity that has the goal of increasing sales and/or foot traffic. Can also refer to product that is affected by these external merchandising mechanisms (i.e., promotion product, cannibalized product, companion product).

Quick Response: The ability to flow goods through the distribution pipeline without excess inventory or costs.

Rack Jobber: A DSD-type with a supplier who brings the product directly to the retail shelf.

Region (Geographic): A geographic grouping of stores.

Requested Product: Product that normally requires early ordering, delivery, and set-up.

Reserve: Product in the stores but not in a sellable location.

Retail: Sales to the consumer.

Returns: See store returns; customer returns.

Safety Stock: Extra product available to insure the targeted service level. Required because of sales and lead time volatility.

Seasons: Sales patterns that regularly repeat each year and within one year. Seasons can be identified year-to-year.

Service level: The mathematical calculation of the percentage of time product is in stock when the customer desires the product.

Shadow Perpetual Inventory: An off-site estimate of the actual perpetual inventory normally kept by a supplier for supplier managed product lines.

Shelf Depth: Number of product units behind one facing.

Shrink: Unexplained reduction of inventory.

Simple Linear Regression: A forecasting method that assumes that within sales plotted over time, a straight line could be plotted, and that future sales would be represented by the slope of this line.

Simple Moving Average: A forecasting method that sums the most recent weeks of product movement, and divides by the number of weeks used.

SKU: Stock Keeping Unit. A SKU is a sellable and orderable unit. Several UPC/EAN bar codes may relate to one SKU.

Slow Movers: Products that do not sell (or turn) rapidly.

Store: A single retail outlet.

Store Demand: Orders generated by or for the stores, the store receipts, or the shipments to the stores.

Store Returns: Product returned by stores to the supplier or the retail distribution center. Products can be returned due to overstock, damage, or incorrect product delivered.

Store Physical Maximum: This term is generally used with planogram product, and refers to facings times depth. If, however, the definition is taken more literally, it can refer to both shelf product and product that is being held in reserve locations in the store.

Suggested Orders: Orders that are reviewed and released by store personnel before order fulfillment.

Supplier Direct: see DSP.

Supplier Partnerships (Managed): Alliances whereby product lines are forecasted by the supplier, using store or distribution center data. The supplier then plans the lines and delivers directly to the retailer.

Supplies: Sellable product used for in-store maintenance or as a component product or ingredient.

Trends: One-time sales increase or decrease. Trend is not recurring.

UPC: Universal Product Code.

Weighted Moving Average: A forecasting technique that weights the most recent weeks more heavily than past weeks. The sum of the sales are divided by the weights of the weeks.

Checklist

The following questionnaire can be used for the overall store or by individual department.

Store Look

Department   _____

What is the Overall Department look?

Planogram

Minimum units per facing is _____

Varies by:

Item rank	_____	_____	_____	_____
Item size	_____	_____	_____	_____
Item cost	_____	_____	_____	_____
Number of facings	_____	_____	_____	_____
Pack size	_____	_____	_____	_____

Non-planogram

Size	minimum:	_____
Color	minimum:	_____
Category	minimum:	_____
Style	minimum:	_____

When is a hole on the shelf acceptable?

Merchandise Mix

Department _____

The goal for each category is to have depth in:			
Sizes	YES	NO	N/A
Price ranges	YES	NO	N/A
Brands	YES	NO	N/A
Color	YES	NO	N/A
Fragrance	YES	NO	N/A
Flavors	YES	NO	N/A
Styles	YES	NO	N/A
Ingredients	YES	NO	N/A

Private label is:	1. The dominant factor
	2. Shares sales with national brands
	3. N/A

_____ _____ is the dominant private label brand is

The expected turns are?
   In-season _____
   Out-of-season _____

Product Characteristics

Department   _____

Percentage of products:	
Basic Products	_____%
Non-Basic Products	_____%
In / Out	_____%

Of the basic products. what % have:	
Reliable Sales History	_____
In-store Cannibalization	_____
Price Sensitivity	_____
Disconnected SKU and bar code	_____

Service Level

Department   _____

Acceptable service level:				
Item rank	_____	_____	_____	_____
Price Ranges	_____	_____	_____	_____
Sizes	_____	_____	_____	_____
Color	_____	_____	_____	_____
Fragrance	_____	_____	_____	_____
Flavor	_____	_____	_____	_____
Private Label	_____	_____	_____	_____
Supplier	_____	_____	_____	_____
Promotion	_____	_____	_____	_____
In-season	_____	_____	_____	_____
End of Season	_____	_____	_____	_____
Out-of-Season	_____	_____	_____	_____

Is it acceptable to be out of one brand if another brand is in stock?

Is it acceptable to be out of one size if another size is in stock?

When is service level by a product group and when is it by an individual item?

Major Ordering Factors

Department   _____

Product is:
    Available ____%

    Requested ____%

Suppliers
Who and where are the product suppliers?

Are there alternate suppliers?

What role are the suppliers currently playing in the product logistics
and what role do they want to play?

Pack
What is the relationship of pack to product turn?

Are there other pack sizes available?

Is variable pack possible?

Major Ordering Factors (continued)

Department   _____

Logistics

What role the suppliers, third parties in the product logistics?

What role do suppliers, third parties want in logistics?

Who are carriers?

What is relationship of order size to supplier/carrier minimums?

Are delivery times fixed days?

Where are the suppliers?

How many distribution centers?

What is the dependability of the suppliers and carriers?

Average Lead Time? _____   Lead Time Variance? _____

Order Cycle?   _____   Review Time? _____

Major Sales Factors

Department _____

Rate (1 - 5) these sales factors:

Store Influences
    Competitive store openings and closings   _____
    Companion store openings and closings   _____
    Street repairs   _____
    Impediments/improvements to transportation   _____
    Weather   _____
    Labor unrest   _____
    Competitive store labor unrest   _____
    Competitive density   _____

Store Layouts
    Store traffic flow   _____
    Product positioning   _____
    Shelf height   _____
    Facings   _____
    Hanging and table products   _____
    Number of locations in the store   _____

Corporate Influences
    Major marketing strategies and promotions   _____
    Pro or adverse press   _____
    Merchandising strategies   _____

Overall Business and Cyclical Economic influences
    Overall business climate   _____
    Cyclical economic influences   _____
    Merchandising strategies   _____

Major Sales Factors (continued)

Department _____

Product Influences
Errors   _____
Trends   •   _____
Seasons   _____
Stocking Levels   _____
Pricing   _____
Promotions   _____
Brand loyalty   _____
Product repackaging   _____
Publicity   _____
Appearance   _____
Fashion   _____

Other Product Influences
Companion marketing   _____
In-store cannibalization   _____
Shared bar-codes across single SKU   _____
Shared items across department   _____
Bonus pack   _____
Special ads / holiday pack   _____
Set sales   _____
Catalytic sales   _____

Demographics
Brand loyalty   _____
Purchasing power   _____
Shopping habits   _____
Age   _____
Education   _____
Family size   _____
Ethnic background   _____
Sex   _____
Income   _____

Major Promotion Factors (Corporate)

Rate (1 - 5) these sales factors:

Store Location
Multiple Locations   _ _ _ _ _
End Rack   _ _ _ _ _
Special Display   _ _ _ _ _
Center Aisle   _ _ _ _ _
Check Out   _ _ _ _ _

Time
Length   _ _ _ _ _
Frequency   _ _ _ _ _
Consecutive   _ _ _ _ _
Activities during   _ _ _ _ _

In-store Promotion Activity
Demonstrations   _ _ _ _ _
FM   _ _ _ _ _
Samples   _ _ _ _ _
TV at POS   _ _ _ _ _

Electronic Marketing

Coupons
Newspaper   _ _ _ _ _
Magazine   _ _ _ _ _
Flyer   _ _ _ _ _
Register   _ _ _ _ _
POS   _ _ _ _ _
Product   _ _ _ _ _

Reduced Price
Advertised   _ _ _ _ _
On Package   _ _ _ _ _
POS   _ _ _ _ _
In-store activity   _ _ _ _ _

Major Promotion Factors (continued)

Advertising - Print

Level

        Feature

        Regular   ____

        Contract   ____

Coverage

        Geographic

        Flyers   ____

Magazines : which? _____

Newspapers: which? _____

        Picture

        Size

        Color   ____

Advertising - Other

TV

        When   ____

        Which

        Type   ____

        Trailer

        Coverage   ____

Radio

        When   ____

        Which

        Coverage   ____

        Type

        Trailer   ____

Packaging

Special packaging

Bonus   ____

Shrink wrapped

Pre-price   ____

Cents-off

Signage

When

Which   ____

Coverage

Type   ____

Number

Size   ____

Implementation Strategies

To implement CAO:

1. Define the environment and its problems, including merchandising philosophy and mix.
2. Define business, industry, and technical directions.
3. Define what the current systems and technologies can and cannot do. Decide what can be postponed, handled manually, and/or improved.
4. Define the steps or phases, and the benefits that will be achieved with each.
5. Provide manual effort to support areas that will not be managed with technology.

The basic premise of this book is that CAO can be achieved in a series of cost-justifiable steps. The benefits will vary by retailer. All retailers do not have the same needs or problems. They will not need to follow the same steps in the same order.

The first diagram shows the implementation of a clean perpetual inventory. The second diagram depicts forecasting. The final diagram illustrates order determination.

Note: This plan does not specifically address the implementation of the top-down strategy program or the integration of planning and planogramming. All this will vary greatly by retailer. In most cases, these changes can best be effected by beginning with a semi-manual version where individual systems access a central database of strategies. It will take some time before functions will be integrated sufficiently to be "driven by" central strategies.

Examples of possible steps are illustrated in diagrams on the pages that follow.

PERPETUAL INVENTORY

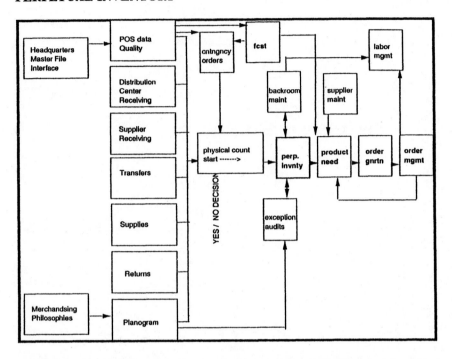

The first step is POS data. This requires a system that can insure complete-ness, edit for reasonability, and audit for questionable transactions. Many things could be done to improve data quality. Among the most effective ones: use of data cleaning systems, use of POS data in-store and in real time, and running ongoing training programs. A major stumbling block for some retailers will be the accuracy of their headquarters file and the relationship of SKU to UPC/EAN. There is no substitute for building a usable master item data base. Data will not be perfect when the project begins but this should not be a reason to delay a CAO project.

Contingency Orders

Contingency orders are an optional part of clean POS data. These are the backup orders for emergency situations.

The next steps are in optional order and will not apply to every retailer.

Distribution Center Receiving

There must be a means to update the perpetual inventory at time of receipt by the store. The receiving must accurately match the shipment notification. If the distribution center shipments are not accurate, it is necessary to fix the systems (computer and manpower) at the distribution center. Communication from the distribution center feeds the store labor management systems.

Supplier Receiving

This is also a two-part solution. The supplier sends advance ship notices to the retailer. Over time, with selected suppliers, only periodic audits are needed to verify the accuracy of the deliveries. Backdoor receiving systems are crucial to the success of supplier receiving.

Transfers

If there are store transfers, systems must perform the following functions:

- Notify headquarters of possible transfer product
- Move affected product from available inventory into transfer status
- Add product to receiving store's inventory upon arrival
- Properly add and subtract costs

Supplies

If there are store supply pulls, procedures for managing these pulls are necessary. If the supplies are a part of normal downward adjustment of inventory, this must be made clear to order determination. Supplies should scan out as supplies, not sales.

Returns

Procedures for customer returns and store returns require procedures and systems to manage adjustment of inventory, transfer status, and aging of transfer inventory.

Planograms

Planograms are not stand-alone systems that do not communicate to the other store systems. They are an integrated and controlling factor. Planograms set the sequence for exception audits and suggested orders.

Physical Count/Start

One by one, by supplier or by planogram, count and start the perpetual inventory. Not all planograms, suppliers, or sections need go on the system in one day. The next steps can take place as other planograms or suppliers are counted.

- Create perpetual inventory
- Create exception audits (in planogram sequence)
- Fix problems as the exception audits expose "holes" in the design

Manage the Back Room

This can mean scanning product out of the back room, tracking product that is kept there, and reviewing back room policies.

Product Need

Using the forecast and the perpetual inventory, calculate product need. At the start, this product need can be used strictly as an audit. If this is for only one supplier or for the retailer's own distribution center, the supplier database and the purchase order management system need not be in place. After more suppliers or products are added, the PO management and supplier databases are created. (Note: If lead time is greater than order cycle, the on-order function must be operative immediately.)

Order Generation

See order generation diagram.

FORECASTING

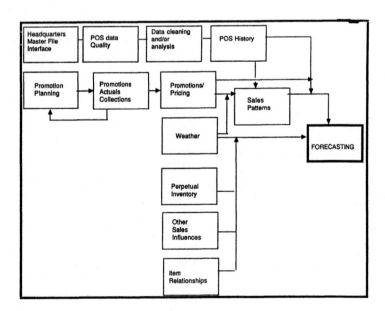

POS Data

Once again, the first step is clean and complete POS data. Do not forecast with bad data. On the other hand, keep in mind that the data does not have to be perfect and probably never will be perfect. If the POS data is uncontrolled and invalidated, its use in forecasting will cause more problems than it will resolve. Data can be good in some Planograms or sections and not in others. Forecasting can be used where the data is usable. (Consider turning off the multiple key.)

POS History

For perpetual inventory, only recent POS data is needed. For creating seasonal and other patterns over time, POS history is required—ideally two years' worth. You should immediately begin collecting the data in-house or through a third party. Lack of history shouldn't keep you from getting started with CAO. But without it, you'd be better off avoiding long-range forecasts or the more advanced order generation models.

Promotions/Pricing

- Plan the promotion/pricing. There must be a system that receives the supplier promotion and cost announcements and lets the merchandisers communicate their promotion plans.
- Collect actuals. Whether in-house or using a third-party provider, collect what actually happened.
- Use promotion/pricing data in the forecast. Depending on the forecasting module, promotion data will be considered a lift to a baseline, a profile, or a part of the overall forecast. The system in some way must account for promotions and price changes.

Weather

Weather is an optional feature depending on the product line. Weather, like promotions and seasons, is described by various systems as a lift, a profile, or a part of the forecast.

Perpetual Inventory

Perpetual inventory isn't imperative unless there are frequent out-of-stocks. Perpetual inventory is used to identify lost sales.

Other Sales Influences

In this book a myriad of other sales influences were identified. Not all play an equal role for every retailer. Those that can be captured can be analyzed by statistical or AI systems to establish their importance in forecasting. If forecast volatility is high, it is worthwhile to investigate what data is missing from the forecast module.

Item Relationships

In previous chapters, this book discussed companion items, cannibalized items, set items, and catalyst items. The ability to tie items together into auxiliary groups is not available in every system. Moreover. merchandisers are not always given the time to establish these ties. But if volatility is unexplained, taking the time to establish these merchandise groups is invaluable.

Forecast and Forecast Volatility

Tune the forecast and identify missing sales influences. If the forecast method is not as good as needed, keep tuning, and initially use an order determination model that is not dependent on forecast quality.

ORDER DETERMINATION

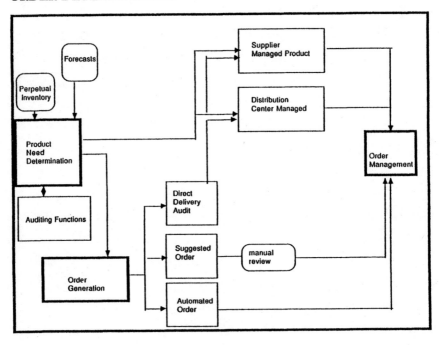

Product Need Determination

This can run for one supplier, one section, or one planogram. Product need determination can feed supplier, distribution center, third-party logistics providers, or order generation. Initially product need determination can feed only the auditing functions.

The next steps depend on where the order generation function is performed, as part of store functions or as part of logistics. As a first step and to get control of the order limits, it is usually best to start outside of the logistics systems. Next step will vary by retailer.

If order generation begins at store level, it produces suggested orders or automatic orders or audits. A good starting place is to either produce audits to the manual orders or suggested orders. When comfort level is high enough, selected sections can be ordered automatically.

APPENDIX D

Planning

The following is by Dr. Terry Donofrio, president of Retail Systems and Services in Waldwick, New Jersey. Dr. Donofrio has created a standard methodology which is used by many retailers to implement automated planning systems.

The merchandise planning function provides both inventory and profitability guidelines for the retail organization. The inventory guidelines are provided based on OTB (Open to Buy) controls and planned inventory levels. The profitability guidelines are provided through gross margin projections based on markup and markdown expectations.

Overall, the planning summary is as follows:

OTB/Inventory Control ($/U)

- Sales Forecast
- Inventory Estimate
- Receipt Plan
- On-order and Resultant OTB

GM Control ($)

- Sales Forecast
- Markup Estimate
- Markdown Estimate
- Gross Margin Plan

These estimates and projections are provided across the various hierarchies that structure the organization. Merchandise plans can be developed as follows:

- Across the merchandise hierarchy: department, class, subclass, etc.
- Across the store hierarchy: store, regions, characteristics
- Across the planning horizon: season, months and weeks

As we have shown in this book, CAO is considered across four disciplines. These elements include:

- Perpetual inventory
- Forecasting
- Order determination
- Logistics

There are various links or natural interfaces between CAO and merchandise planning. These links provide the overall control that the merchandise planning process provides for the ordering of merchandise. However, as we have seen the CAO process also provides planning with some very necessary elements for plan completion and ongoing analysis.

Let's consider the interaction between the two processes in terms of the four elements of CAO.

Perpetual Inventory

Perpetual inventory provides various inputs to the planning process including:

- The ability to track *in-season plan versus actual in-season results* as the season progresses. The CAO process provides the item level store input that can be combined with the planning information to generate plan versus actual comparisons. These comparisons can be provided based on the lowest planning level (e.g., subclass by store).
- *Historical sales and inventory,* which are essential elements of CAO, can be used to support the generation of the initial plan. In a bottom-up approach or strategy, store level sales and inventory history by category would drive the initial plan. During the season the historical sales and inventory position can help generate in-season planning modifications or replanning.
- The perpetual inventory process also provides the various *actual information* which helps evaluate the effectiveness of the overall CAO process and its ability to function within the merchandise plan.

Forecasting

The planning system can provide various inputs to forecasting:

- The *category plans* developed in merchandise planning can provide the basis for the initial forecasts developed in CAO. Category plans at a total merchandise level (not by store) can provide initial guidelines to forecasting, while store level category plans can provide the actual forecast for CAO.

- The forecasting in CAO will be dependent on actions and operations performed by the merchandise division. Promotions is a key area of input for the merchandise division. The *promotional plans* developed as part of the overall merchandise plan provide the quantitative effect of promotions on sales plans at various levels in the merchandise hierarchy. If the promotional plans are defined by store, the input to CAO is even more direct.

- The *merchandise plan* defines the overall merchandise mix planned for the organization. Sales, inventory, and gross margin estimates at various merchandise levels generate the mix for the company. The forecasting process within CAO must consider the overall hierarchy relationships as the lower level forecasts are being developed. If a given category represents X% of a class, then the forecasting process within CAO should be in line with that estimate.

- The assortment plan defines the product definition structure and items that will compose the presentation of merchandise to the consumer. Price ranges, brands, fabric, key items, and so on are all part of the assortment plan. These concepts are also an input to the forecast developed in CAO. Items to be forecast are based on the assortment plan including the timing of the item startup and transition from one season to the next.

The inputs from forecasting to planning are:

- Initial projections for pre-season sales plans can be provided. These initial projections can be derived by chain at various levels in the merchandise hierarchy. Projections can also be derived by store and then combined to form total chain plans.

- In-season sales projections can be provided based on the assessment of plan versus actual results. These projections are used to replan on a regular basis (e.g., monthly) throughout the season. Projections can be drawn at a total chain or store-by-store basis.

- The effect of promotions on sales plans can be estimated based on statistical forecasting-techniques. The merchandise influence on the promotion can also be part of the overall analysis.

- Very detailed sales estimates at the item or category-level can be generated by the forecasting module. These lower level estimates can provide assortment input or help generate bottom-up plans.

The inputs from planning to order determination include:

- The item-level plan provides the basis for the items being replenished. The order determination module can utilize various parameters from the basic item plan such as WOS or Stock/Sales ratio. Order quantities are thereby kept "in sync" with the overall merchandise plan.

- The OTB controls that are based upon the inventory and receipt plans provide the guidelines for order determination (e.g., the OTB established for basic items provides limits for order quantity calculations).

Order Determination

The inputs from order determination to planning include:

- Once the order quantity is determined, the on-order position is updated and OTB is adjusted.
- Very often, order determination generates needs and results in overall buying strategy.

Logistics

The inputs from planning to logistics include:

- Based on the planned receipts and resultant distribution plans, the DC personnel requirements can be estimated based on various productivity standards.
- Store-level receipt plans provide the basis for defining store personnel requirements (staffing levels and timing).

The inputs from logistics to planning include:

- The optimum plan may need to be modified based on capacity limitations (e.g., although optimum receipt flow calls for higher receipt quantities in November, DC capacity limitations may require spreading the receipts across October and November).

In summary, as automation is applied to both planning and CAO, the interfaces can be defined and implemented. These interfaces can now be defined as part of both the planning and CAO systems.

Planograms

The following is by Bob Cohen, president of Beta Data in Dallas, Texas. Mr. Cohen was the author of the Spaceman space management system.

Computer Aided Ordering achieves its maximum return when applied at the store level. The ability to tailor the selection to individual stores and to respond to the business conditions of those stores is the goal of the entire process.

The most effective and concise method of representing retail conditions is the planogram. At a glance, a properly constructed planogram shows how a section should be laid out, how it should be priced, and how it should be replenished. Store-level planograms are a prerequisite to doing store-level merchandising and replenishment.

Planograms are the end result of the entire retail merchandising process. A properly constructed planogram takes into account virtually all of the decision points required in retail merchandising. A simple homily: If the planogram isn't right, the process isn't right.

Planograms are more than elementary pictures of products on shelves. They are a visual synonym for a myriad of quantitative data as well. Developing both the correct location and quantity for a given product requires an accurate forecast of future demand, on-target pricing analysis, efficient replenishment scheduling, and so forth.

Traditionally, however, planograms have existed as a separated sub-task within the merchandising process. Since the advent of the personal computer the stereotypical image of planogramming is that of an individual analyst sitting at a keyboard moving product images about a display screen with the aid of one or another pointing devices. The pricing functions, the planning functions, and the replenishment functions are carried out by other parts of the organization, with practically no communication to the planogrammer other than by bits of paper. Question: If the planogrammer doesn't have easy access to the forecast and replenishment numbers, how does he know how many facings of the product are required to achieve a given customer satisfaction level?

The simple answer is that he doesn't! In fact, the planogram developed under this conventional scenario doesn't really reflect any particular store at all; it usually reflects a store-wide average and at best an average for a typical size and/or grouping of stores. The reality of the situation is that planograms have traditionally served only as rough guidelines for store managers to override at will.

The breakdown between the planogram and the store is a direct consequence of the breakdown between the planogram and the rest of the merchandising process. There are two reasons for this breakdown: Lack of integrated interdepartmental data flows and lack of personnel.

Management's attempt to solve this strangulation at the center often leads them to ask the following question: "What tools can I give my store managers so that they can merchandise their stores more efficiently? After all, he's the man on the spot." The flip answer is: "Not much! Your store managers don't have either the time or the expertise."

Store managers traditionally manage the top 20% of their selection very well. But it is a fallacy that they handle the other 80% just as effectively. They simply don't have the time and the traditional retailing model won't give it to them.

What store managers do have, however, is a fundamental knowledge of the business conditions that affect their individual locations. Store-level merchandising will be achieved with large-scale central systems massaging enormous amounts of detailed data, coupled with rapid response remote systems that allow in-store personnel to participate integrally in the process.

The role of planogramming within such a system now takes on a different aspect. Instead of being just another element within the process, it now becomes the focal point of the process. The goal becomes the production of a correct store-level planogram. All of the individual merchandising decisions become truly integrated such that the location of product in the set, its pricing and its quantity reflect the exact needs of the particular store for which it was produced.

APPENDIX F

Strategic Alliances

The following is by Donald R. Mowery, director of Customer Response/ ECR, Ralston Purina Company, St. Louis, Missouri.

Key to the successful implementation of computer assisted ordering is the development of strategic alliances. The goal of CAO is to effectively execute merchandising plans while reducing operating and inventory costs and maintaining or improving service to the customer. With reliance on computer systems to order products to achieve this goal, it is vital that each player involved understand their role and how it relates to all other roles. Only by using this knowledge to work together can this goal be achieved.

The most obvious need for alliance is between the retailer and its suppliers. But, it is equally as important to develop this same level of alliance between functions within the retailer. For example, effective execution of CAO will require a coordinated and concerted effort between the retailer's merchandising, retail operations, transportation, and distribution center operations functions. And, don't forget the need for an alliance with information systems to make all of this work correctly.

First, look at the logistics needed to accomplish the goals of CAO. Most order determination models include lead time as a factor. Anything that prevents orders from getting to the retail shelf on time will have a negative impact on service level and on achieving the merchandising plan. A change made by the manufacturer in the labeling of the product can result in delays in receiving this product at the retailer's distribution center. This delay will result in the shipment not being posted into available inventory and not being able to fill retail orders. The result is retail out-of-stocks, perhaps at a critical time in the merchandising plan. This could have been prevented had the manufacturer known the retailer's receiving processes and communicated the change in product labeling. To prevent problems such as this it is crucial that all players, manufacturer, supplier, and retailer, understand the complete order-shipping-receiving process. In this way each can anticipate the response to any change or discrepancy and prevent or minimize the impact on the merchandising plan.

Another logistic function that requires a different relationship than before CAO is transportation. As computer assisted ordering reduces the days-of-supply of inventory, the timing of deliveries becomes more important. To ensure orders are delivered on time, it is often necessary to use only one or two highly reliable carriers. It is also often desirable to have preset delivery appointments, that is a delivery time that will be used every day, every week, etc. This requires developing strong alliances between the shipper, the carrier and the receiver.

Often, for retail orders, all of these functions belong to the retailer and the existence of a strong alliance is assumed. But that may not be the case. Because of differing key performance measures applied to the different functions, they may have a relationship that is more adversarial than alliance. For example, a key measure for retail is usually labor cost. As a result, orders are often received when the other workload is light, but the exact time when that will occur is unknown. So, to have preset delivery appointments may require scheduling additional employees or paying overtime or shift premiums. It is critical that attention be paid to these alliances even when they are internal functions.

Alliances are also critical for the execution of promotions. Procurement and distribution of merchandise for promotions can be accomplished in several ways with CAO. However, any of the ways can cause problems if there is not full understanding of the promotional plan and its execution among all participants. One method frequently used is for the category manager to enter both the retail and manufacturer orders for the promotion. If the item being promoted is also regularly carried, this can cause problems. If the promotion orders are cross-docked through the distribution center rather than received into inventory, a large quantity of retail inventory was positioned without the CAO system seeing demand on distribution center inventory. The system will think demand for the item has stopped and will stop creating manufacturer orders. Once the promotional merchandise is exhausted, the demand on the distribution center reappears. Depending on the order lead time, the system may not be able to respond fast enough. This will result in low service levels to retail and retail out-of-stocks. By having a strong alliance between those responsible for merchandising planning, promotional procurement, and staple stock procurement, these situations can be prevented. This alliance will allow the plan to be communicated and executed without residual effects.

The more accurate the forecast, the more effective CAO can achieve its goal. And, forecasting is another area that benefits greatly from alliances. Many factors can affect the forecast, and it is impossible for one person, or function, to have all the information. For example, the merchandising manager knows about national or regional promotions and advertising plans. Other needed information, such as seasonality and store traffic volumes, may come from another source. All of these factors can affect the forecast. By combining the information and efforts, the forecast can be improved. For the forecast to be really useful, it is critical that all parties who use it should understand how the accuracy of the forecast changes over time and what the critical planning horizons are.

Just knowing the importance of alliances is not enough. It is necessary to know what they are and how to develop them. An alliance is two or more parties working together to achieve a common goal. The first step in developing alliances is to determine the goal, or goals, to be achieved, and the parties needed to achieve them. The second, and most critical, step is for the parties in the alliance to ensure they agree on the common goal and agree to share accountability for achieving it. Then, they need to identify the measures that will tell them of their progress. These measures are key. Without them the parties in the alliance will be driven by their own goals and measures rather than toward the common goal. These measures should be put on a scoreboard to be shared by all parties in the alliance. The next step is to develop a common understanding of the roles each party is to play and what processes they use in their roles. From this understanding, it is possible to identify what information needs to be shared between the parties and to develop a plan for communicating that information. Finally, the parties in the alliance need to develop a schedule for meetings. The purpose of these meetings is to review the scorecard to determine progress toward the goal and to plan improvements to the processes to achieve still better results.

Computer assisted ordering is not just a system. It is major change to a business process, or rather a number of business processes. Successful implementation cannot be achieved by one person, or even by one business function. Success will require a concerted effort of many parties toward a common goal. In other words, it requires strategic alliances with common goals and measures, shared information, frequent communications, and shared accountability for results.

Additional Reading List

Andersen Consulting. *Wholesale Food Distribution Today & Tomorrow*. Falls Church, VA: National-American Wholesale Grocers' Association, 1993.

Anderson, Barbara. *Computer Assisted Ordering Coursenotes*. Waldwick, NJ: Retail Systems & Services, 1995.

Anonymous. *Computer Assisted Ordering Practices and Benefits*. Washington, DC: Joint Industry Project on Efficient Consumer Response, 1994.

Anonymous. *Retail Systems Handbook A Guide to Systems Strategies*. Newton, MA: Retail Systems Alert, 1995.

Anonymous. *Retail Systems 95 Proceedings*. Newton, MA: Retail Systems Conferences, 1995.

Category Management: Positioning Your Organization to Win. Chicago: NTC Business Books, 1992.

Donofrio, Terry J. *Basic Concepts Seminar Merchandise Planning Coursenotes*. Waldwick, NJ: Retail Systems & Services, 1994.

Donofrio, Terry J. *Comprehensive Seminar Merchandise Planning Coursenotes*. Waldwick, NJ: Retail Systems & Services, 1995.

Donofrio, Terry J. *Merchandise Planning Systems: An Insider's Guide to Selection and Implementation*. Newton, MA: Retail Systems Alert, 1991.

Freedman, David & Lane, David. *Mathematical Methods in Statistics: A Workbook*. New York: W.W. Norton & Company, 1981.

Kochersperger, Richard H. *Food Warehousing and Transportation*. New York: Chain Store Publishing Corp., 1978.

Kurt Salmon Associates, Inc. *Efficient Consumer Response*. Washington, DC: The Research Department, Food Marketing Institute, 1993.

Leed, Theodore W. & German, Gene A. *Food Merchandising Principles and Practices*. New York: Chain Store Publishing Corporation, 1973.

Nelson, Marilyn McCord & Illingworth, W.T. *A Practical Guide to Neural Nets*. Reading, MA: Addison-Wesley Publishing Company, 1991.

Neville, A.M. & Kennedy, J.B. *Basic Statistical Methods for Engineers and Scientists*. Scranton, PA: International Textbook Company, 1964.

Quinn, Feargal. *Crowning the Customer: How to Become Customer-Driven*. Dublin, Ireland: The O'Brien Press, 1990.

Under the Microscope: Putting the Total Store in Focus. Stamford, CT: Maclean Hunter Media, 1992.

Wheelwright, Steven C. & Makridakis, Spyros. *Forecasting Methods for Management.* New York: John Wiley & Sons, 1977.

Winston, Patrick Henry. *Artificial Intelligence.* Reading, MA: Addison-Wesley, 1992.

Index

About the Author

BARBARA V. ANDERSON is an international consultant and president of Bvac Incorporated, San Carlos, California. With nearly twenty years of experience in the design of major replenishment and forecasting systems, Ms. Anderson is an adviser to major retail systems vendors, particularly on matters relating to computer assisted ordering (CAO), pricing, promotion management, and item and vendor file design. She is a frequent speaker at seminars for retailers, wholesalers, and manufacturers on all aspects of CAO and is currently presenting her own seminars on CAO. This is her first book.